———————— AN AUTOBIC

LEARNING TO LISTEN
THE JAZZ JOURNEY OF
GARY BURTON

EDITED BY NEIL TESSER

Berklee Press
Boston, MA

For Steph and Sam, so they'll know what I've been up to all these years

Berklee Press

Editor in Chief: Jonathan Feist
Vice President of Online Learning and Continuing Education: Debbie Cavalier
Assistant Vice President of Operations for Berklee Media: Robert F. Green
Assistant Vice President of Marketing and Recruitment for Berklee Media: Mike King
Dean of Continuing Education: Carin Nuernberg
Editorial Assistants: Matthew Dunkle, Amy Kaminski, Sarah Walk
Cover Design: Small Mammoth Designs
Cover Photos: Jimmy Katz, courtesy of Mack Ave Records (Top);
David Redfern, Getty Images (Bottom Center); Bill Gallery (Bottom Right)
About the Author Photo: Michael Murphy

ISBN 978-0-87639-140-2

DISTRIBUTED BY

1140 Boylston Street
Boston, MA 02215-3693 USA
(617) 747-2146

Visit Berklee Press Online at
www.berkleepress.com

HAL•LEONARD®
CORPORATION
7777 W. BLUEMOUND RD. P.O. BOX 13819
MILWAUKEE, WISCONSIN 53213

Visit Hal Leonard Online at
www.halleonard.com

Berklee Press, a publishing activity of Berklee College of Music, is a not-for-profit educational publisher.
Available proceeds from the sales of our products are contributed to the scholarship funds of the college.

CONTENTS

ACKNOWLEDGMENT

I started this project about a dozen years ago, but after telling the story of the first half of my life, I hit a wall. In retrospect, I now think I needed more distance from many of the major events in my life. I hadn't gotten far enough past them to fully understand their meaning and impact. Finally, a couple years ago, the logjam broke open, and I wrote 90 percent of the book over a week holed up in a Los Angeles hotel room. It was as if everything I wanted to say had been bubbling under for all that time and had now reached the right moment to come to the surface.

With my history of making records, I am used to projects requiring the involvement of a number of people, and in that sense, writing a book is no different. I shared early drafts with a handful of trusted friends and family whose feedback proved invaluable. In particular, I would like to thank my partner in life, Jonathan Chong, and my partner in business, my long-time manager Ted Kurland, for their constant encouragement. Much needed help with factual details and perspective came from Jeanine Blessing, Catherine Goldwyn, Ed Underhill, my mother, Pat Metheny, Steve Swallow, and Chick Corea. A special thanks goes to my editor, jazz expert and journalist Neil Tesser, who patiently advised me over these dozen years and who fact-checked many details in the narrative. And finally, I greatly appreciate the support and expertise of Debbie Cavalier, head of Berklee Press, and its editor in chief, Jonathan Feist, who found every missing comma and typo.

Gary Burton

INTRO

"So, you have recently come out; has that
affected your playing or your career?"

—Terry Gross, NPR's *Fresh Air*, 1994

As I heard the words "come out," I thought, "Is she asking about *that*?" To me, the pause before my answer seemed a lot longer than it probably was, as my mind rushed through a series of frantic calculations.

You see, I had only recently started to tell a few friends and musicians I worked with about an important self-discovery—that I had finally figured out I was gay. Looking ahead, I presumed that someone in the press would ask me about this during an interview someday—perhaps a writer for a jazz magazine or a local newspaper. I just wasn't expecting it to be on National Public Radio with Terry Gross!

As a musician, I get a lot of requests for interviews, usually to promote a recent record or an upcoming concert. So, it didn't strike me as unusual to be contacted about an interview with Terry for her NPR program, *Fresh Air*. When it comes to interviewing, Terry is as good as it gets, and I definitely treated the request differently than if it had come from some local radio station or newspaper. I was especially looking forward to the interview because I knew Terry was knowledgeable about jazz. She is married to Francis Davis, then the jazz writer for *The Atlantic Monthly* (now jazz critic for the *Village Voice*) and author of numerous articles and books about jazz.

Since Terry does her show in Philadelphia and I lived in Boston, I went to a broadcasting studio near my office that had a high-quality phone connection; this made it seem like we were in the same studio (and avoided that low-fi "telephone voice" on the air). As we got underway, things followed a familiar direction. After hundreds of interviews over the years, I have discovered that mostly the same questions come up over and over: how did you start playing, why did you choose the vibraphone, tell us about your new record, etc. Nonetheless, the discussion was on a pretty high level: Terry has a way of phrasing questions that elicits more specific answers. So, instead of asking, "What was it like playing with Stan Getz," she asked, "I hear Stan Getz was a very difficult character. How was it touring with him?" That left me free to comment on Stan's drinking problems and personality quirks—as well as his genius as a saxophone player—without being the first to bring it up.

I thought the interview would last thirty minutes, the usual length for a "Fresh Air" segment. But after a half-hour, Terry suggested we take a break before continuing. I thought that maybe she wanted some extra material in case they decided to edit our conversation, but then Terry said something strange: "If I ask you anything you're uncomfortable talking about, just say so, and we can stop the tape." I couldn't imagine what she was referring to, but I quickly found out.

Terry's first question of the second half-hour was, "So, you have recently come out; has that affected your playing or your career?"

Around the time I began to come out, I spent a few days in a Vancouver recording studio working with singer k.d. lang on her *Ingenue* album. During that period, she was avoiding public discussion of her sexuality, and we talked some about the problems this entailed. I had been wondering whether it would be better to just avoid the issue or to be totally open about it. But in Vancouver, I pretty much decided that whenever the question "officially" came up, I would be ready to talk about being gay. Now, I just had to take a deep breath before diving in.

Terry and I spent the second half-hour talking about the acceptance of homosexuality (or lack thereof) by other jazz musicians, by the music business, and by jazz audiences. One of the things I told Terry was that I considered myself a jazz musician first, who happened to be gay.

These days I often think it might be the other way around. After all, I can go for hours and sometimes days at a time without thinking that much about music. But every moment of every day, I am aware of being gay.

I'm definitely not the kind of musician who wakes up each morning singing a song, or listens to music all the time, or practices every day. I don't hang out with other musicians talking about last night's gig or someone's new record. In fact, I almost never listen to records at all, and if I do, it's likely to be classical music, tango, or historic jazz. As for practicing, well, my approach always confuses people. I haven't practiced the vibraphone since high school. Maybe I'm like Itzhak Perlman, who says he only takes his violin out of its case when he has a concert or to learn new music. I practice only to run over new pieces or to prepare for a record project.

I did practice regularly when I was first learning to play, but not with any sort of regimented approach. My parents didn't push me to be a musician or insist on a set amount of practice time each day. And for all but the first couple of years, I didn't even have a teacher assigning weekly lessons. I became known for my ten-minute practice sessions. Every time I walked through the living room where the piano and vibes were, I would stop and play a tune or two, then head on out to play basketball or something else. I probably did this five or six times a day, getting in an hour of practice my own way, I suppose. On the other hand, when I would go off to my grandfather's farm or to YMCA camp for the summers, I might not even think about music for a couple of months. (A comment attributed to the famed classical guitarist Andres Segovia, "Anyone who says they practice eight hours a day is either a liar or an ass," remains one of my favorites.)

I will freely admit that I have a kind of love/hate relationship with music. Some instinct, whether healthy or not, tells me not to get too close to music—to keep it at arm's length and avoid being overwhelmed by it, as if it were a tidal wave that might drown me. Not being immersed in music all the time makes the experience fresher and more intense when I do play. This may not be the best way to live with music, but it is my way. Every artist finds what works for him or her.

Life is a process of getting to know oneself, and this is especially true for artists, who struggle to find answers to so many questions. In the case of musicians, we want to turn those answers into song through our creative processes. And that requires learning who you are and discovering how to have a kind of dialogue with the unconscious self—what I call my "inner player." This is true of all musicians, but especially so of jazz musicians (who not only interpret but also compose, through the process of improvisation).

When we want to see what we look like, we stand in front of a mirror. But there is no mirror to reflect a true image of our inner selves. Instead we stitch together a composite picture of who we are. We listen carefully to others and sort out what rings true for us; we look at what we have created and try to see ourselves in it. We artists get to know that inner self, the unconscious, in ways that other people might never imagine. After decades of self-observation and reflection, I believe that this communication with my unconscious has shaped my creative abilities and taught me a great deal about myself. But there is always more to know, another layer of revelation, another insight into how things work.

What Terry Gross did *not* ask in that 1994 interview was why it took so long to figure out my sexuality. I often wonder if my life would have taken a different path if I could have been openly gay from the beginning. But I grew up in an Indiana farm town in the 1940s and '50s, a very different world from the one I live in now. I was supposed to get married and have a family, and I struggled for half my life to do so, overriding my innate identity—so much so that I didn't find my true self until well into my forties. Growing up was like that for many from my generation.

Looking back, it's hard to believe this gay, white, Hoosier farm kid managed to find his way in the macho, cosmopolitan world of jazz. This is the story of my journey—as a gay jazz musician or as a jazz-playing gay man, whichever you prefer.

CHAPTER 1

What's a Vibraphone?

The oldest trophy on my library shelf is a little brass cup (now with a broken handle) naming me first-place winner at the 1951 National Marimba Camp. I was eight, but I had already been a musician for two years. My grandfather and my parents took me to DuQuoin, to the Illinois State Fairgrounds, for what was the largest gathering of mallet percussionists up till that time; there were about fifty entrants in the competition.

I realized that it is intensely satisfying when a group of people sits and watches as you do something they can't—and having them applaud is even better. Winning that trophy was my first indication that some ability of mine just might take me somewhere.

And even at eight, my instincts were already telling me that rural Indiana might not be the place for me.

My parents, Wayne Burton and Bernice Aishe, married in 1934, in their teens, and were together sixty-four years, till the death of my father. Though he managed to work his way through college and graduated as a chemical engineer, his first job was shoveling gravel for $9 a week, working for my mother's father. For economic reasons, my parents waited until after the Great Depression before starting a family. I was born James Gary Burton on January 23, 1943, the middle child of three.

My earliest memories of life with my family take place at 2207 Delaware Street in Anderson, Indiana, where we lived until I was nine. The house was rather small for a family of five, but my parents rented it for just $11 a month. Our car was a thirteen-year-old Ford with holes worn through the floorboard; you could look down at your feet and watch the street passing underneath. We weren't exactly poor, but life was pretty basic. My dad had worked at a General Motors factory in Anderson for about ten years, but by the time the kids came along, he had started his own plastics company in a rented building a few blocks from our house. In spite of our modest circumstances, my folks—typical of parents who had grown up during the Depression—wanted their children to have the things they had missed in their youth. And that included music lessons.

My parents actually had some musical ability, and my father always wished he could have studied music. Strangely, I only discovered their musical backgrounds later in life; for some still unfathomable reason, they kept their own musical histories a secret. When I went to visit them once in the late 1990s, I was given the usual tour of the house, and I noticed an old photograph of a group of teenage boys holding music instruments. I took a closer look and my mother casually said, "Oh, that's your father's band from when he was in high school." He was in the front row holding a trumpet! And if that weren't enough, another room contained an old silver trombone in the corner. I asked where *that* came from, and my father said, "It's your mother's. She used to play it in the high school band." And she still had it!

Where had she kept a trombone in the house all those years without anyone ever noticing it? They had never told any of us kids about their musical pasts. I asked my brother if he knew anything about Mom's trombone or Dad's trumpet, and he thought I was making it up.

I don't want to give the idea that my parents were eccentric—far from it. They were absolutely your typical midwestern parents, as grounded as any parents could be, and they structured their lives around the interests of us children. I can only guess that they didn't want us to feel any expectations from them when it came to our own experiences with music. (When I asked my mother about it, she said they just didn't think it was all that important to talk about.)

People sometimes wonder if I inherited my talent, but other than my parents' youthful encounters with the trumpet and trombone, the family had no other musicians as far back as I have been able to determine. My maternal grandfather, Cecil Aishe, lived his whole life in Odon, Indiana, a small, mostly Amish town where my parents met as teenagers. When I released my first album in 1961, he bought his very first phonograph, just to play my record; I'm sure he had never previously listened to any music. From then on, when I visited his house, I always thought it was funny seeing that little record player on the dining-room table with my one record laying beside it.

When we were small, my brother Phil and I spent our summers at Grandpa's farm, which had a dairy operation and fields of corn and soybean. Nearer to his house was a fairly substantial horse and pony farm, which was his pride and joy. Phil and I were expected to ride in the local horse shows and county-fair competitions and add to his collection of blue ribbons and trophies. Phil was more into the riding part than I was, but we both became familiar with life on the farm— feeding the animals, collecting eggs from the henhouse, helping with the gardening. Some days, Grandpa would drive us around in his old pickup, or just leave us to explore the barns and play with the ponies on our own.

I saw the grandparents from my father's side less often. Hamilton Burton started life as a farmer, then one day came in from the field and said the Lord had called him to preach the gospel. He became a Methodist minister, as would two of my uncles and one of my cousins; in fact, my father was the only male in his immediate family who wasn't a preacher. So, it came as no surprise that Grandpa Burton's reaction to my life in jazz was one of disapproval. When I was in high school and started playing in nightclubs, my parents insisted on keeping this a secret from him. I don't think he found out about my career until I was well along. After he moved to a retirement home, he saw me playing on *The Mike Douglas Show* on television and wrote me a sharply worded letter telling me to cut my hair and shave off my mustache.

Considering all this, I'd say that the music genome in our family began with my parents. My mother told me that when I was about four or five, she brought home a set of 78-rpm records of *The Nutcracker Suite,* and that I would sit and listen to them over and over. When my sister Ann, two years older, started piano lessons, I began to watch her play and soon figured out the notes for myself. One day, when she played a wrong note, I yelled from the kitchen, "No, that's an E-flat, not an E-natural!" Hearing that, my father decided I should be getting music lessons, too.

My folks started trying to find an instrument for me. At that age, I didn't even know what the choices were, so the first step was to investigate the range of options by attending some local performances.

One of these was a recital by Evelyn Tucker, a marimba and vibraphone teacher. I don't really remember this experience— or even the fact that I apparently showed sufficient interest to convince my parents this was the instrument I wanted to play. My mother recalled that when she took me for my first lesson, I was so scared I just sat on the chair, and despite all efforts to get me to try playing, I refused to budge or even speak. Evelyn told my mother that I was probably too young and that we should come back in a couple of years. But as soon as we got home, I started nagging my mother to go back, and after a few weeks of carrying on, another lesson was scheduled. This time, I was ready. (What a metaphor for my life! As with many things, I wanted to check it out and think it through before diving in.)

I do remember that second lesson distinctly. It was in Evelyn's living room, and I learned "Twinkle, Twinkle, Little Star." Being able to learn a complete tune in the first lesson was a real plus, however insignificant the song may have been. Many instruments require a considerable amount of practice before a beginner can even produce usable sounds. The mallet instruments, however, offer the possibility of instant gratification.

So, in 1949, at age six, I started my life in music, with Evelyn as my guide. She was an enterprising lady who had built up a clientele of about fifty students on primarily marimba and vibraphone, but also piano and what she referred to as "dramatic readings." (This latter category seemed to have been created exclusively for three blind girls known as the Heiny Sisters.)

Each year, Evelyn would work everyone into a frenzy, staging a big recital that featured all of her students. This annual ritual required a huge space: getting all those marimbas and vibraphones together wasn't easy, and the image of thirty or forty instruments spread across the floor of a high school gym remains a vivid memory for me. At my first recital, I played "The Parade of the Wooden Soldiers" on a little marimba—a beginner's model, scaled to fit a six-year old. And there was always a finale with all the students playing together; at my first recital, we finished with that staple of the accordion world, "Lady of Spain."

Evelyn was a vaudevillian at heart, and she always tried to spice up the shows with costumes and comedy patter of the corniest nature. Even as a child, I was embarrassed at the gags we had to deliver. There might be a "Tribute to Uncle Sam," or a Carmen Miranda-style number with fruit-laden hats, etc. Evelyn would make us all wear make-up—lipstick and rouge—which, for the boys, was totally weird. But we did it for Evelyn because she overwhelmed everyone with her charm and energy.

The important thing was that her lessons were anchored in good, basic musicianship. Probably unknown to her, this included just what I needed to start improvising later on. Evelyn taught me to read music and introduced me to the concept of playing with four mallets instead of just two. She didn't know a whole lot about music theory, but she knew the basic chord structures, and she would always explain to me the foundation of what I was playing.

Just as important, she encouraged me to begin making things up. Due to the shortage of material written for mallet instruments, I learned a lot of songs from sheet music published for piano, and Evelyn had me create new introductions, endings, interludes, chord voicings, and so on. This was my start at improvising. Years later, when I first heard solos on jazz records, I recognized that this was a more extended form of what I had already been doing under Evelyn's tutelage. I think that's one reason I was eventually drawn to jazz.

After I had practiced the marimba for the first year, Evelyn suggested I also add the vibes to my lessons. And consequently, my grandparents came up with the money to buy not only a new vibraphone but also the matching model of marimba. No more kids' models—these were the real things—but I wasn't yet tall enough to reach the keys. In order for me to play, my father had to build a platform the length of the instrument for me to stand on.

I found out years later that Evelyn was one of the biggest dealers of mallet instruments in the world during the 1950s, because she had so many students, and they all bought instruments through her. Admittedly, it was a small market. Musser, the largest manufacturer of mallet instruments, typically sold only about 150 vibraphones per year in the 1950s. I had presumed there were teachers like Evelyn in every town in America, but I eventually realized she was almost unique in this regard. I just happened to be in the right place at the right time.

Also around then, my father discovered I had perfect pitch. Each note in the scale sounded unique to me. Even as a six-year-old, it took no effort at all to name any note I heard. I've read that only about five percent of musicians have this kind of "pitch memory." It wasn't something I learned from studying music: it was there from the beginning.

My father delighted in showing this off to visitors. He would have me turn away from the piano and would then just strike any random handful of notes, and I would rattle off the name of each pitch. I suppose this "gift" has been helpful to me. But then again, there are thousands of great musicians who don't have perfect pitch, and several musicians I have known with perfect pitch turned out to be very mediocre players. In the end, it doesn't seem to make a big difference.

Evelyn was an inspiring teacher. She reacted very emotionally to everything. When I played a particularly rich harmony, for instance, or got all the way through a difficult piece without making mistakes, she would sigh and say she had goose bumps, making me feel I had done something just short of miraculous.

In the two years I studied with Evelyn, I made a lot of progress, and thanks to her efforts, acquired enough experience to carry on by myself after our family moved. My father was offered a good-paying job in Princeton, down in the southwest corner of Indiana, and we settled into a comfortable house near the center of town. Princeton was much smaller than Anderson and a couple hundred miles away, so the move meant that I never had a vibes teacher again. But I kept on playing, mostly classical-music transcriptions on the marimba and popular standards on the vibes. My father ordered the music from Frank's Drum Shop in Chicago, long known as a haven for anything to do with percussion.

Princeton has a few claims to fame. When I was growing up, the world's largest popcorn farm was just outside of town; Orville Redenbacher got his start there. The daughter of the local Pontiac dealer was married to comedian/pianist Victor Borge (though the great man never visited, as far as anyone knew). Dave Thomas, who founded the Wendy's fast-food empire, was adopted by a couple in Princeton and spent some of his early years there. And it was in Princeton that Gary Burton went into the music business.

After winning the National Marimba Contest at age eight, I entered a television talent contest, the *Morris B. Sachs Amateur Hour,* broadcast from Chicago. It was modeled after the nationally known *Ted Mack's Original Amateur Hour* and featured the usual assortment of tap dancers and novelty acts. For my appearance on the show, I played "Twelfth Street Rag," a popular standard written in 1914 and familiar even to casual listeners.

This was my first visit to a big city and my first stay in a hotel. The show was broadcast from the local ABC station, and I still have a posed studio-promotion photograph of me standing in front of a microphone. I won top prize in the first round: a Gruen wristwatch and $75. This also meant a return trip to Chicago for the final round, which was fine with me. I loved the traveling and the excitement of being in a city. In the final round, I took second place, but that didn't really faze me, because by then, I was starting to gig with some regularity.

At first, I was invited to play at church events and for groups like the Lions Club and the Rotary Club. I could play about a half-hour of pieces ranging from classical excerpts to popular songs with a piano accompanist hired by my parents. It was a chore for my dad to load up a marimba and vibraphone and drive to nearby towns for these appearances, but he never complained. Word began to spread, and soon, I was playing up to a hundred dates a year. (I have more or less continued working at this same pace through most of my career. The music changed, but the schedule remained.)

We made a trip to the Indiana State Fair when I was ten. My performance (once again, "Twelfth Street Rag") was part of a daylong variety show featuring mostly Indiana entertainers but headlined by the marvelous singer Nat King Cole. I remember sitting in the cavernous locker room underneath the arena while my father talked with Mr. Cole about my playing; he was very gracious and encouraging, and it meant a lot to my father. Cole would later become one of my idols. I credit many hours of listening to his records as an important influence, particularly with regards to his melodic phrasing.

Before long, we brought my sister Ann onboard to replace the hired piano accompanist. Ann was comfortable playing the classical pieces that had written parts. But I also needed someone to accompany me on the standards—someone who could "comp," in jazz lingo, without having all the notes written out beforehand.

I had managed to gradually teach myself to play piano, because the keyboard is laid out similarly to the vibes. Since my father was chauffering me around anyway, the obvious solution was to teach him enough piano to accompany me. (He proved to be a willing student.) This freed my sister to play a couple of tunes on the trombone, her instrument in the high school band. The "Burton Family" band was starting to take shape. Next, I decided that my brother should join in.

Phil was a year younger than me and had begun playing bass and also clarinet. We tried a duet performance, me on piano and Phil on bass, at a Cub Scout talent night where we sang and played "Down Yonder," a song from the '20s made famous by Al Jolson. We were a hit, and the family troupe had added another member.

Up until I was fourteen, "The Burton Family" performed nearly every weekend; in a typical December, we worked practically every night playing Christmas parties. We traveled mostly in Indiana, Illinois, and Kentucky, but got as far north as Chicago, and once played a week in Miami. My father maintained his day job as a consulting engineer, but my parents devoted their spare time to driving us all over the place to perform.

Over the years we added comedy, more instruments—I taught myself trumpet and drums—and even tap dancing; I took tap lessons for several years and got pretty good at it. In our show, I did a few dance numbers, including one where I simultaneously tap-danced while playing "Bye Bye Blues" on the marimba. Once, during a power failure at the house, just for the fun of it, I stumbled over to the marimba to see if I could play in the dark. I discovered that one of the new pieces I was working on—the Rimsky-Korsakov novelty piece "Flight of the Bumblebee"—was actually easy to play without looking, because it was mostly chromatic with only a few leaps around the keyboard. Naturally, *that* became a part of the show. Mom made me a blindfold, and I played the piece night after night without missing a note. We also had several black-light numbers featuring glow-in-the-dark mallets and costumes. Anytime we saw something on television that we could use, we would add it to the act. We did seasonal medleys for Christmas, Halloween, Fourth of July, etc. Mom made the costumes, and Dad kept fitting out ever-larger trailers to haul all this stuff around.

We were among the folks helping keep vaudeville alive—or at least on life support—in the form of rural talent shows and novelty acts. During those years, we played with all kinds of entertainers. Some of them were aging show-business veterans still doing well-worn acts, and some were kids like us. Among the regulars were a sword swallower, a roller-skating act, a guy who rattled bones and spoons, an old fellow who chewed up broken glass and razor blades, and quite a few barbershop quartets. We got acquainted with several other families with show-business kids, too, mostly dancers and singers but even some acrobats.

The Burton Family band came to an end when I discovered jazz. It was destined to end anyway, because my sister had by then entered high school, and her interests had turned to other things: mainly, angora sweaters and boys. Still, the family band provided us a wonderful experience. We had traveled a lot and had become extremely close and supportive. I learned the essentials of how to write and arrange music and how to rehearse a group. And what I learned about how to communicate with audiences was just as valuable as anything I learned about music.

In spite of the enthusiasm from my parents and all the performing we did as a family, they were hardly the stereotypical "stage parents." It was never their intention that any of their children would go into a career in music. They thought the life of a musician was a poor one with little prospect for a happy and successful life; in this respect, they were quite different from those parents who dreamed of stardom for their kids and relentlessly pushed them to practice and audition. For the Burtons, music was just family fun.

CHAPTER 2

"After You've Gone"

What was the first jazz record I heard? When I was thirteen, my brother, sister, and I chipped in to buy a record player and started to collect recordings of '50s pop music. Then, I somehow came across a Benny Goodman record. It was a ten-inch disc, and the leadoff tune was "After You've Gone," a swing-era standard that I would record myself some thirty-five years later in a tribute to Goodman and the vibes player in his band, Lionel Hampton. What a hot, exciting thing that Goodman record was! I was enthralled. I started searching for jazz records and soon had a collection covering everything from the west-coast cool of Dave Brubeck to the east-coast hothouse of Charles Mingus. Art Blakey's groups with pianist Horace Silver were a particular favorite. Using every spare moment, I began to work on learning jazz tunes and improvising.

Around that time, my father read in the paper that Lionel Hampton's band would be playing at a dance in nearby Evansville. He wanted to take me, but we couldn't go in the evening because I was too young to be admitted. So, we drove over that afternoon and arrived just as the band was finishing their sound check. My father, always enthusiastic about my playing, went up on stage, introduced himself, and explained to Hamp that his son played the vibes. Hamp waved me up on stage, handed me his mallets, and had some of his musicians play along with me on two or three tunes. He was very encouraging. Thinking back, I'm sure the band wasn't that thrilled to delay their dinner while some kid struggled through a couple of songs. (When I met Hampton years later, I reminded him that I had played for him back in 1956, but he had no recollection of it.)

The other thing I remember about that afternoon was the condition of his vibraphone, all beat up from months of one-nighters on the road—a clue that there were some less glamorous aspects to the jazz life waiting for me.

LIONEL HAMPTON: FATHER OF THE VIBES

For years, whenever someone looked at me with a puzzled face and asked, "What's a vibraphone?" I would just answer: "What Lionel Hampton plays." Hampton was the musician who popularized the vibraphone. He took up the instrument in its earliest years and came to national prominence working with Benny Goodman in the '30s, when Goodman led the top jazz band in the country.

I think of Hamp as a very uncomplicated person who led a very complicated life. He was a natural showman and entertainer, clearly driven to succeed. Some have called him a better entertainer than musician, especially in his later years. (Of course, many early jazz performers borrowed their stagecraft from vaudeville. Louis Armstrong suffered criticism for his handkerchief and his mugging, and in early movie clips of Duke Ellington, you might be surprised by his flamboyant excesses at the piano.) Born in 1908, Hampton played drums growing up in Chicago; in his teens, he also took xylophone lessons. In the late 1920s, Hampton struck out on his own and moved to Los Angeles. It was during this period that he began to practice the newly invented vibraphone. During an L.A. engagement with Armstrong in 1930, the trumpeter recalled that "Hamp would occasionally play on some bell-like thing next to the drum set, and he was really swinging." Armstrong scheduled a recording and asked Hamp to play a couple of tunes on the vibes, and "Memories of You" and "Shine" became the first recordings of the vibraphone.

Hamp's years with Goodman (1936–40) launched him to national fame. In a conversation we had in the mid-1970s, Hamp complained that people still went on about the Goodman band as if he had been with Benny for decades, instead of just five years. Hamp worried he wasn't getting enough credit for his own efforts as a bandleader—not that his bandleading was in any way forgettable. On stage, he was a dynamo, and at times almost manic. In a typical performance, he would play vibes, drums, and even a little piano. He often sang, too, and kept adding bits of show business to his performances. Trumpet player Herb Pomeroy, who toured with the band, told me Hamp was always pushing the guys to try outrageous stunts, such as bribing one band member to wear a parachute and jump off the balconies of theaters when they played "Flying Home," Hamp's theme song. And then there's the story of Hampton's band sharing a gig with Louis Armstrong's group at a Long Island resort. Armstrong dominated in the first set, leaving Hamp determined to steal the show after intermission—which he did by ordering his brass section to jump into the swimming pool during the finale of their set.

There are plenty of instances of producers trying to get him off the stage so they could end a show; he couldn't resist an encore. As jazz writer Gary Giddins once wrote, "Hamp didn't go gently into the wings."

Hamp always seemed to have a fairly loose grip on what was going on around him. I figure his tendency to tune things out explained his relation-ship with his wife Gladys, who was also his business manager. She actually managed practically *everything* in his life—she handled the money, hired the musicians, arranged the tours—and she was a tyrant to everyone, including Hamp. She was famous for spending most of the money on herself. She had a lot of expensive jewelry and a large collection of fur coats, but she kept Hamp on an allowance of $25 a week! Gladys almost always traveled with the band, and she brought along her own hair stylist—and for a while, her four poodles. Herb Pomeroy told me that once, going into Canada, the band sat on the bus for hours while a Canadian veterinarian was brought in to clear the dogs before they could cross the border.

It struck me as odd that Hampton, who made sure he was the star of any performance, would end up in a marriage where he was totally subservient. But he professed that he was totally in love with Gladys. In his autobiography, he said that after her death in 1971, he would go to her closet and look at her fur coats; it made him feel she was still close. He lived for three decades after losing Gladys, but he never remarried.

While he remained firmly based in the swing style, Hampton managed to play with a wide assortment of musicians. He hired young players who later became prominent on their own, and played in all-star collaborations with unlikely players from the modern era. Chick Corea tells of being invited to Hamp's apartment to discuss jamming on some tunes for a 1978 concert in Cannes, France. Hamp wanted to learn "La Fiesta," one of Chick's tunes, though that didn't make it onto the concert (a recording of which was released later that year).

To me, the most incongruous aspect of Hamp's personal life was his life-long involvement with the Republican party. Most musicians tend to avoid politics entirely, or at least identify with more liberal viewpoints, but not Hamp. He was active in both national and state politics and maintained friendships with such prominent Republicans as Nelson Rockefeller, Richard Nixon, Ronald Reagan, and George H.W. Bush. During the Watergate hearings on television in 1973, the testimony included a list of expenditures from a secret slush fund the Nixon White House kept for things they wanted to keep from the public, and in the midst of this long list of payoffs and bribes, I suddenly heard, "$15,000 to the Lionel Hampton Orchestra." Apparently, the band had played at some campaign event and was paid out of the secret fund! But in spite of all the scandals, Hampton remained a loyal Republican to the end of his life.

Ironically, after decades of worldwide fame and popular success, Hampton was virtually broke at the time of Gladys's death. A new manager took it upon himself to rebuild Hampton's career and financial status with a grueling work schedule that suited Hamp just fine. The last thing he wanted was to hang around his New York apartment with nothing to do. It was around this time that Hampton's stinginess as a paymaster became public knowledge. Previously, everyone had attributed the band members' meager salaries to

Gladys's tight-fisted management; hell, even Hamp was underpaid. But in the '80s, his new band members decided to go public about their low pay and even went on strike for a brief while. You'd think it would be embarrassing for such a legendary artist to be exposed as a cheapskate, but as far as I know, nothing really changed. He just found other musicians and kept on going.

As Hamp's career became less relevant to jazz, he received more and more recognition. He is practically a deity in France, in the same way Jerry Lewis is considered a giant of cinema there. If you stroll around the city park in Nice, you'll come across the life-size bronze statue of Hamp. Of course, he was often honored at home, too. In 1986, he received the BMI "One of a Kind" Award at a New York event where we played together and talked for quite a while about the future of the vibes, among other things. (That was around the time he started referring to me as his protégé—even though I was already in my mid-forties!) One of Hamp's greatest accolades came in 1992 when he received the Kennedy Center Honors along with actors Paul Newman, Joanne Woodward, and Ginger Rogers, and cellist Mstislav Rostropovich. At Hamp's request, Milt Jackson and I both played vibes on the national telecast of the event. Hamp didn't perform, since he was an honoree, but he got his chance at the afterparty. True to form, they couldn't get him to stop till the wee hours.

I last saw Hamp at a jazz festival in northern Japan in the mid-'90s. He had already suffered the first of several strokes, but was still going out on tours. Backstage, I was shocked to see how stiff and awkward his movements were. He seemed lost in another world, and I was worried as he slowly shuffled out on stage toward his vibes. But within a couple of tunes, it was like he was twenty years younger. He still wasn't able to really get around on the instrument; his arms were too arthritic. He hit the keys occasionally, but mostly just waved the mallets around and sort of conducted the band. Still, the effect he had on the audience was amazing. Having already sat through many hours of music, they got excited right along with him, and by the end of his set, they were all standing and swaying with the music, clapping and yelling.

He was a true survivor, outliving his contemporaries—Armstrong, Ellington, Goodman, and all the rest. Lionel Hampton passed away in 2002 at the age of ninety-four, the longest lived of all vibraphonists.

Princeton High School offered boys a choice of two educational paths. One was the so-called "Industrial Arts" path. (The girls presumably could choose "Home Economics;" keep in mind that this was a rural town in the 1950s.) The other option was a program aimed at preparing for college, including courses in Latin and Spanish. I thought to myself, "I'll never be going anywhere they speak a foreign language," and I liked the hands-on nature of the "Industrial Arts" courses. So, I took Mechanical Drawing and Architecture, and learned basic skills like electrical wiring, concrete fabrication—I made a birdbath that finally crumbled away after three decades in various backyards where I have lived—and woodworking. (I still have a stool I made in my freshman year that comes in very handy around the house.) I had no idea that a music career was in my future.

Many gay men say that even from childhood, they knew they were gay. For me, it was around high school age that I first sensed confusion about sex. Along with discovering sexuality, as everyone does at puberty, I also felt certain I was somehow different from the other boys. I didn't know what, if anything, to do about it; I had no clue what was going on with that part of my life, and there was no one to ask for advice. I coped with the confusion as best I could, given that I was growing up in '50s rural Indiana.

I was also confused about music. Getting further into jazz, I started trying to figure out the rich, dissonant chords I was hearing on records, but again, I had no idea what I was doing. Good fortune came along when my father noticed a sign advertising "Instruction in Modern Harmony" in a music-store window in Evansville, about an hour south of Princeton. The next Saturday afternoon, we went to check it out. The sign belonged to Loren Blake, a local pianist who taught jazz piano with a strong emphasis on chord theory. I explained that I played piano only a little—with my own self-taught technique—and that my main instrument was the vibes. He agreed to take me on as a piano student, with a focus on teaching me songs and jazz styles.

Loren turned out to be a wonderful teacher. He taught me correct fingering technique for the piano as well as the basics of jazz harmony, and also guided me toward records I should look for. (Jazz records were scarce, so I had to look diligently.) His first recommendation was Erroll Garner, then George Shearing; I remember analyzing the harmonies in a number of Shearing's published piano arrangements. It was an excellent learning experience. Later, when I found myself working with Shearing himself, I remembered a lot of his harmonizations from dissecting those piano arrangements.

Through Loren, I began to make contact with other teen-aged jazz musicians around town. Evansville fielded a handful of modestly talented but enthusiastic young players, enough to make up a combo, so we would often get together at each other's houses on Sunday afternoons for jam sessions. Finally, I had some other musicians to play with!

My junior year, the Duke Ellington band played at my high school. I still can hardly believe they came to our little town in southern Indiana for a gig. (Princeton's population in the 1950s was 1726 families.) It was a major event for me—my first live concert by a famous jazz band. Being a member of the high-school band (I played snare drum so that I could go on the football trips), I was invited to help out with the hospitality backstage. The first thing I noticed when they arrived and came off the bus was that they didn't have the appearance of ordinary people. They wore suits, and they seemed so cool; they just *looked* the way I thought jazz musicians should look. Duke had a valet traveling with him who brought in clothing racks loaded with different suits, sport coats, shirts, rows of shoes, etc. As people who saw the Ellington band during that period will recall, Duke repeatedly left the stage during his concerts and changed into one outfit after another, each more outrageous than before. It was wonderful to watch him breeze into the locker room and with a flourish select this or that jacket, shirt, and so on, improvising an ensemble from his colorful wardrobe. Seeing him in action and hearing the band inspired me tremendously. And the music was incredible—the amazing compositions, all the great soloists, the swing feel of the band. My opinion of the jazz life rose considerably that night. I was buzzing for weeks afterward.

Meanwhile, I started playing local gigs in Evansville. Instead of playing with the family, I was now sitting in at clubs, dances, whatever I was offered. I accompanied singers, played for tap dance revues, performed in churches. I wasn't yet sixteen, so my father drove me to the gigs and sat at a table sipping a Coke waiting to drive me home afterward, usually midnight or later. It must have been a great relief for him when I finally was old enough to get my driver's license.

One of my more unusual gigs was playing piano for Joe O'Neil, a retired vaudeville tap dancer who had somehow ended up living in Princeton. Joe had students scattered around small towns in southern Indiana and Illinois. He would pick me up in his old Ford on Saturdays and drive us to whatever town was on the schedule for that week, and I would play piano as his students practiced their tap dance routines. It was kind of fun, actually, because Joe was full of stories about show biz life. By the end of the day, he would have pretty much emptied his pocket flask, and we'd make the woozy drive back to Princeton driving at about half the speed of the morning trip.

Life changed in a big way for me the summer of 1959. I saw an ad in *Down Beat* magazine for something called the Stan Kenton Stage Band Camp. The jazz camp industry has proliferated since then, offering intensive workshops to students around the country, but this was the first-ever such event. Luckily for me, it was taking place at Indiana University, a couple of hours from home.

For the first time I found myself surrounded by a community of musicians who loved jazz. There were kids from all over the U.S. and professional musicians who served as teachers, and we played and talked and listened from dawn to the late hours of the night. I was in heaven. I was assigned to play piano in a band led by saxophonist John LaPorta, a charismatic teacher who had played with Woody Herman, Charles Mingus, and others, and who would later become a friend and colleague when we taught together at Berklee College of Music. One of my favorite musicians, Shelly Manne, was the camp's drum teacher. Four years later, I would record with Shelly, and would also play regularly at the jazz club he established in Los Angeles. (Shelly gave me some of the best advice I ever got: "Listen to the drummer. Let the drummer be in charge of the time feel. Don't try to lead the band when you solo.")

The highlight came at the end of the week when our student band got an invitation to open a concert at the jazz festival held in nearby French Lick, IN. French Lick was home to a famous resort hotel that was then fading, but during this particular summer weekend, it became the site of a major jazz festival, with people attending from Indianapolis, Chicago, Louisville, and other Midwestern cities. Ironically, until that time, there had never been a person of color allowed to stay at the hotel. (This was still a few years before the enactment of civil rights laws, but the times were beginning to change.)

Playing in a student band may seem like an inauspicious start, but the French Lick Jazz Festival was the first of many festivals produced by George Wein where I would perform during my career. Backstage offered a magical scene for a sixteen-year old newcomer. The group headlining that night was the Miles Davis Sextet—simply the most important and innovative jazz band of its time. That same year, they recorded

Kind of Blue, the most iconic of all jazz records. I didn't yet relate much to Miles' music; jazz was still rather new to me. But I thought he had an awesome presence. As he paced around on the grass behind the stage I snapped his photo with my Brownie camera, flashing the bulb in his face, to which he simply replied, sarcastically, "Thanks, kid."

The person who made the most lasting impression on me that night was Wein himself. During the concert, he stood in the wings talking with the performers as they came on and off the stage, and at times took a very direct part in the performance. At one point, singer Dakota Staton was on and her group started the intro to a ballad, but George yelled out, "No, play something up," and the group abruptly shifted into a medium blues. I was amazed at his audacity, but also at his obvious knowledge of what was going on. I couldn't know it at the time, but George would play a major role in my career in the years ahead.

I stayed on for the remaining day of the festival and saw Dizzy Gillespie, Gerry Mulligan, and the writer Leonard Feather present a panel discussion about jazz. These were all people I knew from reading *Down Beat* magazine. The final concert featured pianist Erroll Garner and then the Ellington band—my second chance to see them play in person. I loved every minute of it.

As I made the trip back to band camp, I began to rethink my career plans. In high school I was a straight-A, honor society student, headed for some kind of traditional career, probably in engineering (like my father) or medicine. I already had sent away for brochures from Indiana University School of Medicine and thought that a career in pathology looked interesting. But the week at jazz camp had totally captivated me. By the end of that incredible week, I knew in my heart that I wanted to be a jazz musician.

And although I didn't realize it at the time, that decision

I made in 1959, to get out of Indiana and become part of the jazz world, also determined how I would deal with my feelings of sexual confusion—because being anything but heterosexual was incompatible with a career in jazz.

I was a newcomer to jazz but I already could tell, from reading about the musicians in *Down Beat* and collecting their records, that the scruffy, gritty jazz life was very masculine and hard-edged. Succeeding in jazz meant, most of all, being welcomed into that community of players, and even at sixteen, I knew being different wasn't going to work.

I also met some musicians my own age at that first jazz camp. I made friends with some guys from Toledo, and after that I would occasionally drive eight hours up to northern Ohio for a weekend of jam sessions. One took place at the Bellman's and Waiter's Club, a sort of social club in the black neighborhood. I was a little leery of crashing the scene without an invitation, but the other guys assured me we would be welcome, and we went inside to ask some of the musicians if we could sit in. They looked skeptically at our motley crew of four white high-school students, but they said it would be okay—though they probably didn't expect a vibraphone to appear. It took several trips to the car for me to bring in all the pieces and further delay to get it all assembled, even as the other musicians started playing. When I finally was ready and struck the first note, the crowd erupted into applause before even hearing me play. I guess just seeing me get it assembled warranted a send-off.

I suppose my parents were surprised and concerned when I excitedly told them about my new plans, but to their credit, they never showed it. Maybe it was easier to accept because I was already having some early success. I was getting plenty of chances to play and making enough money to put away some serious savings. In fact, when I was sixteen, my father borrowed two thousand dollars from me so he could bid on a contract to manufacture some kind of specialized lubricant for the U.S. Navy. He paid me back before my departure for college and operated that business for a couple of years to make extra money.

My philosophy was that the future would take care of itself if you took care of business today, and by the time I entered my last year of high school, I had it all mapped out. My plan was to go to music college and then on to New York—and then, if I was lucky, someday I might get to be on a record.

CHAPTER 3

The Local Scene

I began to explore the musician subculture. Evansville actually had one: it wasn't a large city, but there were some decent musicians and an enthusiastic little jazz scene. (This is uniquely true about Indiana in general; a disproportionate number of important jazz musicians have come from Indiana, despite its lack of any major jazz center. These include the innovative trumpeter Freddie Hubbard, the great bebop trombonist J.J. Johnson, and Wes Montgomery—one of the most influential guitarists in history.)

I got my driver's license and promptly bought a new white Volkswagen convertible with money I had saved from gigging. This allowed me to spend more time socializing and checking out the nightlife. My typical Saturday schedule began with a visit to F's Steak House at 6 p.m., right when they opened, for a steak dinner before going on to my gig. (I actually had never eaten steak before. Not that our family was struggling financially; it just wasn't something on the menu at our house.) After work came the after-hours hangouts at the McCurdy Hotel coffee shop, where local musicians gathered after their Saturday night gigs to order breakfast at four in the morning, laughing and swapping anecdotes.

Not all my gigs were in upscale surroundings. Sometimes, I played on a bandstand enclosed in chicken wire, so the crowd couldn't throw anything at the musicians. Just outside the town of Vincennes, I played a "river club," so called because it was along the Wabash River, in a strip of honky-tonk establishments catering to an unsophisticated crowd. It was a weekend gig, so I left my vibes on the bandstand overnight. The next morning, I got a call from the bandleader saying the police had closed the club for some liquor-law violation; the rest of the weekend was cancelled.

I didn't know what to do about my instrument. Since it was a sunny spring day I decided to drive the half-hour to Vincennes to check it out. Sure enough, the place was deserted and there was a big iron bar padlocked across the door. I thought it might take weeks or longer to get my vibes back. I thought I might even lose them entirely in some kind of legal action. I looked around back for another door. There wasn't one, but I saw a window, which I jimmied open to climb inside. The club was dark and gloomy, but I could see the vibes still on the bandstand. I took them apart and carefully tossed each piece out the window until I had it all on the ground, then managed to pack everything into my car and get back on the highway without anyone noticing. The musician's life can be glamorous; sometimes, it's a bit dangerous, too.

I joined the Evansville musician's union, located in a rambling house in a residential neighborhood. The atmosphere was supplied by the older musicians, who hung out there playing cards and telling stories. There were also Saturday-afternoon porn movies provided by a local saxophone player. I started working a steady trio gig at the Pal Steak House, doubling on vibes and piano from nine to one, after which I'd drive home to get a few hours sleep before school the next morning.

Then I decided to take up a daytime trade, tuning pianos. (Like I didn't have enough to do already.) Having perfect pitch, I realized piano tuning should come easy, and after taking a mail-order course, I built up a steady business tuning and repairing pianos. Fortunately, my high school principal was very understanding. I had already completed all but two of the courses required for graduation, so he allowed me to attend school just two hours a day during my senior year. That meant I could tune pianos three or four afternoons a week and work five nights a week at the steakhouse. I didn't have much time for anything else, but I was having a ball. And it felt good, making enough money to be independent.

Not everyone approved of the direction my life was taking, however. Mr. Downey, a neighbor who taught history at the school, lectured me severely about the dangers of drink and moral corruption and advised me to give up my night-crawling schedule. But he was too late; I was already on my way to the jazz life. I can't speak to the topic of moral corruption, but Mr. Downey needn't have worried about the alcohol. I didn't take my first drink until I was in my thirties, although it had nothing to do with his advice. It was because I remembered playing, as a kid, at company parties and similar events where drunk people would try to talk to me after we performed, and they scared me half to death.

Working nights and most afternoons left little time for the typical life of a high school student. I did squeeze in occasional pickup basketball games with friends; this was Indiana, after all, the most basketball-crazy place on earth. And I usually had a girlfriend, although I now realize that from puberty on (like all gay men), I knew I was somehow different. But I was desperate *not* to be different; it was out of the question. I couldn't be "different" and still be Gary Burton, the kid musician that people admired and respected.

Of course, I couldn't totally bury my feelings either. One of my school friends introduced me to sex, and until the end of high school, we would occasionally have sleepovers where we experimented, although we convinced ourselves we were nonetheless straight. He *was* straight, as far as I know, and

I was determined to be, even though I was being pulled in another direction.

As I neared graduation in the spring of 1960, I began to focus on the goals I had set: go to music college, get a degree, and then try my hand in New York. If that plan didn't work out, I could always get a job as a music teacher somewhere. I always have a plan. Life has a way of taking you somewhere else, but I always have a plan, anyway.

I got a sense of the big time when bass trumpeter Cy Touff, a well-known Chicago musician, needed a backup band for some concerts in Illinois and Kentucky. He was opening some shows for comedian Shelley Berman—a huge star at the time, who traveled with his own valet—and I got the call to play in the band. The group included the best that Evansville had to offer, and the gigs went well. I watched everything that went on: how we traveled, the experience of staying in a different hotel each day, the protocols of the backstage scene. My first "tour" lasted just five days, and then I was back home in Princeton, but I had gotten a taste of the musician's life, and I liked it.

That last year playing gigs around Evansville provided what some might call my "big break." Honestly, I've never believed in that concept; I think that it's usually lots of little breaks that happen along the way. But if I ever had a break that led to much bigger things, this was it.

It started with saxophonist Boots Randolph, who was on his way to becoming a major name in pop music. (He had his big hit a few years later, in 1963, with "Yakety Sax," which became a staple of British comedian Benny Hill's television show some years later.) Boots was originally from Paducah, Kentucky, but his wife was from Evansville, so he was based there for a while. I got acquainted with Boots at the Blue Bar, his regular gig in Evansville. Even though I was underage, I would venture into the club for Saturday-afternoon jam sessions. Once you got past his novelty numbers, Boots was actually a good saxophonist. His idol was the classic tenor man Coleman Hawkins, and on a straight-ahead ballad, Boots captured that sound awfully well. And in 1960, Boots did me a big, big favor.

Boots had recently broken into the Nashville studio scene (just a few hours' drive from Evansville), performing on records with Elvis Presley, Connie Francis, and many other pop stars. In Nashville, he'd gotten to know guitarist Hank Garland—probably the most respected of the studio musicians there—who had come up through country music, achieving a reputation as a prodigy guitar player. At the age of sixteen, Garland had a million-selling hit called "Sugarfoot Rag," and by the mid '50s, he had recorded on literally hundreds of country records with most of Nashville's biggest names. Along the way, he also discovered jazz. His heroes were Tal Farlow, Barney Kessel, and Barry Galbraith, three of the best jazz guitarists of the time. Hank worked as hard on his jazz playing as he did at everything else, and now he wanted to try making a jazz record. It took a serious effort on his part to persuade Columbia, his record company, to let him depart country music for jazz, but he eventually won them over. And he was looking for a vibes player.

There weren't any vibists in Nashville, however, so Hank was on the verge of using some other lineup. That's when Boots heard him mention the vibes and recommended me. I was a month away from graduation.

I remember riding down to Nashville in Boots's Cadillac with my vibes piled in the back. I set up my instrument at the recording studio owned by the legendary Nashville producer Owen Bradley and waited for Hank to arrive. He came in with a bass player and a drummer, and we jammed a few tunes. I thought it went well enough, and afterwards, we talked a bit, and I explained my plan to finish high school and go on to Boston for college in the fall. Then Hank blew me away by suggesting I move to Nashville for the summer to play with him at a local club while we prepared to record his jazz album.

VIBRAPHONE OR VIBRAHARP?

As if it weren't challenging enough to play an instrument most people have never heard of, the people who *have* heard of it can't agree on what to call it. When the instrument was first introduced, different manufacturers employed different names. The Deagan Company was probably the first to use "vibraharp," and later, the Musser Company also used that name. (Claire Musser founded his company after leaving his job as plant manager at Deagan. I was told that he left Deagan following the discovery that he was having an affair with Mrs. Deagan.)

A company called Leedy Manufacturing had used "vibraphone" for an earlier and less sophisticated version of the instrument, and for whatever reason, that eventually became the established name. In the 1950s movie *The Benny Goodman Story,* Lionel Hampton referred to his instrument as a vibraharp, and that's what I called it as a kid. But by the time I started my professional career, I was more used to hearing "vibraphone" or simply "vibes." When I called it a vibraharp, people seemed to picture some kind of electric harp rather than a mallet instrument. So, vibraphone it is.

Of course, many people still come up to me and tell me I'm a really good xylophone player.

THE MARIMBA

The concept of a mallet instrument is extremely basic: some version of it was probably among the first musical instruments of early humans. You find a piece of hard wood that, when struck with a stick, makes a musical tone; line up several different-sized pieces of wood, and you've got a crude mallet instrument. In time, someone placed an empty gourd or bowl beneath each wooden bar, providing a resonating chamber that would increase the volume.

Today's marimbas use metal tubes as resonating chambers, and each bar is tuned to a precise pitch by sanding down the underside. But primitive wooden-key instruments have existed for thousands of years and are native to many cultures. The marimba is popular in Mexico and is practically the national instrument of Guatemala, where you commonly find marimba ensembles featuring a half-dozen players (with two or three sharing each instrument). Wooden-key mallet instruments pop up in many African cultures, as well as in Asia; on my first visit to Thailand, I became acquainted with their version of the marimba, the *ranat*. Meanwhile, over the past fifty or sixty years, a classical repertoire has gradually developed for the marimba, performed by a growing number of internationally recognized soloists.

Xylophones and marimbas both use wooden bars, played with rather hard mallets for the xylophone and softer mallets for the marimba. The xylophone's bars are uniformly thick, while the underside of the marimba's bars are sanded down in the middle to about a quarter-inch thickness; this gives the marimba a mellow, woody quality compared to the xylophone's shrill sound. Today's audiences know the xylophone primarily as a staple in cartoon music—heard, for instance, when Tom and Jerry fall down the stairs. But in the 1920s, xylophones were very popular for ragtime and a humorous musical genre known as "novelty music."

The typical mallet for these instruments is a rubber ball glued on the end of a stick, usually made of rattan and thus slightly flexible. Some players prefer dowel rods or plastic sticks, but rattan remains the most common. The rubber balls come in different degrees of hardness and are often wrapped with yarn to soften the attack.

THE VIBRAPHONE

Most musical instruments have been around in some form or other for a couple of hundred years; the vibraphone didn't arrive till the late 1920s, when instrument companies began experimenting with new versions of mallet instruments. The idea was to make a metal xylophone.

The first metal-keyed instrument that we would consider a vibraphone went on sale in 1929. The most intriguing aspect of this instrument was the addition of motor-driven rotating blades in the resonator tubes. By sequentially opening and closing the tubes, these blades create a tremolo effect, which is often erroneously described as vibrato. Technically speaking, "vibrato" describes an up-and-down fluctuation in pitch; "tremolo" occurs when the volume level fluctuates, which is what happens as the blades rotate in the vibraphone's resonators. (I guess the name "tremolophone" didn't exactly roll off the tongue.) The vibes world is divided fifty-fifty about whether to play the instrument with the motor on or off; I belong to the latter group, though at first I did use the motor most of the time. After all, I paid for that motor when I bought the instrument, so I wanted to get my money's worth.

The first vibraphones had bars made of steel. A dampening pad, made of felt and running the length of the instrument, was soon added, connected to a foot pedal that allowed the player to control the ringing of the bars. A few years later, manufacturers determined that an alloy of aluminum and nickel (usually 95 percent aluminum, 5 percent nickel) provided a better material than steel: cheaper, lighter, and readily available in wartime.

Not surprisingly, the first jazz musicians to try the vibes were xylophone players, such as Lionel Hampton and Red Norvo. By the time I started playing in 1949, the instrument was barely twenty years old, and the technical and musical possibilities had just begun to emerge, giving me the rare opportunity to grow up with my instrument. I had the chance to pioneer several technical and musical breakthroughs (such as four-mallet playing) that expanded the vibraphone's possibilities and built my own reputation as well. I consider all this as lucky timing on my part; if not me, someone else would have explored these possibilities in due time.

When I speak to groups of vibraphone students, I usually start by pointing out what makes the vibraphone the easiest of all instruments to learn. I'm not kidding. It takes several years to develop a pleasant tone on a wind or string instrument; same goes for playing in tune. But from the time you strike your first note on vibes, it sounds professional, and it's always in tune. With most instruments, one has to learn some kind of fingering system for, say, the keys on a saxophone or the valves on a trumpet. Pianists must learn to coordinate their ten fingers to play scales and arpeggios without getting all tangled up. By comparison, the vibraphone represents the ultimate in simplicity. All the notes are laid out in front of you, just like a piano keyboard. Using two or even four sticks, one requires only modest skill to execute melodic passages. Most players can manage to play a simple song or two immediately, which is very encouraging to the beginner. One reason that so many vibes players have transferred over from other instruments is that they found vibes so easy to master quickly.

That's the easy part. The hard part is making the instrument sound alive. It lacks the natural phrasing of brass and woodwinds and even string instruments, which more closely copy the human voice. The voice remains the role model for musical phrasing; with mechanical instruments like vibraphone and even piano, the big challenge is to attain "vocal phrasing," something that comes quite naturally to horn players.

You may wonder why more people don't play vibes, given the initial ease of playing. I can think of three reasons. First, a vibraphone is fairly expensive compared to buying an entry-level guitar or trumpet—thousands of dollars instead of a few hundred. Second, it's big and clumsy, so you need a van, and you'd better be prepared to carry around heavy cases wherever you travel. Finally, since the instrument has attained real visibility only in jazz, you almost never see one on television. No rock bands or pop groups feature the vibes, and young musicians are drawn to what they see: guitars, keyboards, drums, saxophones, etc.

Still, the vibraphone has established itself as a legitimate instrument, here to stay, and maybe someday it will gain more popularity outside the jazz world. I've tried to do my part by recording at various times with pop and country artists. But so far, it hasn't spurred that torrential wave of vibraphone popularity I know you've all been expecting.

So, the day after graduation, I loaded the vibes into my Volkswagen and headed south. The first chore was to find a place to live. At seventeen, I was still a minor, so Hank helped me look. This Nashville star, one of the busiest studio musicians in town, spent several days helping me answer ads for apartments. Most of the places I could afford were crummy, but as we drove around checking them out, I discovered that Hank possessed a wealth of country music stories, and he spent the time pointing out spots all over town where he or some other famous musicians used to live or work. (We finally found an apartment near a strip mall, where my next-door neighbor turned out to be Johnny Rivers, an aspiring singer who had a hit record a few years later with the television show theme "Secret Agent Man.")

I soon adopted a daily routine of tagging along with Hank

as he played studio sessions or went to the Grand Old Opry. No one seemed to mind him bringing a visitor along, and in fact, everyone made me feel welcome. I watched traditional country artists like Hank Snow and Cowboy Copas make records. I went to the Opry with Hank and spent an evening backstage arguing with singer Faron Young, "the Hillbilly Heartthrob," over whether steel guitar or violin was more difficult to play. (I thought it was violin, Faron sided with the steel guitar.) I once spent two hours in a back room at Owen Bradley's studio, talking with Phil Everly, the younger of the Everly Brothers, about jazz musicians he had heard in New York. And Hank and I began playing weekends at the Carousel Club.

The Carousel was a famous Nashville nightspot owned by a colorful guy named Jimmy Hyde, who always parked his Cadillac Eldorado convertible in the middle of Printer's Alley, the strip of clubs at the heart of Nashville's nightlife. Because of Hank's popularity, many famous country musicians came in to see our little jazz trio. One was singer Jim Reeves, a regular at the Carousel who liked to give me advice about the music business. He told me that every time he made a record for his label, RCA Records, he also made one for himself and put the tapes away at home; he called it "his insurance" to support his family after he was gone. As it turned out, he died at age forty, when the plane he was piloting crashed in bad weather, and I noticed that for a long time after, new Jim Reeves records kept hitting the market every year. So, I guess his plan worked.

Another Carousel regular was country music legend Chet Atkins, known both for his unique guitar playing and for his many years as a producer for RCA. When I arrived in Nashville in 1960, Chet was head of RCA's Nashville division, and he had brought a number of major talents to the label. One of those, pianist Floyd Cramer, asked me to play on his first album; the hit single from that record, "Last Date," launched Floyd's solo career and was my first appearance on a record that went gold. I only had to play a few easy chords in the background, but I was proud to be on it. (Several times in my career, I have played small roles on top-selling commercial records. It's a strange sensation. After working your tail off to achieve modest success with your own music, you play something of little consequence on someone else's record, and it sells millions. That tends to mess with your head a little.)

As the summer progressed, Hank's little group continued to get noticed. Then came the next break: jazz impresario George Wein passed through Nashville and someone brought him by the Carousel to hear us. He liked what he heard, and that night he invited us, along with some other Nashville musicians, to play a few weeks later at the Newport Jazz Festival in Rhode Island—merely the most important jazz festival in the world.

So, on the July 4th weekend, eight Nashville musicians, including Hank Garland, Chet Atkins, and Floyd Cramer—and me—flew north. Arriving in Newport, we knew something was not quite right; we saw evidence of street violence and heard rumors of trouble. We left our bags at our small bed-and-breakfast and started walking toward the park to catch the last of that evening's concert, but we had only covered a couple of blocks before getting caught between a drunken mob and an advancing police line. Being a bunch of country yokels, we looked so out of place that the police just sent us back to our hotel instead of running us off with the rest of the crowd, and from the safety of our rooms, we heard the sounds of rioting and breaking glass all through the night.

What followed is now part of jazz history. Way too many people had showed up for the festival and, unable to enter the park, had gotten unruly. The state police eventually arrived and fought with this crowd through the night. The riot resulted in much damage to property, the remainder of the festival was called off, and we were stuck in Newport for several days before we could get transportation out of town.

As it turned out, a lot of RCA people were also in Newport, because the company had provided the remote recording facilities for the festival. With so much time to kill, somebody got the idea to move the recording equipment to a large house where the RCA people were staying, to record an afternoon jam session. So, my very first record was an unplanned jazz party of country musicians—titled, appropriately, *After the Riot*. I rarely mention this as my first recording because it was a pretty strange effort—all those country players doing their best to play jazz, although it wasn't their usual thing. I cringe now when listening to it. But without question, the whole experience made for one heck of a weekend.

When we finally got out of Newport, Hank suggested that the two of us stop over in New York for a couple of days. He wanted to visit his friend Barry Galbraith and hit some jazz clubs. Despite the typical New York summer weather, Hank insisted on wearing a dark suit and tie; he said that in New York, he felt like he always had to be dressed in a dark suit to fit in. So, the both of us sweltered in our suits for two days. This was my first visit to New York. We went to Birdland, one of the most famous clubs, and we rode the subway out to Queens to spend an afternoon at Galbraith's house. Hank showed me how people on New York subways folded their newspapers into quarters so as not to take up much room in the crowded cars. I found it all fascinating.

When we got back to Nashville, we resumed our weekends at the Carousel and started planning Hank's record. Hank wanted Joe Morello, Dave Brubeck's drummer, for the record. They had met as youngsters, traveling through New England with a country music show, and Hank was confident that once he figured out how to call him, Joe would agree to do the record. I thought he was dreaming; Morello was a major player and Brubeck's group had a very busy schedule.

Eventually, Hank did reach Joe and talked him into it.

It must have sounded awfully crazy to Joe, flying down to Nashville to record with a country guitarist he hadn't seen in ten years, not to mention the inclusion of an unknown seventeen-year-old vibes player. (I wish I could have overheard that conversation.) But Joe said yes, and he even brought along bassist Joe Benjamin, who had previously played in Brubeck's quartet. Due to segregation, however, Benjamin had to stay in a separate African-American owned hotel.

Hank and I chose pieces from the repertoire we had been playing at the club—some jazz standards and a couple of originals. Our producer was Don Law, a legendary figure in the record business, and we recorded over two evenings at Owen Bradley's studio. Everything came together quite easily. By this time, I had played on several country sessions and had spent the summer watching Hank play on other dates, so I was somewhat familiar with studio routines. I hoped I didn't come off as too inexperienced; in any case, Morello was impressed with my playing. He suggested that I stay in touch when I moved to the East Coast, and he proved to be a tremendous help to me over the next few years.

Hank's record was titled *Jazz Winds from a New Direction*, and the cover photo showed Hank sitting in his MG sports car with his collection of guitars. Through the years, I've heard many comments about this album; in fact, almost every guitar player I have known is a fan of that record. George Benson told me it inspired him to take up the guitar in the first place.

I hadn't paid much attention to country music growing up, and once I discovered jazz, I had become a real "jazz snob" who disdained just about everything else. But my summer in Nashville opened my eyes to a world of truly talented people. Actually, country music has much in common with jazz: both are rhythmically powerful, both feature improvised solos, and in both, the musicians have an enormous respect for instrumental skill and creativity. Granted, country is different from jazz in many ways, but it covers a stylistic range—from traditional and purist to fairly commercial—quite similar to that of jazz.

The best surprise of my Nashville summer came at the very end, when Chet Atkins convinced RCA to offer me my own record contract. Even for Chet, this couldn't have been easy, since the label didn't expect to find a jazz musician in Nashville. What's more, I was only seventeen.

And then, through no intention on my part, I discovered my first lesson about record companies: there's no such thing as a "standard" contract.

I was back home in Princeton, packing for college, when RCA mailed me an offer with lots of legal language. Frankly, neither my father nor I knew what to do with it. I was afraid to sign it without getting some advice, but I didn't know whom to ask. So, I just let it lay there on the kitchen table for a week. Then, out of the blue, another contract arrived from RCA, this one offering more money—plus some special considerations in light of my college plans. Without even trying to bargain, my lack of a response to the first contract had motivated them to increase their offer.

I decided not to wait any longer—though if I had, who knows if I might have gotten an even better deal. But what they offered was already pretty enticing. First, RCA would provide weekly checks to help cover my living expenses as long as I was in college. In the meantime, I would begin making a record per year—with a cash advance for each—and then two records per year after I finished school. It was a wonderful deal, and I took it, fearing it might go away as magically as it had appeared. In today's recording industry, you would never see such a generous contract. Providing an artist's living expenses for several years of college would be unthinkable. Today, things happen at a much faster pace and artists, especially new ones, have to show quick results to remain with a label. (I went on to record twelve albums for RCA over the next eight years.)

By September of 1960, not yet old enough to vote, I had accomplished the third of my three goals from a year earlier. I had not only been on a record, I had been on several—and now I even had my own contract with a major label! Of course, I still hadn't tackled the first two goals: going to school and getting a degree. I knew I had a lot to learn; I knew I'd had an amazing run of luck, something I couldn't assume would always be the case. I needed to get answers to lots of questions, musical and otherwise, along with a lot more experience. I packed up my newest car—a Triumph TR-3 I'd bought my last week in Nashville—and with a small trailer attached to carry the vibes, departed for Boston.

CHAPTER 4

College Bound

I drove into Boston during the Friday evening rush hour. I had no idea how to find Newbury Street, where the Berklee School of Music was located. In addition, this was my first encounter with big city driving. But with a helping of beginner's luck, I somehow ended up at the right address.

At first glance, Berklee wasn't very impressive, and even less so after a prolonged look. It was much smaller than I expected; the entire college occupied a single brownstone. I had only seen two other colleges, each with a large sprawling campus: Indiana University in Bloomington, where I had gone to jazz camp, and North Texas State College in Denton, which my father and I had visited because it had the only other college jazz program in the country (besides Berklee). But Denton, with the occasional tumbleweed rolling down the street, was even more forlorn than Bloomington. So I chose Berklee, sight unseen, mostly out of confidence that a large city held the best opportunities. I met up with my jazz-camp friends from Toledo, and we found an apartment down the block from the school. The rent was $9 a week for each of us.

Boston was somewhat quaint in 1960. The Back Bay area was still essentially residential, and Newbury Street—which is now the most upscale shopping area in town—consisted mostly of rooming houses. In them lived a hundred or so

Berklee students, who practiced and had jam sessions at all hours. I was in heaven again: it was like jazz camp, only going on year-round.

Whatever Berklee lacked in appearances, it made up for in substance. Then as now, the school hired first-rate teachers, and the small student body included wonderful musicians, many of whom went on to successful careers as players and educators. And it was all about the music—every day, as much as I could find time for. I soon realized that, being mostly self-taught, I suffered from a music-information shortage. While I could play plenty of things on my instrument, I usually couldn't explain what I was doing. But Berklee's faculty got me caught up in short order, teaching me counterpoint, composition, harmony, arranging, the fundamentals of other instruments, and so on. I was in three different rehearsal bands, so I rarely lacked an opportunity to play.

I was disappointed at first to learn that Berklee had no vibes instructor. (The drum teacher, Alan Dawson, had only recently gotten a set of vibes himself and had just started to play.) I had to choose either piano or drums as my primary instrument, though I could play vibes in the various ensembles. For one year, I took both piano *and* drum lessons, but soon realized I had little interest in drums. From then on, I studied piano exclusively, which proved immensely helpful to my vibraphone playing.

I studied jazz piano but also gained a great deal from a classical piano teacher, Alfred Lee. Just as I had earlier opened my ears to country music, I now found classical music to be a new source of inspiration. Alfred also taught me ear training and sight-reading. Because I had perfect pitch, I could easily play back or write down anything I heard, but he gave me exercises that raised my skills to another level. Thanks to him, I became an excellent sight-reader, which has served me well in my career.

My favorite teacher was trumpeter Herb Pomeroy, a Boston legend and a hero at Berklee for more than forty years. I studied improvisation with Herb and also played in the ensemble he directed. But just as important, I got to work regularly with him at "The Stables," the club he operated in partnership with some other local musicians. (Its actual name was the Jazz Workshop, but since it occupied the basement room of a bar called The Stables, that's what everyone called it.) Herb played there six nights a week. The audience comprised mostly music students and serious jazz fans, especially the two nights a week when Herb led his big band. A lot of innovative writing and playing took place at The Stables, and I was fortunate to enjoy it on a regular basis, both as a listener and as a performer.

The Stables had a relaxed and almost comical air about it, thanks to the fact that musicians ran the place. There was none of the tension that often exists between club owners and musicians. The occasional intrusion of a drunk from the upstairs bar contributed to the atmosphere. To get to the jazz club downstairs, customers had to walk through the bar and down a steep ramp to the swinging doors marking the club entrance. Unfortunately, the men's room was halfway down that same ramp. About once a week, some lush would start down the ramp, find himself unable to negotiate the turn into the men's room, and hurtle to the bottom, crashing through the double doors and landing in the first row of seats. It happened so frequently that after a while, the musicians barely noticed the commotion.

Those first months at Berklee were so exciting that I practically forgot everything else. I had not even bothered to call or write home to let my folks know I was okay. They didn't want to be interfering parents, so they waited a couple of months before finally telephoning the college—just to ask if I was still there! I was called in to the office and told that I ought to phone home occasionally. I felt so guilty that I started calling every week.

One night during that first winter, I got a call to rush down to Storyville, the jazz club in Boston owned by George Wein. Singer Anita O'Day was opening that night, but her band had missed their plane, and she needed a trio to back her up. I met two other students at the club, and we rehearsed with her for a couple of hours to learn her music. Anita's road manager promised us $50 each and told us to get some dinner and be back in time for the first set. We returned to discover that her musicians had managed to arrive and we wouldn't be needed after all.

The three of us sat through Anita's first set, waiting for the road manager to pay us. We didn't know if we would get the full amount or only part of it, but we had spent the afternoon rehearsing and were ready to play, so we assumed we would get *something*. Finally, the manager came over to offer us complimentary copies of Anita's latest album—and that was it! No fifty bucks, not even fifty cents. I was furious but too shy to protest. We left the club and tossed the records into the first trash barrel we saw.

Years later, while reading Anita's autobiography, I learned that during those years she was a hardcore heroin junkie, which explains her stinginess. (For a junkie, it's mandatory to hang on to every dollar for the next score.) I also learned something else about her that explains why I never warmed to her singing.

There are two "instruments" one can play without any knowledge of music, using just intuition: drums and vocals. Any other instrument requires some knowledge of music fundamentals—such as chords, scales, how harmonies move— and most often, learning to read music. But there are quite a few drummers and singers that have had successful careers in the jazz field (and in pop and rock, certainly) simply performing "by ear," without benefit of actually knowing these fundamentals.

Anita was one of the "ear" vocalists, and finding this

out helped me understand my lack of interest in her style. Although renowned for her vocal improvising (also called "scat singing"), Anita didn't know what was happening in the underlying compositions, and to me her choice of notes and phrases sounded like guesswork—as opposed to the great vocal scat singing of, say, Ella Fitzgerald or Sarah Vaughan, who knew the structure of the music inside out.

Also that winter, I organized my first record session for RCA in New York. At a loss for which musicians to choose, I started by calling the only New York musicians I knew: Joe Morello and Joe Benjamin (who had played drums and bass on the Hank Garland record). I asked Herb Pomeroy to come down from Boston, and with Herb's assistance I added two more New Yorkers, pianist Steve Kuhn and guitarist Jim Hall. In retrospect, it was an odd assortment of players, in terms of their different styles, but they were all excellent musicians.

We gathered to record about a dozen tunes at RCA's 23rd Street Studio in January, 1961, just one week before my eighteenth birthday. Things went wrong from the start. A major blizzard on the first day caused Morello, coming by car from New Jersey, to arrive four hours late. When he finally got there, he didn't have any drums with him, so we got almost nothing done. The next day, Benjamin was the problem. I was going to record several familiar standards but hadn't written out individual parts for the musicians. I assumed they would already know the tunes or could use a standard lead sheet (a page showing the melody and chords). But Benjamin refused to play anything without a written bass part, so I had to waste valuable time scribbling bass lines for each song. When we finally did start recording, we all tried our best, but it just never came together. I was so disappointed that I asked the company to shelve it, and I've always been glad this was not the first record released under my name.

In the next few months, as I got more entrenched at

Berklee, I began playing with an assortment of student groups that worked at clubs around town. At one of the regular places, Connelly's—a dingy bar in the mostly black section called Roxbury—I heard drummer Roy Haynes' New York band for the first time. Roy exemplified cool; when he performed at the club, he parked his yellow convertible by the front door. He was terrific, and if you had told me I would be playing with him just a few years later, I'd have said you were crazy.

Connelly's often brought in solo acts and hired a local rhythm section to accompany them, and one weekend, I got a call to play with trombonist Matthew Gee. Gee wasn't that big a name in jazz, but he had worked in the Ellington band for a while, and trading on that, he had gotten a booking at Connelly's.

Our local group (vibes, bass, and drums) arrived and set up, but when Gee got there, I could see we were in for a rough night; he was already pretty drunk before playing a note. I had worried about what tunes he would call. Would I know enough songs for him? Would he want to play standards or originals? As it turned out, my concerns were misplaced.

To start the first set, Gee called for a "blues in F"—basic and easy. Then he suggested "Poor Butterfly," a song so simple that, although I barely knew it, we played it without a hitch. Curiously, Gee followed this with another blues in F; after that, he paused a bit and then just launched into "Poor Butterfly" again. I found this a little bizarre, but we were just getting started. For the rest of the night, he went back and forth between those same two songs, the blues in F and "Poor Butterfly," over and over.

Normally, a set would run no longer than maybe 45 or 50 minutes. After an hour and a half, as it became clear that Gee would continue playing these two songs indefinitely, the club owner came up and stopped us. I thought Gee might try something different when we began the second set, but it was right back to "blues in F" and "Poor Butterfly." As the evening wore on, he got more and more wasted until he was having trouble just standing. For my part, I was fascinated by the audience reaction to this spectacle. I was especially surprised that no one seemed to notice we were repeating the same two songs all night. I didn't know what to make of that.

Fortunately, the crowd had thinned out by the end of the second set, when Gee finally fell completely apart. Extending his arm, he lost his grip on the trombone slide, which went sailing into the audience. Gee stared at what was now half a trombone as if he had never seen such a thing, and then began to weave precariously. As he fell, he reached out to grab the vibraphone for support, managing to take my entire instrument with him into the front row of chairs.

I looked down on a tangle of resonator tubes, trombone parts, wooden folding chairs, and two customers buried in the pileup. No one was hurt and the vibes survived without major damage, but the trombone was totaled. This didn't really matter, however, because the club owner came up to announce that we were finished for the night—and for the remainder of the weekend as well.

Despite a few of these less-than-inspiring experiences, my first year in Boston was incredibly productive. Thanks to Berklee and the Boston music scene, I was learning music as fast as I could take it in. And after I got established around Boston, I started getting occasional calls to work at a couple of local recording studios, for $10 per session. Usually these involved advertising jingles for local businesses, or background music for local singers. One time, a radio station hired me to play sound effects simulating different atmospheric conditions for the weather reports. But one session sticks out as an object lesson in jazz economics.

I got a call early one Sunday morning to come "right over" to the studio for a session. It was odd for a session to be scheduled early on a Sunday, and even odder to get the call only minutes in advance. In addition, this particular studio was a nuisance: it was situated up two flights of stairs, and I had to make several trips to transport my vibraphone. But $10 was a week's rent, so I loaded up the vibes and went over.

The session had already begun, and I noticed immediately that it was some kind of jazz project instead of the usual jingle session. Through the control-room window I could see my teacher Alan Dawson, the best drummer in town, along with a few other musicians I didn't recognize. I watched for a while as I caught my breath from the stair-climbing, and I began to notice that it sounded exceptionally good. They were playing in a less familiar key, one not so common for jazz groups of the day, which the tenor saxophonist negotiated with impressive fluency. When the tune ended, I went in to set up the vibes, and that's when I recognized the tenor player as Paul Gonsalves, the star sax soloist with Duke Ellington's band!

I was amazed. Here was a jazz legend, recording with local players early on a Sunday morning, in a little jingle studio in Boston. We played about a half-dozen songs that morning. I never got a copy of it; I don't even know if it was ever released.

This was the first (but hardly the last) time I would witness a major musician taking an unimportant, low-paying gig to make some needed cash. It always saddens me to think of how often it happens—how often it *has* to happen. In this case, the Ellington band had played a concert in town the previous night, and someone had approached Gonsalves with an offer to stay over and record the next morning, probably for a very modest payment. He had no idea which other musicians would take part or what would happen to the recording after they finished; it was just some extra spending money.

Sometimes, we play because we really want to play; sometimes we play as a favor for another musician; and sometimes, it's just because we need the money. Despite countless hours of practice and concentration to elevate our art, we all too often have to put that aside because of circumstances.

Jazz has always occupied a curious middle ground between high art—the world of classical music, museums, and theater—and popular culture, which appeals to the masses. Classical music, which tastemakers hold in very high esteem, benefits from considerable financial subsidies; pop music often fails to achieve artistic respect but makes up for that with greater commercial success. Jazz musicians live somewhere in the middle. We survive with fewer subsidies than classical music and less commercial success than pop stars. Particularly in the earlier days of jazz, even the best-known jazz stars often lived rather modestly. The situation had improved quite a lot by the 1970s and '80s. But for many jazz musicians, life remains a daily struggle between what they believe in and what they must do to survive.

STEVE MARCUS

One of my best friends during my Berklee years was tenor saxophonist Steve Marcus, who would later play with Stan Kenton, Woody Herman, and Buddy Rich. Steve hailed from New Jersey and came to Boston to attend Berklee, but never actually got in. He couldn't pass the entry requirements, one of which was being able to read music. Despite attempts by myself and others to help him, he had a mental block about it, and played entirely by ear. None of this really slowed him down, though. He found a place to live near the school, made friends with the more talented students, and then played with them in jam sessions day after day, getting some benefit of their Berklee experience by osmosis.

Steve was truly eccentric in a lot of ways; I found him delightful. He always dressed like the typical slob, in old ragged clothes and worn-out boots. But one day when I was at his apartment listening to records, we got into a discussion about clothes, at which point Steve pulled out a couple of drawers and displayed a haberdashery's worth of never-worn dress shirts, ties, and sweaters. Then he opened a closet full of suits, a houndstooth sports coat, and several pairs of elegant leather shoes—none of them ever worn, all still in their protective plastic bags. I was incredulous. What on earth was going on?

He explained that until he had achieved enough success and fame to lead his own band on real jazz gigs, he didn't deserve to wear these nice clothes. But he was ready for whenever that moment arrived.

And that moment did arrive a year or so later, when Herb Pomeroy asked Steve to put a group together for a night at The Stables. Those of us who had only seen him dressed in his moth-eaten sweater were stunned at the sight of the new Marcus. Living out his fantasy, he had arrived an hour early to stand in front of the club, posing as casually as he could, in his finery, smoking a cigarette—just a typical jazz musician waiting for his gig to start. That night, we dubbed him the Count of Marcus, and the nickname stayed with him: when he formed a jazz-rock band in the late '60s, he called it Count's Rock Band.

Our friendship continued when Steve and I both moved to New York in 1962. He had a regular weekend gig at a Jewish country club in Brooklyn, and as the holidays approached, he asked my advice about finding a piano player for New Year's Eve. This was a problem, because every musician who can carry a tune gets booked early for New Year's Eve. I suggested some names to call, but no one was available. Then, we got the idea that it might be a hoot if *I* came and played piano. (By then I was touring with Stan Getz, but we were off during the holidays.) Steve told me the leader was a Gary Burton fan; I told him I couldn't deal with having this guy go on about playing with me for a local New Year's club date. So, we came up with a cover story. I would be "Eddie Grayson," a friend of Steve's from Boston who just happened to be in town for the holidays.

The evening was one of those gigs from an alternate universe (as New Years' gigs often are). It started with a cocktail hour by the indoor pool, then moved into the main room as we played background music for dining; so far, so good. But these people had paid for a whole package of dinner, booze, and a floorshow, and that's where things got sketchy. The floorshow was a dance troupe, and they were late—*really* late. We were forced to keep playing set after set as the crowd became restive and then belligerent. Midnight came and went—we did play "Auld Lang Syne"—and then it was 1 A.M., and still no dancers. By now, several members of the audience, who had paid hundreds of dollars for tickets, were in open rebellion, demanding their money back and threatening to break the furniture.

Finally around 1:30, word came that the dancers had arrived—a Harlem dance troupe called "Mama Lou Parker's Sepia Frolics" (no kidding). They stumbled off the bus; it was their third (and last) show of the night, and the girls were clearly exhausted. They asked us to play for them and requested "Night Train"—a bump-and-grind sort of blues that had been a hit in the '50s—which we dutifully repeated for about an hour, while the sweaty dancers in their skimpy outfits did their kicks and shimmies. At about 3 A.M., things wound down. The ladies boarded their bus, and we got paid and headed back through the tunnel to Manhattan.

Steve informed me a few days later that the bandleader was very pleased with my work and wondered if I could stick around and work a few more weekends. I instructed Steve to say that unfortunately, Eddie Grayson had already gone back to Boston. Steve soon got the call to join Stan Kenton, his long awaited chance to work with a name band. He had almost everything he needed, from the clothes to the horn, and he was a first-rate soloist. But he still hadn't gotten used to reading music. Later, I asked him how he had managed that. He said he got through the first gigs by just pretending to play during the sax ensemble sections and only playing for real when he was featured; apparently, Kenton didn't notice the missing sax part. After a few weeks of this, Steve gradually learned his parts by ear and could finally play the entire set.

One of my favorite Count Marcus stories concerns his first travel day with the Kenton band. The departure call was an early one, 6 A.M., and the bus was out front of their Chicago hotel with the luggage doors open, waiting for the musicians to stagger down to the lobby. Steve was so excited that he arrived a half-hour early. He had his toiletries in their usual small leather bag, which he was kind of swinging around as he excitedly paced back and forth in front of the bus, daydreaming about the thrill of joining the famous Kenton band, when suddenly he felt a *thunk!* and saw Kenton lying on the ground. Kenton had been stowing his suitcase in the luggage compartment, and just as he was standing up, Steve had socked him with his toiletries bag, knocking him out. (Kenton's collapse was no doubt exacerbated by his regular morning hangover; he never had a drink before a performance, but as soon as the gig was over, he would get hammered as fast as possible.) Steve didn't know what to do; on his first day, he had just knocked his famous bandleader unconscious. He quickly jumped on the bus and sat in the back, pretending he had been there all along, and watched from the window as Kenton gradually sat up, bewildered, and looked around. Steve said he appeared to think he'd hit his head on the door of the luggage bin and never knew he'd been slammed by his new recruit.

Steve finally found his true home in Buddy Rich's band. He became Buddy's confidant, court jester, and right-hand man, as well as the band's tenor soloist. I saw Steve years later, when Buddy was nearly seventy, and asked what he thought he'd do when Buddy retired or was no longer around. Steve's flip reply was that Buddy would never quit and would live forever. But within the year, Buddy had suffered a stroke and died. Steve retreated to his home in New Hope, PA. He made a few tries at starting a band and even talked of reviving Buddy's band for some touring, but his career was never really that active again. The Count of Marcus died of a heart attack in 2005, a week after his sixty-sixth birthday. I regretted his passing, and also the fact that he hadn't found a fulfilling musical outlet after the halcyon years with Buddy.

CHAPTER 5

New Adventure

During my summer off from school in 1961, I had two records to make in New York: one for myself and one for Joe Morello. RCA had contracted Joe to lead his own project, to be titled *It's About Time*, and he asked me to play on it. The other featured soloist was saxophonist Phil Woods, a childhood friend of Joe's and one of my idols. Phil would arrange half the songs for a quintet, and the widely respected composer/arranger Manny Albam would write big-band charts for the others.

At the first rehearsal, I quickly sensed Phil's lack of enthusiasm about an unknown teenager being included in the project. He had written some quite challenging music, which I didn't see till the first rehearsal. I think he half expected I'd be unable to keep up, and he could then get Joe to drop me from the lineup. Fortunately for me, the first day, we concentrated on Joe's drum parts. We had barely begun rehearsing the whole quintet before our time was up for the day, so I managed to escape without having to play more than a few notes.

I went back to my hotel room and spent five or six hours frantically practicing my parts, pounding my mallets on the bed as I imagined the vibes laid out in front of me. The next day, I played everything almost perfectly the first time through. Phil gave me a big smile, and in the years that followed, he played on several of my own records. Along with a few other musicians (notably Bob Brookmeyer and Jim Hall), Phil was particularly encouraging when I moved to New York the following year.

Joe himself was incredibly supportive when I first came on the scene—introducing me to key people and playing on my first records—and also a lot of fun to hang out with. At the time, he still had one of the most high-profile jobs in jazz, touring with Dave Brubeck. But when Brubeck broke up his band several years later, I found myself in a position to return Joe's kindness by offering advice and support to *him*.

He was thinking of starting a group of his own, and since by then, I had successfully launched my own band, Joe asked me several times about the process I went through. I encouraged him by saying that his visibility in Brubeck's group should make it fairly easy to succeed on his own. But I also cautioned him that it would mean working a year or two for modest fees, probably not making much profit, and taking whatever jobs he could get, until the group got fully established. (It seems to go that way for almost everyone who starts a band.) Joe wasn't comfortable with the idea of working at a loss, though, and while he tried a few gigs with some local players around New York, he never actually committed himself to starting a full-time band. He just couldn't pull the trigger. I have little doubt he would have ultimately succeeded with a band of his own. Then again, not everybody is cut out to be a leader.

Since my attempt at leading my own record date the previous winter had gone so dismally, I was taking no chances with my next shot. I kept it simple by organizing a trio record with Morello on drums and bassist Gene Cherico. We recorded at Webster Hall, an old ballroom on 11th Street that RCA regularly used as a studio because of its excellent acoustics. (Today, it survives as a popular dance club, its history as a recording venue long forgotten.) The album, titled *New Vibe Man in Town*, came out a few months later, in the fall of '61.

In those days, artists didn't have much say in the production of their records, so I didn't get to choose the title or, for that matter, the corny cover photo. It features a hired model walking along a New York street, a string of vibraphone bars hanging over his shoulder, his face turned away from the camera (allowing record buyers to assume I was the guy in the photo). But in spite of the cover, I was pleased with how the music turned out, and thrilled to have finally released my debut recording as a leader.

One more record date in 1961—one that did *not* take place—would have reunited me with my Nashville benefactor Hank Garland.

I had stayed in touch with Hank during my first year at college, and we even got together midyear to play at a record-industry convention in Washington, D.C. Hank started planning a second studio session for us that summer, but we never got the chance. What happened next was something out of a soap opera—or, more appropriately, a country-music lyric. I heard the details from Boots Randolph later that year.

Hank discovered that his wife, who was ten years older, had started seeing other men. At one point, he even hired a detective, and learned that she had also had a previous husband—whom she had never divorced! In the midst of this turmoil, he came home one day to find that she had run off to a motel with a lover. Hank jumped into their old station wagon and headed off to find her.

Hank was well-known as a pretty wild driver in the best of circumstances, often getting pulled over by the Nashville police (though they usually let him off once they found out he was a country music star). So, we can assume that in his fevered state of mind, he was driving even faster and more recklessly than usual when a wheel came off the old car, and it went careening into a bridge. Hank suffered massive injuries and lay in a coma for a couple of weeks.

He partially recovered over time, but because of his brain injuries, he could never resume his career. In the first year after the accident, his musician friends concocted a plan to help cover his medical bills. (Like many musicians, Hank had no insurance.) Normally, studio musicians fill out a W-4 form at the end of each recording session and then receive a check a couple of weeks later. To help Hank, about once a week, each of his Nashville buddies would sign a W-4 with Hank's name, and that check would go to Hank's family. Eventually, Hank moved with his wife and two daughters to Wisconsin to live near her family. Coincidentally, she herself died in a late-night single-car accident sometime later. After that, Hank lived quietly in Florida with his parents and other relatives till his death in 2004, always a legend to guitarists and fans.

I consider Hank my first real mentor. He was generous with his time and freely offered his knowledge of music and the music business, and he opened a number of doors for me. Because of all that, I found it hard to stay in touch with him after the accident. I was extremely conflicted by the knowledge that he was still alive but not really the same person with whom I had formed such a bond.

About ten years later, at the request of his family, I spoke to Hank on the telephone—an incredibly painful experience. Hank spoke about the record we had made as if it had been last week, and he grew emotional and agitated as we talked. He told me, "I had a conversation with Hank Williams yesterday, and we talked about a lot of things—and he's been dead for twenty years!" He couldn't keep the passage of time clear in his mind, even though he seemed aware of it. All these years later, I still miss the Hank Garland I knew that long ago summer in Nashville. Somehow, the earliest experiences in one's music career leave the most vivid memories.

Those memories contrast sharply with *Crazy,* a movie version of Hank's life story. I managed to catch a screening in

2008, and I was dismayed by the factual inaccuracies. The film distorted (or simply lied about) practically everything I had witnessed during the time I knew Hank. Why the filmmakers needed to change the facts so drastically is anyone's guess; the real story would have easily sufficed. In any case, Hank's biopic was poorly received and never made it into movie theaters, though you can get it as a DVD rental.

Still, I was flattered that the movie did include a segment about the historic recording sessions I made with Hank. They even found a vibes player in Los Angeles to play me. (And how many of us get to see an actor portray himself in a movie?)

When I returned for my second year at Berklee, I started working a regular trio gig near Suffolk Downs Racetrack in East Boston. (I mostly played piano, using the vibes only occasionally. Until I moved to New York, I worked more often as a pianist.) The club was the 1233 Lounge, run by a nefarious character named Rocky, and its operation was something of a mystery, since it never drew much of a crowd except for a handful of Rocky's friends. We eventually realized it was actually a front to launder money from the racetrack across the street.

But Rocky loved our music, and although the club had few customers, he kept us on for a whole year. He hired singers to come up from New York for weekends, requiring us to learn new music each week. We backed the Italian novelty-tune singer Lou Monte, and fading popular stars like the Ink Spots. Sometimes, we played for sexy female singers who looked like Playboy bunnies but had less than impressive musical skills. Week after week, it provided just the kind of experience I needed: rehearsing, reading new music, adjusting to new styles, and working with lots of different people. And I was getting paid for it, too.

That year, I placed in a couple of magazine polls. I finished second among vibists in the *Down Beat* "Talent Deserving Wider Recognition" poll; I showed up in the *Playboy* Jazz Poll, too. Rocky thought that was terrific and had a sign printed with my picture to put in the window.

Meanwhile, I had begun to play occasional jazz dates around Boston with a group of Berklee students—a quartet featuring trombone, vibes, bass, and drums—which surprisingly received an invitation to perform at a jazz festival in Uruguay during the winter break. The Uruguayan Jazz Society wanted to bring in a band from the States, but figured they could only afford a student group. So, they contacted the famed Berklee School of Music, and they in turn asked if I wanted to take the gig. Since I had already made a record—which had even gotten a review in *Down Beat*—the Uruguayans were thrilled to have us.

We were excited to go. None of us had ever traveled outside the country, let alone to the bottom of South America, and the trip was scheduled to last a full month. And while January meant cold and snow in Boston, it was summer in the southern hemisphere. We anticipated a real adventure. We were not disappointed.

We flew first to Miami to connect with a flight on Ini Airlines, an Argentine carrier. The aircraft was an old DC-6, a pre-jet propeller plane, and the flight was completely full; we had to leave the bass and vibes behind for the next day's flight, because they would have overloaded the plane. There were no other North Americans on board. Not even the flight attendants spoke English.

The flight required several stops for refueling and took twenty-four hours to reach Buenos Aires, and the passengers spent the first few hours partying hard—some more than others. At one point, I stood up in the aisle to stretch, and an elderly gentleman, who had been drinking heavily, tried to pass me and tripped over my foot, falling flat on his face; he didn't even put his hands out to break his fall. Then, he just lay motionless in the aisle. Amazingly, no one had noticed:

people were sitting nearby reading papers or dozing, but no one saw him on the floor. I thought he would start to get up any minute, but he didn't.

My first impulse was to try to tell someone about it, until I realized no one spoke English. Besides, I had no idea what would happen. I had read a travel book warning of legal hassles in Latin American countries, and I was afraid of where this might lead, so I just sat down again. As the minutes slowly passed, I glanced every now and then to see if he was still there. Then, I started to imagine myself explaining to the authorities how I had accidentally killed this guy. After a while, another passenger finally noticed him on the floor and hailed the stewardess. She brought out an oxygen tank and tried to revive him, but nothing seemed to help. I now began picturing my next few months in an Argentine jail.

But the old guy finally did come around, and spent the rest of the trip hooked up to the oxygen with cold compresses on his head. I was feeling kind of shaky myself by the time we finally arrived in Buenos Aires—and I still had no idea of the surprises that lay ahead.

The next night, we traveled from Buenos Aires by river-boat across the thirty-mile width of the Rio de la Plata to Montevideo, the capital of Uruguay. The boat was an aged paddle-wheeler that took twelve hours to make the crossing, churning all night through choppy water. The rough sailing made the communal sleeping quarters below deck too scary to contemplate, so we spent the night hanging out with the ship's crew on deck, sampling maté, the local tea.

In Montevideo, we got into the leisurely pace of the South American summer. We stayed in a small hotel and ate at a local businessmen's club that donated our meals. Most afternoons, we rented bicycles and rode to the beach. The Uruguayan Jazz Society had scheduled concerts for us about once a week in Montevideo and Punta del Este, a resort area to the east.

Between gigs, we played jam sessions at the jazz society's headquarters. We had to use a borrowed bass, since the bass and vibes we'd left behind in Miami had still not shown up. I played mostly piano until the organizers managed to locate an ancient vibraphone.

Our concerts featured several South American jazz groups, too, including one from Brazil led by a young pianist, Sérgio Mendes. His band had just started to promote a new Brazilian music called *bossa nova*. A few years later, they adopted the name Brazil '66, and Sérgio became a major star in the United States, as bossa nova captured the attention of American jazz artists and audiences. (By then, the bossa nova had played an important part in my career as well.)

The concerts were going nicely for us, but not so great for the organizers. Previous festivals had drawn well, but in 1961, because of political unrest and other reasons, attendance was way down. As we got to the end of our stay, I started worrying about the finances. I was owed nearly a thousand dollars for expenses I had covered with my own money, and we still hadn't seen the plane tickets for the trip home. Then, after several days of stalling, the man in charge simply left town, stranding us without explanation.

Some of the people we'd met in Montevideo decided they had to at least get us back to Buenos Aires, if only to avoid indefinite responsibility for our welfare. So, they chipped in and flew us back to Buenos Aires, where I attempted to get us on the first Ini Airlines flight back to the States. By this time, I was running low on cash, so we checked into the cheapest hotel we could find, which was basically a brothel; we were the only guests with luggage. Surprised to have actual tourists staying there, the hotel offered a special rate: instead of the usual $2 a night for a double room, we paid just $1.50. We found a restaurant nearby where we could get a steak dinner for a dollar each, and we allotted our remaining cash to see us through the rest of our trip.

Now, we just needed to find out how long that would be. I called Ini every day, only to be told that the plane was "under repair." I eventually learned that the entire airline consisted of only two planes—the DC-6 we'd already flown on and an even smaller DC-4—and that both planes were, indeed, getting repaired.

The delay dragged on for almost a week, so we cut back our expenditures even further. We started sitting in at local clubs and meeting local musicians, who proved wonderfully hospitable, bringing us to their homes for dinners and showing us Buenos Aires during the day. Despite our worries about getting home, we were having the time of our lives. But I still spent part of each day searching for the missing vibes and bass.

At last, Ini informed us that we could leave two days later— and that's when I finally located the vibes. A local musician, who had been helping me try to track down my instrument, called to tell me that the cases were being held in a customs building in downtown Buenos Aires—where I learned it would take about a month to get them cleared for release. (When I returned home, I did something I would consider foolhardy now: I sent $300 to that guy, an almost total stranger, to get my instrument out of customs and freight it back to me in Boston. And this kindhearted soul went through all the hassles this must have entailed; my instrument arrived in Boston about six weeks later.)

Then, after fighting our way through the crowd at the airport to check in for our flight, we saw the bass standing in a corner near the counter! It had been there the whole month! The staff said they were wondering who it belonged to. I must have called them a half-dozen times asking about it, but no one ever mentioned it was right there—even though they probably walked past it each day.

This time, we got to take the bass with us on the flight, despite the fact that we were on the airline's smaller plane, the

DC-4. The first leg of the trip required flying over the Andes Mountains, so everyone had to wear oxygen masks. (Only about half of them were working, but no one passed out.) Since the plane was slower, this trip took even longer than the flight down—thirty hours to get to Miami, with four fueling stops along the way. The plane had only one menu item, a chicken-and-green-bean box meal, and no facility for heating it, so they served it cold, every four hours, like clockwork.

When we arrived in Miami, we discovered that we'd have to wait seven hours for the next available flight to Boston. We were down to only a few dollars by this time, and we needed to save some cash for cab fare once we got to Boston. We had just enough to each order a piece of pie in the airport restaurant. When I finally paid the taxi on Newbury Street early the next morning, I had 25 cents left—a fitting conclusion to our amazing South American adventure.

A few months after we got home, I saw in the news that the old paddle-wheeler we'd taken across the Rio de la Plata had gone down in a storm, drowning all on board. We had made it out just in time.

I returned to my routine of playing the 1233 Lounge most nights and sitting in with Herb Pomeroy at The Stables when I could. It was also around this time that I began to notice something new in my improvising. Maybe once a night, as I was soloing on some familiar song, I would play a brief melodic phrase or two that I hadn't seen coming. This was momentarily disorienting, like hitting a patch of ice on the highway. I would get a chill down my back and my heart would race, as I played something I'd never played before—and hadn't even consciously conceived before my hands just took over on their own. When this first happened, I thought maybe I was just imagining it. But as it happened more and more, I tried to analyze it, and what I discovered remains one of my biggest breakthroughs—as a musician, but especially as an improviser.

In considering this phenomenon, I had two realizations: whatever I played in that spontaneous state was very different from my usual playing, and these moments of music were the best I played the whole night. I made it my goal to trust this new experience whenever it occurred and to see if I could let it continue, instead of feeling the need to jump back in and retake control. I was just beginning to understand the role of the unconscious mind in playing music.

From then on, I gained increasing respect for the capabilities of my "inner player." I embarked on a lifetime effort to build rapport with my intuitions, my instincts, and my unconscious mind. While I have learned a tremendous amount from reading, watching, and listening to others—as well as from the sheer quantity of my experiences over the decades—I think the most important things I have learned have come from within myself.

PART II.
APPRENTICESHIP

CHAPTER 6

"Autumn in New York"

I had just turned nineteen when Berklee's spring semester started in 1962, and even though I had not quite completed my college education, I was beginning to feel restless at school. Yes, I was still learning a lot, and yes, I had a comfortable niche in Boston's bustling music scene, which included working steadily at the 1233 Lounge and playing good jazz gigs fairly often. But I grew increasingly anxious to try my hand in New York, the Jazz Mecca. I resolved to spend the summer making my move. I figured, if I couldn't find work, I could always go back to school in the fall.

At the end of the semester, I returned to Indiana to organize my stuff and to get a new automobile—something more practical than a British sports car—and in July, I drove my newly acquired Ford station wagon to New York. For the first few weeks, I stayed on the Upper West Side at the apartment of trumpeter Danny Stiles, originally from Evansville, whom I had met during one of his visits home.

Coincidentally, Danny lived in the same building as my idol, Bill Evans, whose piano poetry and new approach to the trio format had already begun to have a major influence on modern jazz. I occasionally saw Bill in the elevator or outside on West End Avenue, but I never spoke to him. This was a dark period in Bill's life, the height of his heroin addiction, and he was in terrible shape. When I moved in, the building super-intendent saw my vibraphone cases, realized I was a musi-cian, and confided his concerns about Bill's declining circum-stances. He was deeply impressed with Bill's reputation, but worried: Bill's electricity had been turned off months earlier, and the super had given him a lantern to use at night. Bill didn't stay in the building much longer, and it took a couple of years before I actually got to meet him officially, at the first of several opportunities we had to play together.

Through Danny, I found out that an apartment was coming available in the neighborhood. It suited my budget and my needs, and ultimately, I moved into Apartment #3A at 34 West 73rd Street. My landlady was a fierce little Lebanese woman named Jesse, who, along with her brother, owned a number of buildings on the block. She used a small basement room in the building next door as her office and spent her days holed up there, fighting with the maintenance people and painters who worked for her. She terrified me. I started out paying the rent in person each month, but I dreaded going down to her little room and getting caught up in a conversation with her. She was always trying to get me to stay and talk, which really meant listening as she complained about everything wrong with the world. Soon I started mailing her the checks rather than walking them next door, just so I could avoid her.

Manhattan of the '60s was a looser, crazier version of today's high-powered scene—a gathering place of creative people who more than anything else exuded vitality. I found it inspiring. I began to spot actors and show-business people on my daily walks to and from the subway, or at the corner bank, or the market. Basil Rathbone, who played Sherlock Holmes in the movies, strolled down my block each evening in his trench coat, very much in character. Another film actor, Robert Ryan, was a regular at the Irish bar around the corner, and I also saw Tony Randall and Maureen Stapleton pretty often.

At the end of the block stood the legendary Dakota apartment building, home to actress Lauren Bacall (and later John Lennon and Yoko Ono). And in the space that had been the Dakota's tennis court, a modern high-rise building was going up. Coming out of the 72nd Street subway station by Central Park and walking past the Dakota, before turning down 73rd Street to my building, it felt like passing through first class to get to the economy section on an airplane. Still, I considered myself fortunate to have landed in this neighborhood as my first New York base. Even before I'd connected with the jazz scene, I had dropped into a show-business enclave, and I found it exhilarating.

This being the first place of my own, I tried to decorate it as nicely as I could—given the fact that I was starting with the bed I'd slept on since the age of three. (I had won it in some church raffle; my parents had entered my name, and the prize was two matching beds and a chest of drawers.) I added more contemporary items purchased in the neighborhood to perk up the place. After four years in that apartment, when I could afford something larger, I asked Jesse if she had anything available. She sent me to see a one-bedroom apartment next door, at 36 W. 73rd. She told me the painters were up there working, and I should just go in and look around.

The previous tenant, also a musician, had been eccentric, to say the least. He'd painted the ceilings purple and the floors black (and had also installed a pay phone in the living room). The painters were having a hell of a time getting the place to look normal, slapping on coat after coat of white paint as they tried to cover the dark colors. As I looked around the kitchen, I heard Jesse come in the front door and launch into a screaming tirade at the painters about how many times they were painting the ceiling and how much it was going to cost, how everyone was trying to cheat her, and so on. Not wanting to have any kind of confrontation, and already intimidated by Jesse, I got more uncomfortable by the minute. So, I just stepped into a nearby closet and hid there in the dark, figuring that eventually she would wear herself out and leave.

After five or ten minutes, the closet door suddenly flew open and there she was. Startled, I thought she was going to yell at me next. But without any apparent surprise at finding me hiding in a dark closet, she just smiled and said, "How do you like the apartment?" In fact, I liked it a lot, so I moved in and stayed in the neighborhood for another few years, and passed it on to my sister when I left.

Because of my own discomfort in her presence, it came as a surprise to learn that Jesse could also be very nurturing. She had a history of spotting talented young performers among her tenants, and when favorite renters hit the big time, she helped them find someplace upscale to move to. I really hadn't expected that degree of kindness and concern from her.

One of Jesse's tenants who got this favored treatment was said to have been Dustin Hoffman. Another up-and-comer was my upstairs neighbor, the newspaper columnist Rex Reed. At the time, I didn't know who he was. But I began to notice packages from the *New York Times* and various magazines in the vestibule downstairs, and I would hear typing for hours at a time, so I figured him for some kind of writer. A few years later, I saw a very complimentary review he had written about one of my albums and recognized his name from the mailbox. Though we lived on adjacent floors, we had never actually met during those four years; we finally met at a taping of the *Mike Douglas Show* in 1968. It sounds odd that we lived in the same building for years without actually meeting, but that's New York for you.

(The most difficult part of that taping was not performing for the cameras, but rather talking with Mike Douglas himself.

This is typical. Over the years, I've appeared on television shows hosted by Merv Griffin, Johnny Carson, David Letterman, etc., and they all had something in common: the questions they ask don't have normal answers. The questions are usually kind of silly, and you're supposed to joke around and come back with some witty reply. On the *Dick Cavett Show* in the late '60s, after I finished playing my song, Cavett walked over to me and asked, "What's it feel like to play the vibes?" I had no idea how to answer that—who would?—so I stumbled and mumbled something that barely made any sense.)

Having settled into my first New York apartment, I needed to find work. Almost immediately, I got a phone call, out of the blue, to play a wedding reception in Queens. I considered this a good omen and gladly accepted, even though I had never played a wedding gig before. But the band had some fine musicians—including the excellent guitarist Gene Bertoncini—and while I didn't know the usual wedding repertoire, I knew I could play along once the tunes started. Since this first gig had come so quickly, I thought others would follow, and I would keep busy. This was not to be; that wedding reception was the only work I got during my first six months in New York, other than one of my own record sessions (and a gig that ended before it really started, as you'll see).

In my anticipation of work to come, I transferred my union membership to New York, Local 802—though not without complications. At that time, the New York local required musicians to live in town for six months before they could join, during which they were restricted from taking any steady work. This helped prevent carpetbaggers from changing locals and grabbing full-time jobs (such as Broadway show gigs) from the hometown players. But it presented quite a problem for young musicians, who could hardly survive for six months in New York without employment. Joe Morello, my mentor from Dave Brubeck's group, came to the rescue. He knew someone at the union who suggested a way around the waiting period. I was to claim that I had moved to the city a year ago, and just now decided to transfer my membership.

In those days, the union had offices in the Roseland Ballroom, a fading dance hall in midtown Manhattan, where each Wednesday afternoon, hundreds of musicians would gather on the dance floor to contract local gigs. I got to witness this crazy scene, called the "hiring floor," when I showed up to meet my contact. Armed with a pile of phony rent receipts, I rehearsed my story with him before he took me in to repeat it for the union secretary. I was scared to death that the secretary would see through this subterfuge and ban me for life, or something like that, but it went okay, and I walked out a full-fledged member. Over the next few years, I called this guy several more times and went through the same routine for friends from Berklee who had just moved to New York and needed to get into the union. It all ended when a union election swept that administration, including my inside guy, out of office.

I also tried hanging out at some of the musicians' bars, particularly the two main ones: Jim & Andy's, and Charlie's Tavern. They were both in Midtown and popular with jazz musicians and studio players, and from midafternoon till after midnight, you could find an assortment of musicians, either on their way to work or just after their sessions, relaxing with a beer and sharing stories. A&R Recording, located just in the next building, had a direct phone line installed to Jim & Andy's. When they needed someone to play a certain instrument, they could call down and usually find whoever they needed.

The pace of musicians' lives seemed much more casual in those days, and social time constituted an important part of the day. But I'm basically a shy person, more comfortable reading a book than hanging out at a bar. I tried going to Charlie's Tavern once, but didn't have the nerve to walk up to anyone and introduce myself. To make matters worse, I also didn't drink, and it seemed a little ridiculous to sit at a bar for several hours nursing a Coke. I'm sure it could have led to some good contacts, and probably some gigs, too, but I just wasn't cut out for that scene.

To this day, I hate schmoozing, but to make it in this business, you need to socialize to some extent. Still, it always strikes me as a waste of time. Sometimes, I wonder how I ended up in a career that involves so much personal interaction; hanging out with other musicians is a primary way of getting work, and also a way to meet new players to collaborate with. I'm certainly not the first introvert to end up in the music world, but "the schmooze" has always posed a challenge because I find it so awkward.

Besides my wedding job, I had one more hilarious gig— well, almost a gig—that first summer in New York. It came about when Joe Morello recommended me to an old friend of his, the guitarist Sal Salvadore, who was putting a band together to work summer weekends at a beach club on the outer end of Long Island. The money wasn't great, but I really needed the work, and while Sal wasn't a major name in the business, I had at least heard of him. Sal's quartet consisted of guitar, vibes, bass, and drums. I don't remember the drummer, but the bassist was Eddie Gomez—only seventeen years old and brand-new to the scene, but already a great talent and destined to leave a lasting influence on jazz. Sal's quartet may not have worked out as hoped, but at least I got to know Eddie, whom I've been privileged to work with a number of times since.

After we'd rehearsed a couple of afternoons at a studio uptown, Sal suggested I drive out to the beach club with the vibraphone in my car, while he brought the rest of the band in his station wagon. Unsure of directions, and excited about my first jazz gig in New York, I left plenty early and arrived in mid-afternoon. I set up my vibes and met the club owner while I waited for the rest of the group. Eventually, customers began to arrive and order drinks as the sun sank into the Atlantic—but no sign of Sal. (We had planned to arrive early enough to squeeze in some more rehearsal, so this was definitely not a good omen.) As the dinner hour got underway and the 8 o'clock start time approached, I began to really worry.

The owner grew increasingly agitated—and seemed to be holding me responsible—when Sal telephoned to say they were en route and would get there soon. This didn't much placate the owner, and at 8:30, he asked me to play the vibes, unaccompanied; people had started to complain about the lack of entertainment. My abilities as a stand-alone soloist were hardly adequate for the situation, but I plodded through a half-hour or so, drawing a poor response from the now testy crowd, who had begun to sense that the band might not arrive at all.

I took a break, hoping to be rescued by Sal's arrival. At this point, the drummer showed up, alone, in his own car, but he didn't know what had happened to Sal and Eddie. We waited at least another hour, watching as patrons walked out (after getting their money back). The owner wouldn't even speak to us by this time. Around 10 P.M., Sal's station wagon finally pulled up to the front door. Before he and Eddie could even unload their equipment, a major argument erupted with the club owner. Sal emerged from the club's office and said that we would play one set, even though what remained of the crowd had grown surly.

But by the time we'd set up, another argument ensued between Sal and the owner, and this time he terminated us. Sal swore he would get us our money. He claimed he would bring the guy up on charges with the musician's union. For months, I called and left messages with Sal, trying to get some money out of him, since in my eyes this was entirely Sal's fault. Four or five years later, I would still get an occasional message from him promising to pay me something. Nothing ever came of it, and truthfully, it would have been a travesty of justice if the club owner had to pay us a cent.

But this was a good lesson: my early experience with Sal helped me clarify my own philosophy about the business relationship between bandleaders and sidemen. In my view, the leader shoulders the responsibility of making the job a success, for which he gets a higher fee than the sidemen. Meanwhile, the musicians deserve to be compensated as agreed upon, even if things don't work out as expected. Most leaders see it this way, but unfortunately, some do not.

With my next record project coming up, I started plotting ways to get some major players to play on it. I contacted Joe Morello and Phil Woods, and both agreed, which gave me some credibility for enlisting others.

Next, I waited outside Rockefeller Center each evening for about a week, trying to catch trumpeter Clark Terry as he finished taping the *Tonight Show* (which then aired from Radio City). When I caught him, at last, he was understandably reticent about being approached on the street for a record date by some nineteen-year-old kid. But I dropped Phil Woods's name, and then I exaggerated a bit—okay, I lied outright—and said I had also hired Tommy Flanagan, one of the most respected pianists in all of jazz. Hearing those familiar names, Clark's face brightened, and he said he would do the session. Then I got Tommy Flanagan's number, called and introduced myself, and told him that Clark and Phil would be on my record—and that convinced *Tommy* to accept. I filled out the band with a Boston bassist, John Neves, and the trombonist from the student band I had taken to Uruguay, Chris Swansen, whom I also asked to write some charts.

We recorded the album in September 1962, and it came together smoothly. I was especially happy with Phil's playing and with Chris's arrangements. RCA decided to title this record

Who Is Gary Burton?, and the cover featured a shadowy silhou-
ette; apparently, I still wasn't deemed worthy to appear on my
own record covers, establishing a pattern that has tended to
continue throughout my career. (I've always preferred having
my photo on my records, though most of the time it ends up
being something else. I don't know why this is so difficult. As
a leader, I've made over sixty records to date, but managed to
have my picture on the covers only about ten times.)

Meanwhile, money remained a problem. Record sessions
provided only a few days of employment, and my college
support checks from RCA had ended when I left Berklee. (One
of the RCA executives went so far as to ask if I was sure I wanted
to leave before graduating; he thought I should wait another
couple of years, even though it would have cost RCA to keep
subsidizing my education. Imagine that happening today!)
But salvation arrived courtesy of pianist Marian McPartland,
with a little help from my guardian angel, Joe Morello.

Joe was a friend of Marian's, having played in her trio
in the '50s, and he took me to meet Marian at the Hickory
House, where she had a steady gig. Marian asked me to sit
in on piano, expecting me to play with two fingers, the
way Lionel Hampton played piano. But when she saw that
I played correctly, and maybe sounded halfway decent, she
was impressed. And even though she had yet to hear me play
the vibraphone, Joe's enthusiasm about me prompted Marian
to call *her* friend (and fellow Brit pianist) George Shearing
and give me a glowing recommendation. Shearing led one of
the few well-known bands that regularly featured vibes, and
sure enough, I soon got a call from the office of John Levy,
Shearing's manager, asking me to come in on Labor Day for
an audition.

CHAPTER 7

On the Job Training

PART ONE

When I got to Shearing's office on Labor Day, 1962, I found the building closed for the holiday (like every other building on 57th Street). It was a blistering hot day in New York, and after standing outside the building for an hour or more, I was about to give up when someone finally came to open the lobby door. And then a car pulled up carrying George Shearing and his road manager.

Once settled upstairs in the office, George and I played a few tunes, just the two of us. He asked me to sight-read some fairly difficult parts, which I managed easily. Perhaps because he had been blind from birth, George always had great respect for good sight-readers. In any case, he certainly seemed impressed and immediately asked me to join his band. There was only one hitch. He was taking a break from touring to attend guide-dog school; he had never owned a guide dog and wanted to see if one could fit into his musician's lifestyle. Because of this, the job wouldn't start until January. In the meantime, I secretly hoped I might find something to start sooner.

I occupied myself by exploring New York on a budget,

riding the subway to every part of town. I also became a regular customer at the New York clubs—the Half Note, Birdland, the Village Vanguard—catching all the current bands. My apartment's former tenant had temporarily left behind his piano, so I got in some work there, too. Even at Berklee, I had always wanted more practice time than my schedule would allow. Now, here I was in New York with absolutely nothing to do but practice to my heart's content. Trouble was that without a job, I was just in too much of a funk to actually do so.

I *almost* got a job with flutist Herbie Mann, who led one of the few groups (besides Shearing's) that featured vibes. Herbie called to say he had heard a lot of good things about me, and he invited me down to Basin Street East, a club on 48th Street. He wanted me to hear his band and discuss replacing his then current vibes player, Dave Pike.

I got to the club, chose an out-of-the-way table, and listened to the band's first set, feeling confident I could fit in with no problem. In fact, it seemed like a better prospect than waiting six months for Shearing's gig to start. But at the set break, to my alarm, Dave Pike headed right toward my table and sat down next to me. He thought he recognized me and asked if I was Tommy Vig (a vibes player about my age from the West Coast). I said no, but Pike persisted that he recognized me, and when I told him who I was, he flew into a rage. He wanted to know if I had been asked to come in, and when I admitted that was the case, he stormed across the room and got into a heated argument with Herbie. I figured this would eliminate any chance of me joining the band, but to my surprise Herbie came over a few minutes later and asked if I could start in a few weeks! I said, "Sure," and he told me to expect a call with further details.

In spite of the awkward circumstances, I was elated. I already had another job offer, and one I deemed even better than Shearing's. But two weeks later, when no call had come,

I began to worry that something had gone wrong. I didn't want to appear anxious, but eventually, I called Herbie's manager, Monte Kay—who didn't seem to know anything about any job offer. (That really *did* make me anxious.) A couple of days later, Herbie finally called with some lame explanation about his decision to keep Dave on after all. He just hadn't bothered to let me know. I thought he'd been serious when he offered me the job, and I was really disappointed—actually, make that "furious." Sometime in the next twenty years or so, I eventually stopped being angry, but I don't think I ever really forgave him.

I continued to look for work in New York while waiting for Shearing's job to start, but nothing else came along. I had to borrow money from my father to pay the rent ($115 a month). But on January 7, 1963—a couple of weeks before my twentieth birthday, and just as promised—I was on a plane to California to join the George Shearing Quintet.

George lived in Los Angeles and had scheduled a couple days' rehearsal out there before our opening gig, at the Santa Monica Civic Center. This was my first trip to California, and I was excited at the prospect of checking out the West Coast jazz scene, which I had followed on records and in *Down Beat* Magazine since I first discovered jazz. Leaving the New York winter, then stepping out into the balmy California afternoon, seemed wonderfully exotic. The guitarist for George's group, Ron Anthony, was also on my flight, and we went directly from the airport to the Vine Lodge Motel in Hollywood, right next door to the recently constructed Capitol Records Tower.

Then as now, Hollywood offered a mix of glamour and sleaze. It still boasted such fabled hangouts as the Brown Derby and Schwab's Drugstore, though these would soon disappear. The Vine Lodge was a different kind of Hollywood landmark: the best-known and most popular residence among traveling musicians, for the simple reason that a room went for about $10 a day.

In the '60s, most jazz bands worked weeklong engagements in large cities, and certain hotels gained a reputation for being "entertainer-friendly." In addition to the Vine Lodge, these included the Croydon and Cass Hotels in Chicago, the Wolverine Hotel in Detroit, and the Bryant Hotel in New York. Bandleaders usually stayed at more upscale hotels, while the sidemen sought out inexpensive digs, since we had to pay for the rooms ourselves. (The practice of bandleaders paying for the musicians' hotel rooms didn't become common until the '70s.) If several bands were in town at the same time, the local "musician's hotel" would become a lively social scene.

I met the rest of Shearing's group soon after arriving in L.A. Chicago bassist Bill Yancey had, like me, just joined the band. The drummer was the legendary Vernel Fournier, whose early work with Ahmad Jamal I had long admired; his light swing and laconic approach to jazz drumming left an indelible impression on me. The group also featured Latin percussionist extraordinaire Armando Peraza, a star in his own right, who had toured with Shearing since the early '50s. As a result, the famous "George Shearing Quintet" had the odd distinction of actually comprising six musicians. Our entourage included the tour manager, Ed Fuerst, and the driver/equipment manager, Chuck Noll. We rehearsed at George's house in Toluca Lake, a comfortable residence presided over by Trixie—Mrs. Shearing—who was also George's business manager.

GEORGE SHEARING

Shearing grew up in England, the youngest child in a family of eight. Like many children born blind, he gravitated toward music, and achieved success playing both piano and accordion. He soon distinguished himself on the British jazz scene and could have easily remained there for the rest of his career. But in 1947, he decided to try his luck in America, universally known as the home of the best players. This was no easy feat. It meant starting from scratch to build his reputation here, which went slowly at first. George formed a new band, characterized by what came to be called "the Shearing Sound," a lush combination of vibes, guitar, and piano that was atypical at a time when horn players dominated the sound of most groups. Even more unusual, his first vibes player was a woman, Marjorie Hyams.

At first, George struggled to keep the group working. John Levy, the bassist in that band (who later became George's manager), told me they really scuffled until the Shearing Sound caught on. But in 1949, George's recording of "September in the Rain" became one of the most successful jazz records of that era, selling over 900,000 copies.

George had a few eccentricities. For instance, he took great pride in his collection of Steuben glass figurines, going so far as to purchase a case with built-in lighting to show them off to visitors. Of course, he couldn't see any of this, but he loved turning on the display lights and asking what you thought of his latest addition to the collection. He also made an effort to woo the ladies when the opportunity presented itself. He would chat up some female fan during a set break, then find his way over to the band members and ask, "Is she hot? What do you think?" He told me about once inviting a potential conquest up to his hotel room to "listen to some records" after a gig, but when they entered the room and George began to get amorous, the lady was shocked. She said she hadn't known he had this in mind. George replied, "Well, you wouldn't expect a blind man to have etchings, would you?"

One of his favorite tricks, when meeting a woman who seemed interesting, was to reach out to shake hands and bump into her breasts to "innocently" cop a feel. At one gig in Los Angeles, the statuesque movie star Jane Russell was in the audience, and sure enough, when George was guided over to meet her, he went a little too far—and thus got to check out the famous Russell cleavage. He couldn't stop talking about it for days.

George was also one of those people who find farting hilarious. On long car trips, it was only a matter of time before someone squeezed one off, and that would initiate a farting contest, with George trying to guess the identity of each contributor.

George continued with his trademark sound for about three decades, but when just the two of us rehearsed new material for the band, I discovered he had a fine singing voice, too. He was especially good on poignant, narrative ballads. I told him he should consider singing in public and maybe on records, and he eventually did so on some of his later albums.

The last time I saw George, at the end of 1997, was a matter of pure luck. I was at Avatar Studios in New York recording the album *Like Minds*, and someone told me that, coincidentally, George was in the next studio recording with Marian McPartland. When we took a break, I went over to say hello. They were on break, too, and George said he would love to come over to hear what I was working on. Then he did something very touching; without hesitation he reached out and took my arm so I could guide him to the next room. A blind person doesn't trust just anyone to lead him, but George remembered I'd had plenty of practice bringing him on and off stage when I played in his band. So, even though some thirty-five years had passed, he was confident grabbing my arm and briskly setting off toward the other studio, with me leading the way.

The rehearsals with George's group went well and our first concert took place on February 16, 1963. (George's label, Capitol Records, recorded the performance and released it later that year under the title *Jazz Concert*.) We then flew to Salt Lake City for a concert at Brigham Young University—Mormon country—where the contract prohibited the use of either alcohol or tobacco anywhere on campus. I remember all the guys who smoked hurrying through their last cigarettes as we neared the university. I also remember pulling off a coup with George that night, although I felt a twinge of guilt about it later.

Ever since my audition, George had been praising my ability to sight-read difficult music; apparently, many of his previous vibes players had been poor readers. This comes as no surprise. Since the vibraphone repertoire is fairly small, vibists often learn by ear and play from memory, instead of developing their reading skills. In any case, my reputation as a sight-reader took a major leap forward that night in Salt Lake City.

George called a number that we hadn't rehearsed, an

original of his named "Conception." In terms of both written melody and harmonic structure, it's a fairly complex piece, and not that famous (even though both Miles Davis and the pioneering bop pianist Bud Powell recorded it in the 1950s). George assumed I wouldn't know it and told me to just play along as best I could. In fact, I knew the piece quite well; I had learned it at Berklee, thanks to the teaching of Herb Pomeroy. But I couldn't resist the temptation to stay mum. When we got into the performance, I played it without missing a note—which left George practically wetting his pants. He didn't stop raving about it for months. And because he did go on about it so much, I never had the nerve to tell him that I'd already known the song and wasn't really playing it for "the first time."

George had a massive repertoire with maybe a hundred or more arrangements that we carried around in large black folders. While he usually stuck to a familiar lineup of a couple dozen tunes, sometimes he chose a piece from his early years— even if we had never rehearsed it. He actually had a perverse tendency to call unrehearsed pieces whenever we were playing an important gig. The results were usually pretty shaky, with the whole group sight-reading together. (On one occasion the group fell apart completely on just such an attempt, and George had to quickly segue into "Bernie's Tune"—a well-worn jam-session piece that everyone knew—to save the performance.) It might have been George's way of breaking the monotony of the road, or relieving the pressure he may have felt before a big performance. Perhaps, it was just his idea of living on the edge.

But even on pieces we rehearsed, reading George's music posed a challenge. Many of his arrangements featured unique and unexpected rhythmic phrasing, which was part of "the Shearing Sound." But over time, through countless performances, George had gradually altered the phrasing so that the music we played no longer matched what was written on the parts. As we would read through a new piece, we had to stay alert to George phrasing a passage differently from how it was written. Then, we had to remember what he did, so we could play it that way the next time. I don't think he ever knew this was going on. I certainly never told him. We all just did our best to adjust to his variations.

Armando Peraza quickly nicknamed me "the Professor," because I always had my nose in a book. But it was Vernel Fournier who provided learning of a different sort—my first real education about race relations. He told me about books by Richard Wright and W.E.B. DuBois, and we would talk about the history of race relations in America for hours in the car when we toured. Vernel had grown up in New Orleans and had a lot of stories, but the evidence was all around us. Civil rights laws were still a few years away, and when we traveled in the South, the black musicians had to stay in hotels that catered only to people of color. If none were available, the concert sponsor had to line up private homes where the black musicians could stay. Some restaurants allowed a racially mixed group to eat together. Others would take our orders but bring the black musicians their food in take-out containers, letting them know they weren't welcome to stay.

As I was growing up in southern Indiana in the 1950s, racism was all around me, but I had little exposure to the hard truths of segregation. The local movie theater did have a section in the balcony reserved for black patrons, and the courthouse in the town square had separate water fountains, but I never gave much thought to the implications of these practices. I do remember when the city decided to build a public swimming pool; the town debated whether it should be "whites-only" or open to all, but "open-to-all" won the day. The schools were already integrated by the time I came along. Even at Berklee, I rarely encountered these issues, and I remained pretty naïve about the history of racism in America.

So, my education on this topic started with the Shearing band. It came a little late, but by the time of the great struggle to pass civil rights laws a year later, I could appreciate its importance. I became very partial to Holiday Inns, which had just started to appear widely in the early '60s. This Memphis-based chain was the first in the nation with a policy of absolute non-discrimination. For years, I stayed at Holiday Inns whenever possible, because I knew there wouldn't be any hassles—and because I appreciated that they were the first hotel chain to do the right thing, even before the law said they had to.

I didn't really need much of a reminder that I was a white guy in a music strongly identified with African-American culture. This was even more striking in the first decade of my career. Most of our gigs took place in nightclubs located in large cities, and the black community made up a good part of the audience. In addition, some in the jazz world continued a racial stereotype, which claims that only black musicians can play "authentic" jazz. Bob Thiele—the head of the influential Impulse Records label in the '60s, who produced many of John Coltrane's seminal recordings as well those of other artists—once told me I had spoiled his long-held belief that the most important jazz players on any given instrument were always black. I was astounded that someone of his experience could have such an antiquated perspective.

But I can honestly say I've never experienced any rejection from black jazz artists. And by the '70s, the equation itself had changed. We were playing fewer club dates and more concerts, often on college campuses, while the jazz education movement in high schools and colleges helped bring the music to a wider, more diverse public.

Oddly, the only time I've been dissed for being white came at the hands of college administrators. In 1998, the Recording Academy—the GRAMMY® organization—offered to send some name musicians, at no cost, to several colleges for one-day workshops aimed at encouraging their jazz programs. The Academy asked me to do one of these at Howard University, the historic black college in Washington, D.C., but a few days later I got another call, saying that Howard refused to have me. I was told they didn't think it was "appropriate" for a white musician to speak on jazz to their students. I thought the jazz world was way past that kind of thinking, but apparently not.

Working with George, I learned a lot about blind people. For starters, I couldn't help noticing his skill at compensating for his lack of sight. As a child, when most musicians were learning to read music, George developed a gift for memorization. He could learn new music incredibly fast. And on the road, where we stayed in different hotels and ate in different restaurants almost every day, George developed an uncanny ability to quickly memorize the layout of his surroundings.

Of course, Shearing still needed a hand when navigating trips to and from the piano. The band's vibist always had the task of leading George on and off stage, and while that would seem an easy enough assignment, I was surprised at how often we would get tangled in microphone cords snaking across the floor, or end up in a cul-de-sac, blocked by instruments, and have to reverse course to find a different route to the piano. The guys in the band broke me up with a story involving my predecessor, Warren Chaisson. One night, as Warren led George to the piano, a button popped off George's coat and Warren let go of George's arm to pick it up. Left adrift, George reached out and found the boom microphone above the piano (which he used for announcements), swinging it around just in time to hit Warren on the head as he came up with the button, and knocking him to the floor—a real Three Stooges moment.

During my year in the band, George traveled with his new guide dog, Lee. George had always regretted being dependent on someone else to lead him around for even the simplest errands, but now with Lee, his Golden Retriever, he

84

could do such things on his own. He told me he got a special thrill that year from buying Christmas presents for his wife and daughter without them accompanying him. He and Lee walked to a shop near his house, where George picked out some china figurines and had them gift-wrapped as surprises for Christmas morning. He knew the shop had plenty of glass items on display, so when he got to the door, he waited for the owner; he didn't want to wander around on his own and accidentally break something. But while he waited, a customer who was leaving noticed the blind man standing there with his guide dog and pressed a quarter into George's hand. He thought that was hilarious.

George loved humor, and particularly humor about being blind. At gigs, alumni band members would sometimes show up unannounced, come on stage, and slide in to play one of the instruments; George would soon notice that someone new had taken over and then try to guess who it was. Once, his old bass player Al McKibbon came up behind George, put his hands over George's eyes, and said, "Guess who!" George loved it.

I discovered something else about blind people from my experiences with George. In conversation, they tend to be much more likely than others to speak frankly, and even harshly. Not seeing another person's shocked or hurt expression, many blind people don't restrain themselves in the way that sighted people usually do. Once, in San Francisco, a family made an appointment to bring their blind daughter to meet George. The little girl played piano and the parents were looking to George for encouragement—maybe even some advice regarding their daughter's future. After introductions, the little girl played a light classical piece at a level typical for her age, and when the piece ended the parents looked expectantly to George. He just barked out, "Forget about it, she doesn't have a future in music." The look on their faces was horrifying; the little girl burst into tears as George just stood there waiting for them to leave. Watching this go down, I was shocked. I turned to Trixie, who noticed the look on my face; she quietly told me George used to be even less tactful at this kind of thing, though I found that hard to imagine.

Trixie handled the business side of things: the publishing, salaries for the band members, dealing with the record company, etc. I could never quite decide whether it was Trixie, George, or both of them who were "funny about money." By the time I joined the band, George had achieved considerable financial success but remained naturally stingy. I suppose that growing up poor in England, and scuffling during the early years, had instilled survival instincts that were hard to change. Sometimes, we would get into a heated debate over something like me getting reimbursed for a $3 taxi fare, which would leave me on the verge of quitting the band. Then, a few days later, George would hand me a gift-boxed cashmere sweater he had bought me as a gift.

After a few months, I learned that the other sidemen were making $300 a week while I was getting just $275. (This was a bigger deal than it looks like; $25 in 1963 had the same buying power as $185 in 2012 dollars.) Granted, I was "the new guy," and maybe, since I was only twenty years old, George didn't think I deserved the same as the others. By the time I discovered this, though, I felt I had proven myself. In fact, I thought I had become the star soloist in the group, aside from George. So, I plucked up my courage and went to ask him for a $25 raise. George seemed surprisingly uncomfortable. After hemming and hawing, he said he would have to talk to Trixie, but that night, just before we performed, he told me I would get the raise.

On the gig, George didn't call any of the songs that included a vibes solo. I wondered if that was a coincidence or whether George could be mad enough to cut out my feature numbers. I got my answer the next night. In fact, three or four nights went by before I once again got to take a solo.

George had one foot in the jazz world and the other in the commercial world. Because of this, his performances differed from those of other jazz bands. Instead of an extended series of improvised choruses, the soloists were each limited to one chorus per song—maybe twenty or thirty seconds of solo space—to keep the music accessible to his audiences. (And on ballads, only George soloed at all.) After my student experiences, this was a drastic change. I had grown accustomed to soloing until I reached some kind of peak, however long it took. At first, I didn't know what the heck to do. I started by trying to squeeze all that I could into that one chorus, using every device that would fit. I soon saw that this wasn't working; it sounded frantic, as if I was throwing in everything *and* the kitchen sink.

Then, I stepped back to look at the situation philosophically. In previous bands, we would play six or seven songs per set. With George, we did a dozen or more, since each tune was relatively short. I concluded that either way, I would be on stage for several hours and would get roughly the same amount of solo space. With George, it was just broken up into smaller chunks. (In a way, it reminded me of my old "ten-minute" practice sessions as a kid in Indiana.) My goal became to say something clear, compelling, and complete in each of these briefer showcases. And these shorter opportunities also cured me of using the first chorus or two of my solos to sort of "warm up," instead of launching right into something interesting for the listener to follow.

(In performance, a lot of jazz musicians play long solos, only to discover that these don't work so well in the recording studio. In the early days of recording, the musicians didn't have much choice; 78-rpm records only ran about three minutes per side, so all of the early jazz records—many of them classics—are that short. Even after the arrival of the 33-rpm LP—what this century's listeners know as "vinyl"—record companies feared that radio stations would ignore albums with long tracks, which in turn would hurt sales. So, up until the '70s, the general rule was to keep tracks under five minutes.)

Having to play short solos in George's band provided me with great discipline. Ever since, when a recording situation or guest appearance requires a short solo, I'm ready and willing. And I learned several other valuable lessons from George as well.

First, I became proficient at playing in all the key signatures. Because of their tuning and construction, different instruments play more easily in different keys. In jazz, we usually gravitate to those keys most popular with the lead instruments; in the '50s and '60s, we played mostly in the keys easiest for the horn players (such as the key of F and the key of Bb), while today we tend to use keys that guitarists find most comfortable (G or A, perhaps). When I joined Shearing's band, I was accustomed to playing in the horn-friendly keys. But George had no such bias. Since he couldn't see and didn't read music, the sharps and flats in the less common key signatures made no difference to him. As a result, his repertoire was about equally divided among all twelve keys. I had to scramble those first few months to get a handle on some of the tunes, but after a year playing his repertoire, I never again had a problem with key signatures.

Second, George convinced me to stop using the vibrato that gives the vibraphone its name. (See chapter 3.) He preferred the instrument without that effect, and though I missed it at first, I came to agree with him. I've played without vibrato ever since, and sometimes also without accompaniment—another trick I learned from George. His unaccompanied solo pieces were often the highlight of our performances, and knowing a good thing when I saw it, I began playing solo pieces myself after I left George's band. In time, this became a trademark of my concerts for several decades.

Third and most important, George was a master of *reharmonization*, the process of finding new and colorful chords to give variety to even familiar melodies. Learning his music was like taking a crash course with a master music theorist. In that way, at least, I felt I hadn't left college after all.

We spent a lot of time on the road—quite literally, in fact. George had a leased Cadillac de Ville and a van with "George Shearing and his Quintet" painted on the side, and we would often drive all night from, say, Chicago to Denver for the next week's engagement. This saved the band members a night's hotel bill; it also fit our nightlife schedule. The musicians took turns at the wheel and received a stipend for driving, although having just turned twenty, I was too young to qualify for the car insurance. I resented missing out on the extra cash, but my youth had an upside. The plan was usually for George to fly from city to city while the band drove, but because he had a fear of flying (especially in bad weather), he often offered me his plane ticket and took my place in the car instead. I made quite a lot of flights traveling under the name "George Shearing"—this was before you needed identification to board a plane—while George opted for those all-night car rides.

Since George was based in L.A. and the band spent a lot of our time there, I bought a used Honda motor scooter ($150) to get around. George highly approved, and one afternoon even insisted on getting behind me and going for a ride around the neighborhood. He loved it. George used to wish he could drive a car someday. This led me to have occasional dreams about him behind the wheel of the band car, careening down the highway and frantically asking me which way to turn.

Road travel has remained a part of my life ever since, though I no longer do much long-distance driving. And I must admit, I've never had my name painted on the side of a vehicle. I once passed a station wagon on the Pennsylvania Turnpike with "The World-Famous Ink Spots" painted along the side—and there they were, all four of them seated neatly inside, wearing suits and ties. I can't imagine having to travel every day like that: being on display, with people staring in the window at you, and having to guard your appearance while wondering what they think of you.

CHAPTER 8

The West Coast Scene

George Shearing's loyal following ensured sizable audiences everywhere, and in large cities, our nightclub engagements usually spanned from one to four weeks. Early in my time with the group, we headed to San Francisco for a month-long booking at the city's leading club, the Blackhawk. I was especially looking forward to this, since I owned records that both Miles Davis and Shelly Manne had recorded there. But except for my time onstage, I got surprisingly little chance to retrace their footsteps.

Shortly before our engagement, the city's nightclubs had gotten into a tussle with the police over the admission of minors. The solution called for each club to create a special section for patrons under twenty-one (much like Birdland, the famous New York jazz club, had done several years earlier). But the Blackhawk had to construct a chicken-wire fence to partition off the minors' section—complete with its own street entrance! Since I had just celebrated my twentieth birthday, the club owner insisted I spend all my break time sitting in the chicken-wire cage with the other underage patrons (on the occasion that any showed up). On weeknights, I was usually the only one back there, reading my book.

I met a lot of remarkable people in San Francisco during that first visit. Several local musicians came to hear us, including the well-known vibist Cal Tjader (who had played in George's band before me). But none of them made as much impact on me as the iconoclastic composer and inventor Harry Partch.

I became acquainted with Harry at the insistence of Emil Richards, another former Shearing vibist. Emil had contacted me while we were still in L.A. to tell me about Harry, saying that I absolutely had to look up this percussion pioneer when the band got to San Francisco. I had no intention of calling a total stranger and inviting myself over (Emil's enthusiasm notwithstanding). But about a week after we arrived, Emil called to say he had just gotten off the phone with Harry, who was now expecting a call from me.

Reluctantly, I rented a car and found my way up to Harry's home in Petaluma, an hour north of San Francisco. Harry met me at the door: a frail white-haired man with a twinkle in his eye. He lived in the office of an abandoned chicken hatchery, surrounded by several huge empty barns. He explained that he needed a lot of room for his instruments, and the hatchery was virtually rent-free. I walked in and discovered the most amazing menagerie of musical instruments. There were marimbas in all sizes. The biggest used an eight-foot plank for its lowest key, pitched below the bottom note on a piano. He also had some odd string instruments, some peculiarly tuned organs, and several alien-looking percussion devices.

Like Alice, I'd stepped through the looking glass, but into Wonderland's music shop.

This actually was not the first time I had encountered homemade instruments. But in almost every case, they were a disappointment. Even if ingenious in concept, they would prove impractical when it came to actual music-making. Over the years, though, Harry had rebuilt his instruments many times, and they offered fascinating possibilities. Early in his life, he had come to the conclusion that conventional instruments, and the tonalities they produced, would not be right for him. He spent the next ten years collecting his theories in a book titled *Genesis of a Music,* and the remainder of his life building instruments, composing music in accordance with his theories, and organizing performances of his works. By the time we met, he had been at it for thirty years and had produced eight records and a small number of concerts. Drawn to large performance settings, somewhat operatic in concept, he only managed to complete a project every few years. But Harry had the respect of the hipper contemporary musicians in both the jazz and classical worlds, and people often traveled considerable distances to attend the premieres of his work. He is sometimes lumped in with his better-known contemporary, the avant-garde composer John Cage. Harry knew Cage, but felt that Cage had not remained true to his music. He dismissed the notoriously experimental Cage as a commercial "sellout," which I found hilarious.

I was particularly impressed with Harry's commitment to such an original and difficult musical path. I had thought jazz musicians were the ones going against the grain, but this was on another level entirely. For example, a Partch performance required that he first teach the musicians his unorthodox systems of notation, as well as how to play his one-of-a-kind instruments. His music did not revolve around virtuosity or star soloists. Instead, it centered on compositional content and the ensemble performance. (That's just the opposite of jazz, where we tend to focus on individual players and their technique; we don't go to hear just "a trumpet player," but to hear a *specific* trumpet player whom we admire.) I found Harry's "non-star" approach a refreshing alternative, and I have enjoyed his music ever since we met. Once you get past the unique instruments and odd tunings, Harry's music has a melodic simplicity and a wonderful sense of humor.

We became friends and began a correspondence that lasted many years, punctuated by my visits whenever I came to the

West Coast. He loved to tell stories about his years wandering the country during the Depression, and how he organized productions of his music. On one of my visits, he told me there had been a break-in the night before. He'd heard noises coming from the cavernous empty barns and guessed it was a gang of teenagers; he feared that if they discovered him, they might harm him—or worse, vandalize his unusual instruments. He didn't know whether to call the police or to hide in a corner and hope they wouldn't find him. But then he got the idea to play one of his pump organs, a quite remarkable beast that he called the "chromelodeon." Tuned to Harry's unusual quarter-tone scale, it sounded even more sinister than the organs you hear in B-movie thrillers. As he pumped his eerie music into the darkness, the intruders took off like bats out of hell—which they probably had pinpointed as the music's source.

I gradually lost touch with Harry after he moved in the late '60s to San Diego—where he died in 1974—but I will always value getting to know him and discovering his work in my formative years. The lessons of his artistic philosophy still serve as an excellent balance for my own perspective on the art of making music.

Between tours, the Shearing band spent most of its time in Los Angeles, and I made some good friends among the local musicians. Among the best were Larry Bunker and his wife Lee. Larry, a drummer and vibist, introduced himself one night when I was sitting in at a local club. Before long, I was staying with the Bunkers (instead of at a hotel) whenever I went to L.A., and Larry would even give me the keys to his Aston Martin for evening drives. He had bought the car after Red Norvo called one day to tell him that the local showroom was making some great deals, and they had both ended up with new cars the same day. Driving Bunker's car, I often wondered if Red was somewhere in town driving his Aston Martin, too—just us two vibists, separated by a couple generations, tooling around in our iconic British roadsters.

Larry was among the busiest studio musicians in town and sometimes recommended me to recording contractors when his own schedule was full. For one such session, I got to play for pianist Martin Denny, who had become popular for his exotic Hawaiian-style instrumentals employing birdcalls and jungle sounds in the background.

The "leader" wasn't actually on hand for the session, however. One of the other musicians told me that Denny was difficult to work with and slowed down the pace, so his producers had taken to scheduling his record sessions while he was out of town. They simply hired another pianist to "ghost" for him. (You could consider him the Milli Vanilli of his time.) Later that year, I met Denny himself, at the London House in Chicago, where I was playing with Shearing. He went on about how much he enjoyed working with me—as if we had actually made the record together! (At least, I played on it; he hadn't even been in the room.)

I occasionally tagged along with Larry on his own studio sessions, which led to my meeting the legendary singer Judy Garland. Larry was playing drums for her 1963 summer TV series, with Mel Tormé serving as arranger and musical director. I attended the final rehearsal for that week's show at CBS Television City, situated between Beverly Hills and Hollywood. Being young and not well versed on singers—or "show biz" in general—I didn't fully appreciate the moment. I now wish I had known more about Garland's status as one of the great American singers when I met her that afternoon. Neither did I know much about Mel Tormé—another monumentally talented vocalist and musician—though I would cross paths with him a few times in later years. (Once, as I performed on a jazz cruise in the Caribbean, Mel sat in on drums and played with great fluency; then again, he had been drumming on stage since his teens, when he occasionally appeared with the band led by comedian Chico Marx, of all people.)

My year with Shearing introduced me to people and places that would figure prominently in my career over the next decade. We played one concert in San Francisco produced by a local promoter named Bill Graham. A few years later, Bill launched a new and influential career promoting rock concerts at the Fillmore Ballroom, where I played with my own band in the late '60s. I also got my first taste of Japan around this time. World War II had ended less than twenty years earlier, and we were among the first American jazz groups to play in Tokyo, to large and receptive crowds. When we arrived, hundreds of people ran onto the airfield just to meet our plane, and I have enjoyed a strong following in Japan ever since.

Those crowds thronged to hear the "Shearing Sound," of course. But by this time (1963), George's trademark style was wearing thin, and we had started to play more modern interpretations of standards, as well as some new jazz compositions. Sometimes, audience members would come up to me and gush about what a genius George was. Then, after a pause for breath, they would complain that we hadn't played enough of their favorites. I always wanted to ask why, if they considered George so gifted, they wouldn't also trust his judgment when it came to choosing material. It taught me that no matter what the artist thinks, most people really just want to hear what they already know.

I made three records with Shearing: two "live" recordings and one unusual project featuring twelve of my own compositions. About halfway through my year in the band, George suggested I try writing something using counterpoint, a la Bach. I titled the piece "J.S. Bop," and he liked it so much that he asked me to write several more for a new record. Incredibly, Capitol Records had never allowed George to record any original compositions—he had always been relegated to familiar standards—so this represented a major development. At first, we planned a half-album's worth: six songs that the group recorded at the Capitol Tower, using a Los Angeles rhythm section (starring drummer Shelly Manne) plus a woodwind quintet. Months later, the label gave the okay to expand it to a full album of originals, so I quickly wrote six more contrapuntal pieces for George.

Titled *Out of the Woods*, it remains my most ambitious effort at composing and arranging. It received excellent reviews, and I take special pride in the fact that this was George's first album of original material after dozens of previous recordings for Capitol. I've never done a lot of composing, so coming up with a full program of originals was no easy matter, and it had its pitfalls. For instance, I didn't know how to write for the alto flute; I assumed it would be the same as writing for the alto saxophone. It isn't, as became immediately clear when we started to play. To save the day, Paul Horn (who had the part) switched from alto flute to the much louder alto saxophone, then played softly enough to blend in with the other woodwinds.

My other recording session in 1963 came in mid-August, when I laid down tracks for my next RCA project at Studio A in New York, an album called *Something's Coming*. I decided to again use guitarist Jim Hall—who had played on my initial, unreleased album attempt—and I brought in Larry Bunker from the West Coast to play drums (with New Yorker Chuck Israels on bass). When the editing was completed a couple months later, I invited Jim to drop by my apartment and hear the finished tracks. In retrospect, I'm surprised that he actually did so; Jim doesn't go out a lot, and I certainly wasn't an important figure in his career.

But to this day I remain glad he made the effort, because he gave me some valuable advice. Around that time, I had developed some doubts about playing an instrument so unfamiliar to most listeners. I was in one of my periodic bouts of soul-searching, and despite my success up to that point,

I wrestled with whether the piano or some other instrument would have been a better choice. I laid my concerns on Jim. "What if the vibraphone turns out to be as unpopular as, say, the accordion?" Jim wisely replied that the instrument didn't matter; it's what you do with it. Then he told me about Astor Piazzolla, a musician I had never heard of, who Jim described as "a sort of accordion player"—and also a monster musician. I recently reminded Jim of this conversation, and he didn't remember any of it—in fact, he expressed surprise that he had even known about Piazzolla that long ago—but it had a huge impact on me. I decided to stop doubting the vibraphone and just focus on the music.

(Coincidentally, I got to meet Piazzolla in Buenos Aires a couple years later, and found that he did in fact play a complicated button-type "sort of accordion"—an instrument called a *bandoneon*, with which he revolutionized tango music. I became a lifelong fan and eventually got to perform and record with Piazzolla. And because of Jim Hall's advice, I have always equated Piazzolla's music with my own commitment to the vibraphone.)

Back in L.A., one late-November morning, I was asleep on the hideaway sofa in the den at the Bunkers' house in Laurel Canyon—my home away from home—when Lee came rushing in to switch on the television. A neighbor had called to tell her about the shooting of President Kennedy in Dallas. We all sat stunned as we watched the day's events unfold. Shearing had scheduled a rehearsal for that afternoon, and he insisted we go through with it, since we had several dates coming up, but everyone was in shock. The whole country came to a halt, and our gigs—along with most other entertainment events— were cancelled for the immediate future. As a quite apolitical twenty-year old, I attached little meaning to Kennedy's assassination; I regarded it mostly as an interruption of my current plans. Within a few years, though, as Vietnam came to dominate the news, I started to realize the effect that world events had on my own little life, and I became much more political—a stance that has only deepened as I've aged.

Larry Bunker and I had scheduled a "live" recording at Shelly's Manne-Hole (the city's most popular club) for the Monday and Tuesday after the assassination, but of course, we delayed it several weeks, until we thought the mourning period would have passed. When the rescheduled date arrived, we got the instruments set up early, tested out the mobile recording van parked in the alley behind the club, and everything was ready to go—everything, that is, but the listening public, who had not yet gotten over the death of the president. That first night, only one person showed up: an elderly fellow with a shopping bag, who apparently heard the music from the sidewalk and wandered in out of curiosity. After a little while, he realized we were trying to make a recording and that he was the entire audience, so he did what he thought we expected: he applauded passionately after each solo. He was ruining our session. We obviously couldn't release a record with the sound of one person clapping after each solo, but we didn't have the heart to stop him. And we couldn't get inspired anyway. The next night, we invited everyone we knew in L.A., and the audience turned the session into our own private jazz party. The record came out well enough, and was issued on an obscure label owned by Fred Astaire: the Ava label, named after Ava Gardner, who would make a brief appearance later in my career.

About this time, I started seeing a therapist, hoping to get some answers about my sexual confusion, but also to help me deal with all the things going on in my life. I was a small-town kid thrown into a fast-moving world that I didn't fully understand. Something told me that if I wasn't careful, I might make some very big mistakes.

I made an instant connection with Bill Fay, the therapist.

Based in New York, he was whip-smart. He also played classical piano, which made it easy to talk about issues involving music. Looking back, I don't know how well I would have survived without his help in dealing with everything coming at me. In a way, I found myself experiencing the kind of adolescent turmoil that one usually goes through at fifteen or sixteen—except that at that age, I was already playing gigs and tuning pianos, living in a world of adults. I had effectively postponed my coming-of-age, and I was struggling to deal with it now, while at the same time handling a full-time career. The main focus of my therapy started with the question of continuing to convince myself I was heterosexual. But as time went on, and I went from being a sideman to leading my own band, career issues occupied a larger portion of my sessions.

For the next five years, I saw Bill whenever I was in New York between tours. During these periods, I often went five days a week. Sometimes, when I was on the road, we scheduled long-distance telephone sessions. This was one of the most productive periods of my life; thanks to Bill, I learned to make the most of it.

Also in 1963, I experienced my first adult relationship. During my regular layovers in California, I had gotten to know the vibraphonist Lynn Blessing. He was also from Indiana, and we hit it off right away. Lynn lived with his wife Jeanine and their one-year-old son in the Silver Lake section of L.A. They invited me to stay with them when I had time off, so in addition to the Bunkers' house, I now could count on the Blessings' hospitality as well.

With Lynn off playing gigs, I found myself spending more and more time with Jeanine, and it soon became clear that we had become more than just friends. But before this turned awkward, Lynn announced that he was seeing someone else and wanted a divorce. That cleared the way for Jeanine and me to begin an off-and-on relationship that lasted several years. Since Jeanine wanted to stay in California to finish college, we relied on old-fashioned handwritten letters and nightime phone calls that cost more than we could really afford. But we were having fun. Whenever I found the time, I would visit Jeanine in L.A., and one time, she used her semester break to stay with me in New York. In time, we both moved past that relationship, but we've maintained an easy friendship to this day.

The Shearing band finished 1963 at the London House in Chicago—a once famous supper club, known for its steaks, which by the '80s had ironically become a Burger King (and is now a bank). It was at the London House that George told us he was breaking up the band. He wanted to stay home in L.A. for a while, and he planned to launch his own radio show. The news made me very unhappy. It seemed like the year had gone by in a flash, and I didn't want it to end. But by Christmas, I was back at my New York apartment.

According to my datebook, I had been away 312 days that year. I had met plenty of fascinating people, made a lot of important contacts, and learned vital lessons about music from fellow musicians (and particularly from George). I also came to realize that I had learned a lot from George's road manager, Ed Fuerst. I couldn't have asked for a better teacher of touring-band secrets, such as how to get a bunch of musicians and a truckload of equipment where they needed to go, on time, while keeping everyone happy.

On my first day back in New York, I headed downtown to sign up for unemployment, unaware that I would remain out of work long enough to collect exactly two checks. To paraphrase a well-known remark made by tenor saxophonist Zoot Sims, a bunch of guys named Stan Getz were about to enter my life.

CHAPTER 9

On the Job Training
PART TWO

As 1964 began, I considered moving to California. Having spent most of the past year there, I knew more musicians in Los Angeles than I did in New York. On the other hand, several friends from Berklee had moved to Manhattan. Two of them, Chris Swansen and Steve Marcus, had settled on my block, so I now had some friends in New York, as well. I had a little money saved, and *Something's Coming* was scheduled for release in a couple of months. I trusted that some kind of work would show up before then.

And sure enough, two weeks into the new year, I got a call from Chuck Israels, the bassist from *Something's Coming.* Chuck had a regular gig with the Bill Evans Trio, but Evans was on one of his periodic extended leaves to deal with his heroin addiction. In the interim, Chuck had gone to work in tenor saxophonist Stan Getz's quartet.

Chuck told me that guitarist Jimmy Raney was planning to leave the band, and that Stan needed another guitarist, or maybe a pianist, to replace him. Stan had called quite a few players but had not found anyone available for the next tour, which was fast approaching. He finally called pianist Lou Levy, an old friend of his in L.A.. Levy had a steady gig with singer Peggy Lee, but it turned out that he had heard me playing at Shelly's Manne Hole just a month or so earlier, on my live recording date with Larry Bunker. Levy mentioned that since I played with four mallets, and could thus play chords, perhaps I might fill the role. Chuck also spoke up for me, so Stan suggested I audition by sitting in with the group for a night.

Stan was performing at Basin St. East, the setting of my unfortunate encounter with Herbie Mann a year and a half earlier, and this occasion proved no less disappointing.

To begin with, I didn't know Stan's music. Even though some of the pieces were familiar standards, Stan's group had their own arrangements, and I had limited success picking up on what to play or when to play it. I assumed that Stan wanted to hear how well I could accompany him, but I didn't really get much chance to try this either. Whenever he soloed, Raney played behind him quite busily, and I was afraid to get in the way. So, I only played behind the guitar solos. On top of that, my own soloing wasn't going too well either, since I didn't know the material, or for that matter, the styles of the players.

As the set continued, I knew I was making a poor impression, but things really turned bad when Stan took umbrage at the fact that I was only accompanying Raney. This became painfully clear when he stopped abruptly about eight bars into one of his own solos, turned to me with an angry red face, and shouted, "Why do you only play for him? What's wrong with *my* playing?" I was so stunned that I could hardly play at all for the rest of the set! At that point, I didn't know Stan at all. I wouldn't discover until later that he was prone to paranoia and could fly off the handle unexpectedly.

In the dressing room afterward, Stan was obviously unhappy about how it had gone, and although he intended it to be halfway humorous, his last words to me were, "Don't call us, we'll call you." Mortified, I packed up the vibes and went back uptown. Those unemployment checks were looking pretty good right about then.

But two weeks later, a subdued Chuck Israels called to say that Stan still had not found a replacement, and now they had just a few days before starting a three-week Canadian tour. So, Stan wanted me to join the group despite my audition. Too embarrassed to call me himself, he had asked Chuck to do it. I hesitated, but Chuck was a friend. Also, the new drummer joining the group was Joe Hunt, a musician I had admired on records. So I entered the world of Stan Getz.

The next day, Chuck and I drove about forty-five minutes north from Manhattan to Stan's house in Irvington, NY, to rehearse before traveling to Montreal. Since I had regularly visited Shearing's home—an upscale, beautifully furnished house in a wealthy section of L.A.—I thought I had a sense of how a successful jazz musician lived. The Getz house, though, fit the classic definition of "mansion." Built at the center of a gated multi-acre estate, it sat atop a hill overlooking the town; the winding road to this manor must have been a quarter-mile long. Stan and his wife Monica had five children—three boys and two girls, ranging in age from 15 to 4—so they actually needed a big house. But this was really dramatic. The bassist Steve Swallow used to call it Toad Hall, after the palatial estate in the fable *The Wind in the Willows*.

While there was plenty of house, there wasn't much *in* the house. The Getzes had lived there for only a year or two and apparently were furnishing the place slowly. The downstairs rooms didn't have carpets, and the bare floors created an echoing ambience throughout the first story. We set up our instruments in the living room while the Getz children peered in through open doorways, curious about what was going on.

The music started out shaky. For starters, Joe Hunt had just gotten out of the Army, and this was the first gigging he had done in a couple of years. And unlike Shearing, who had hundreds of arrangements for his group, Stan didn't have anything in the way of written music. We spent the day cobbling together arrangements, as we tried out various tunes, mostly standards. Stan also wanted me to learn several songs from his recent recordings, but he had no music for them. I had to listen to the records, learn the songs by ear, and quickly memorize them.

At that time, I didn't know much about Stan's music. I just recognized him as a famous name from the '40s and '50s—a saxophonist who had spent much of the last decade in Europe, who had recently repatriated and put out a successful bossa nova album. I had little knowledge of his role in jazz history or his considerable abilities. I soon learned what I had been missing.

We left the following day for two bookings: a week in Montreal and two weeks in Toronto. This was in late January, with Canada in the icy grip of winter—and with the Brazilian singer João Gilberto, who had just recorded with Stan for an upcoming album, joining us as guest artist. The first few nights did not go well. Stan drank pretty heavily and would only play the first set each evening, leaving the rest of us to play the second show without him. (This actually worked to my advantage, since we could play tunes that I knew without worrying about Stan's reactions.) But João was terribly unhappy. Severely reclusive, he would rarely leave his apartment even in New York; performing every night in this sub-zero climate was alien to his Brazilian psyche. In addition, he spoke only Portuguese, so we had a lot of trouble communicating with him. Fortunately, Chuck was quite quick with languages, and within the first week had picked up enough Portuguese to manage some basics.

Somehow, we got through the week and moved on to Toronto. Instead of the small audiences we'd had in Montreal, we played to full houses in Toronto, which motivated Stan to give better performances. I was beginning to get a handle on the songs, at last, but still hadn't learned much about how to replace the pianist when accompanying a solo. Having only occasionally tried this on the vibes, I certainly wasn't ready to accompany one of the most finicky soloists that music has ever known. Stan would try telling me what to do but would get frustrated half the time and just yell, "Stroll!" which meant to drop out and let him play alone with just the bass and drums. (Stan's anger made it seem more like "Take a hike!")

But as the two weeks went by in Toronto, things gradually came together, and by the end of the engagement the group had found a blend. To my surprise, and probably Stan's as well, he asked me to stay on with the group for a few more concerts. Those "few concerts" eventually stretched into three more years. During that time, he mostly called me "Youngblood" whenever he was in a good mood—I was twenty-one when I started with Stan—and various other things when he wasn't.

Today, Stan would probably be considered bipolar. He swung between being very "up" and exhibiting extreme paranoia; he frequently thought everyone was out to take advantage of him. He was compulsive, as exemplified by his obsession with saxophone reeds. Every few weeks or so, he would retreat from the world around him and spend hours sorting reeds and trying them out, one after another, setting them up in rows on the dressing-room table until there was no space left. He would go through ten boxes at a time, all the while complaining that there just were no good reeds anymore, they were all useless, and so on.

On a typical "reed night," he would continue to test them throughout the show. Some nights, he had dozens of reeds lined up on the end of my vibraphone so he could try them out, tooting a few notes on each as the rest of us played our solos. It was distracting and disrespectful, but in one of his reed frenzies, Stan was oblivious to just about everything.

When we played a club, Stan would routinely drink eight to ten shots of scotch per night, after polishing off a quart of Dewar's before even getting to the club. Most mornings, he sent me to buy him a bottle and bring it to his room. By my second year in the band, he alternated between bouts of drinking and sobriety, often going to health retreats in either North Carolina or Minnesota to dry out during breaks in our schedule. Stan owned a luxurious Jaguar, but because of his drinking, he rarely drove it himself; I became the designated driver. (The car was always breaking down, though, and after a while, he started hiring a limo to drive him from the Irvington house into New York for gigs.)

Stan found a way to work comments of questionable taste into any conversation; the most common were either anti-Semitic or anti-gay. (He seemed embarrassed about being Jewish and also committed to proving his manhood.) And he constantly made crude sexual remarks to anyone and everyone. He would often remark that a handsome man looked "good enough to eat," with a salacious tone in his voice; with women it was even more exaggerated. Once, at an after-concert reception in Europe, Stan, his wife Monica, and I were in conversation with some dignitary and his wife. Stan began to stare conspicuously at the low-cut cleavage of the dignitary's wife. After some minutes of this, he growled in a low voice, "I'd like to suck your tits." For something like that, you would expect someone to get arrested—or at least punched in the nose. But Stan could get away with it. Monica just said, "Oh, Stan," and everyone else just stood there shell-shocked.

Stan himself once punched an airplane stewardess when she reached to adjust his seat belt. They did throw him off the plane for that one.

STAN GETZ

Stan Getz had grown up fighting to survive, and I suspect that fighting reassured him that he was still alive. (What a way to live.) His way of relating to friends and family was to constantly challenge and try to hurt them; if they put up with this, it proved to him they must really care about him. (What a way to love.)

But whatever his personal failings, Stan Getz had a natural genius for music. He came from a poor family in the Bronx and started playing woodwind instruments in middle school. One of his first instruments in the school band was the notoriously difficult bassoon, which requires an unusually strong embouchure. Stan credited this for helping him develop a good sound on saxophone—first alto, then tenor. He developed so quickly that when he was fifteen, the veteran bandleader Jack Teagarden heard him and immediately hired him for his band. This posed a problem because Stan was not yet of legal age to leave school or home. Consequently, Teagarden filled out papers to become his legal guardian, and Stan left school after freshman year to begin his professional life.

Stan told me the year he toured with Teagarden was idyllic. Teagarden and his wife were very calm and considerate and treated Stan as their son. While the rest of the band traveled separately, Stan rode with the Teagardens in their Chrysler station wagon. Jack loved fishing, and would frequently pull over whenever he spotted a nice lake, drag out his fishing gear, and relax for a while.

While still a teenager, Stan emerged as a rising star in the bands of Woody Herman and Stan Kenton. He also became a serious heroin junkie. His decade-long drug habit ended when he got arrested for trying to hold up a drug store in Seattle. After a brief jail stay, he decided the best course of action was to leave the country, since the Internal Revenue Service was also after him. Living the life of an irresponsible junkie musician, Stan had never filed a tax return in his life.

Stan's first marriage ended in divorce, and incredibly, he gained custody of his three children (since his wife Beverly was in even worse shape than Stan at the time). His second wife, Monica, came from a prominent Swedish family, and the Getzes lived for nearly ten years in Denmark while Stan played throughout Europe and got his life together. Stan and Monica also had two more children, so they had a fairly large blended family by the time they decided to return to the States—where they found the IRS waiting. The IRS estimated the taxes Stan would likely have owed from those early years, and then required him to turn over most of the income from his subsequent gigs, leaving him less than enough to even pay the salaries of his musicians.

Stan told me that after six months of this, he had used up most of his savings and was close to giving up and returning to Europe. Around that time, though, he got a call from Verve, his record label, saying that guitarist Charlie Byrd was making a record featuring the new music from South America called "bossa nova," which combined jazz and samba. Verve thought that adding Stan to the record would increase commercial appeal and jazz credibility, since Charlie had little recognition outside his hometown of Washington, D.C. Stan desperately needed the extra money, so he took the date.

Jazz Samba with the Charlie Byrd Trio became a big seller, reaching number 1 on the *Billboard* pop chart. It established Byrd as a national artist and elevated Stan's status as well. And it started the bossa nova craze in the U.S.

Stan knew nothing about Brazilian music prior to that record session, and he found the level of musicianship in Byrd's trio lacking—a fact he expressed to me several times. But that opportunity served a number of purposes. It led Stan into a new kind of music, which would ultimately prove immensely successful for him, and it resolved his immediate financial problem. Ironically, he didn't actually see any of the royalties from that record; the money turned out to be almost the exact amount needed to settle his tax bill. But while the royalties went to the government, Stan could substantially increase his fees for concerts and club dates until he was at last making a living typical of a major jazz star.

Stan was full of contradictions, among them a great insecurity about his playing. Despite his success, he had no formal musical training, and he feared that any day, he would be exposed as a fraud. Nonetheless, he liked to hire highly educated players for his bands. I think they challenged him; but also, by surrounding himself with smart, knowledgeable players, he reassured himself that he belonged in their company. He didn't sight-read well, and he had only limited knowledge of music theory—the knowledge of how and why the harmonies follow each other in a composition—which limited him somewhat as an improviser and as a composer. He was an "ear" player (similar to the "ear" singers, like Anita O'Day). Instead of reading music and knowing what notes each chord contained, Stan just listened and tried to find notes that would work. As "ear" players go, he was extremely good at it, and very few people noticed—not even many other musicians. But playing with him on a nightly basis, I quickly became aware of it.

Stan seemed to sense this weakness, and in response, he pushed himself to keep trying new and challenging pieces. Pianist Jim McNeely, who played with Stan long after I left the band, told me this continued when he was in the group. If you brought in some songs for Stan to consider, he would usually go for the hard ones, instead of picking the easier ones that he could learn quickly. That meant playing them over and over till Stan could get comfortable with the song structures.

One of Stan's most beloved records was *Focus,* a project he did in 1961 with composer Eddie Sauter. It called for Sauter to write a program of music for just Stan and a string section—a bold move, since Stan didn't read well and Sauter's music was very sophisticated. Fate played into Stan's hands, however, when his mother passed away on the eve of the recording sessions. Because of this, the strings were recorded first, and Stan came into the studio a few weeks later to add his parts. This made it possible for him to repeatedly listen to the strings and try out a lot of things before recording his solos, instead of having to improvise his parts on the spot. On one piece, he felt that the rhythmic energy called for more than just tenor sax, so he called in drummer Roy Haynes to play along, using just brushes on a snare drum (which Roy, of course, did beautifully).

The record remains a masterpiece, and Stan was always especially proud of it. As I listen to it closely, I can hear Stan playing "by ear," waiting for the strings and reacting to what they play, rather than leading the music by anticipating what the strings will do next. But it doesn't matter. He sounds so good, and Sauter's writing was such a good fit, that it all worked anyway.

Stan developed one of the warmest, richest sounds ever on the instrument, and he had a natural feel for lyrical melodies. I have often said that I learned about harmony from George Shearing and melody from Stan Getz. I also learned from Stan a lot about the music business—in many cases, what not to do. He was a larger-than-life character who brought a lot of trouble upon himself and the people close to him, but he was a classic survivor. In his youth, he was the worst kind of heroin junkie, and later, an equally bad alcoholic. I don't think he ever stayed sober for more than a few days at a time until he turned fifty, and it took a terrible toll on his health and his loved ones. But he got through it all, maintaining his career the whole time. Even when diagnosed with cancer at age fifty-nine, he continued to tour and play until he lost the battle five years later.

When his friend, trumpeter Herb Alpert (the legendary record producer and label owner), contacted Berklee about establishing some kind of memorial at the college, I knew exactly what to recommend. At the time, we were rebuilding and expanding the library, and it is now named the Stan Getz Library and Media Center. Stan always felt inadequate because he didn't get the kind of education he so respected. He would have loved the idea of a library named in his honor.

When we returned from Canada to New York, it was clear that João would not continue performing with the group. As in Montreal, he'd been very unhappy in Toronto. Most of the time, we couldn't get him to leave his hotel room. For two weeks, the maid could never get in to clean. He bought food from a grocery on the corner and ate in his room, only emerging for the gigs—and a couple of nights, he didn't even do that.

(Throughout his career, João has continued to struggle with performing in public. A few years ago, I played Carnegie Hall and one of the stagehands told me that João had played there the previous night. He was staying at the Meridien Hotel, conveniently located about one hundred feet from the Carnegie Hall stage door on West 56th Street, but the first challenge was getting him out of his hotel room. Lengthy conversations took place between the promoter in the hallway and João, in his room, claiming he wasn't quite ready. Once informed of the delay, most of the sold-out crowd headed for the lobby bar, soon consuming the entire inventory. At the one-hour mark, doubts arose whether the show could take place at all, given the hall curfew. When João at last emerged from his room, he was led quickly to the hotel entrance, where he refused to make the thirty-second stroll to the stage door; he insisted on being driven by a limo! Since 56th is a one-way street leading *away* from the stage door, this would have meant going around the block in midtown Manhattan, which can take a good chunk of time. But the driver had a great idea. As soon as João settled into the car, he just backed up 56th Street to the stage door, and João got his limo ride—all one hundred feet of it! João then realized he was wearing his sunglasses and wanted to go back to his room for his regular eyeglasses, but the promoter knew enough to send someone else, fearing João would once again lock himself in his room. Ultimately, the concert started seventy-five minutes late, just in time to avoid cancellation. I was told the audience loved every minute of it, although the promoter probably needed a vacation after it ended.)

Getz/Gilberto, the new bossa nova record by Stan and João, wasn't due for release for another couple of months. Nonetheless, and despite João's absence, we started playing some tunes from the album on our gigs, mixing them in with the jazz standards. And during this time—and especially on the *bossa nova* material—I began to notice things about Stan's playing that made me re-examine my own approach to soloing.

I had always tried to play something new and different each time I soloed. I made it a point of pride to avoid repeating ideas, or using phrases that might be perceived as clichés. But Stan would play practically the same solo every night on certain pieces. And sometimes, he didn't improvise at all; he just played the melody, but always with great feeling and expression. I had never before heard anyone do so much with dynamics and expression. At first, I reacted to Stan's approach by dismissing it, criticizing him for his lack of adventure. But then, I saw the way he communicated with audiences. He completely captivated them with these often simple but powerful melodies. As an improviser, he was a poet.

This really opened my eyes. It forced me to rethink my concept of the jazz solo. At the same time, as the band's only chord-instrument player, I saw a chance to further develop my four-mallet technique, something I had only begun to explore till then. The combination of my new insights on improvising, plus my evolving technique, forever changed the way I play music.

Long before I felt ready, Stan decided to record the quartet "live" at the Cafe Au Go Go in New York. Then the record company, with the help of Stan's wife, persuaded him to include João's wife, Astrud Gilberto, on a couple of songs for this recording. Since João no longer wanted to perform this music after his difficult Canadian experience, this allowed Stan to continue the format of collaborating with a Brazilian vocalist. But Astrud didn't have any repertoire; for the week at the Go Go, she quickly learned two songs (a bossa nova arrangement of the standard "It Might as Well Be Spring," plus a new piece called "The Telephone Song"). In fact, she had never sung professionally at all, except for one chorus on one song on the just-released *Getz/Gilberto*.

That one song, though, was "The Girl from Ipanema," which became a massive hit. When it was edited down for radio play, João's vocal (in Portuguese) was gone; only Astrud's (in English) remained, and it launched her career. As the story goes, Astrud's addition on *Getz/Gilberto* was a spur-of-the-moment idea at the recording session, suggested by either Stan's wife, or the producer, or the engineer, or by Stan himself—everyone involved eventually claimed credit! Astrud has said the idea came from her husband, though I have trouble picturing João bringing it up, since he didn't speak a word of English.

Astrud Gilberto was supposedly this alluring beauty. I didn't see it at all; I thought her rather plain. But she seemed to think she was irresistible. She flirted with most men (including me), constantly asking them to do her favors, as if to suggest that a woman of her great beauty would simply expect such treatment. She once asked our bass player to pick up some magazines for her. To his astonishment, she also expected him to pay for them.

I didn't respond to her flirtations; I just didn't find her attractive, or even personable. I later found out that she had complained to Stan about me, telling him that I must be gay, since I was the only man she knew who hadn't come on to her. When Stan told me this, we had a laugh over it, but later I wondered if Stan sensed something about my orientation. I also suspected that he himself was sometimes attracted to men. He constantly commented on good-looking guys and tended to make more "faggot" remarks than anyone I'd ever met. I wondered if this was a kind of protest or defense against confused feelings of his own. Meanwhile, he had a voracious appetite for sex and chased after almost any woman that showed the slightest interest in him.

But my real reason for disliking Astrud was that she just didn't sing well. She had no musical training and no performing experience before she started touring with us. It hurt my pride to have her in the group.

Stan planned to record two nights at the Go Go. Frankly, the whole group was still too inexperienced to try a "live" record, and Stan was very nervous about the project. Adding an untested singer to the program increased the challenge, and none of us in the band went into it with much confidence. The venue didn't help. The Go Go was not exclusively a jazz club; it also booked comedians and theatrical performers, taking it out of the jazz "comfort zone." And just two months before our appearance, the club had gained new notoriety when comedian Lenny Bruce got arrested there, leading to his famous obscenity trial. But the audiences at the Go Go had a reputation for being especially responsive and supportive. And word had gotten around that Stan would present some "new Brazilian music," which lent an air of anticipation when we took the stage.

The first night did not go well. About half an hour before show time, Stan ripped the seat of his expensive tailored trousers, and a temporary repair job involving safety pins was all that could be managed. Playing in front of an audience with your pants torn apart would unnerve many people; for Stan, this sort of thing could literally alter his state of mind. Fortunately, things came together on the second night, and almost all the tracks on the record came from that performance. We didn't get a good version of "The Telephone Song" on either night, since we didn't know it too well, so a couple days later, we arrived at Rudy Van Gelder's recording studio to record that one tune again.

Van Gelder had become something of a jazz legend in the '50s, thanks to the distinctive sound of his recordings for such storied jazz labels as Blue Note, Prestige, Savoy, and others. In 1959, he opened a brand-new studio in Englewood Cliffs, New Jersey, and a great many jazz musicians made the pilgrimage out there to record. He was extremely particular about the studio and his equipment, always wearing white gloves when he sat at the console so as not to leave fingerprints on the knobs. He had a strict no-smoking policy, too. In those days, many if not most musicians were smokers, but they willingly abstained in order to record at Van Gelder's. Not Stan, though. Creed Taylor, the record's producer, pressured Rudy to make an exception. We arrived to find a chair and a microphone in the middle of the studio, with an ashtray on a stand next to it.

Van Gelder told Stan he could smoke only at that spot. That's how we completed the recording *Getz Au Go Go,* which was released in late 1964.

But even as we finished the Go Go recording, *Getz/ Gilberto* had started to get noticed. The album had come out a couple months earlier, and Astrud's feature on "The Girl from Ipanema" was getting a lot of airplay. About that time, I remember waking up early one spring morning in my apartment on West 73rd Street; the windows were open, and I could hear the cars and people on the street below. I was used to this, and had gotten to the point where I could usually sleep through most of the street sounds—even the guy who sang opera as he delivered groceries in the mornings. But that morning at about 6, I woke with a start when I heard someone whistling the bridge to "Ipanema." The single had only been out a few weeks, and I realized then that something big was happening. By midsummer Stan and Astrud's version of "The Girl from Ipanema" had peaked at number 2 on Billboard's pop charts. Only the Beatles kept the record out of first place.

People clamored for the music from the record, and it became obvious that it would be good for business if Astrud joined our touring group. Unfortunately, we couldn't easily replicate the recording with a jazz quartet. The record featured a group of Brazilian musicians with quite different instrumentation. In particular, it was built around João's guitar playing; we didn't have a guitar in the band, though I simulated João's comping as best I could. What's more, Stan had already grown disdainful toward the bossa nova. I think he feared getting trapped into playing it full time. So, we continued to focus on jazz, playing just a couple of Brazilian tunes at the end of each performance.

In May 1964, Astrud joined the group for a week in Washington, D.C. and then toured with us the rest of the year. That gig also marked my elevation to tour manager. Stan was notoriously disorganized when it came to things like travel arrangements and business responsibilities. For example, we had arrived in Washington without hotel reservations or local transport to the gig, causing a major inconvenience for everyone. I offered to take care of these things, and Stan put me in charge from then on.

The Washington gig got only rockier with the addition of Astrud to the quartet. As a novice performer, she knew only a few songs. She also didn't know the etiquette of road travel, something that veteran musicians take seriously. Admittedly, it wasn't easy for her, suddenly thrust into the spotlight, having to learn everything as she went along, and the sudden success of the record created all kinds of additional stress. We began working every day of the week, filling the off days with extra concerts—sometimes two a day, if time permitted. We sold out every date, and wherever we went, Stan and Astrud were besieged with requests for press interviews.

Things got even more stressful (not to mention complicated) when Stan and Astrud began having an affair a few weeks after she joined the band. Though it started rather discreetly, they eventually made little effort to disguise it. Once I went to Stan's room to give him some contracts to sign. I assumed he was alone, but as I turned to leave, I caught a glimpse of Astrud standing naked behind the bathroom door. After bassist Gene Cherico joined the band, he told me that as he was driving one of the rental cars back from a concert, Stan and Astrud were having sex in the back seat. The situation got especially tense whenever Stan's wife Monica flew out to travel with the band for a few days, forcing the lovers to pretend nothing was going on.

To promote the record, we appeared in two movies that summer. The first was *The Hanged Man,* only the second made-for-TV movie, and well reviewed at the time. It starred Edmond O'Brien, Vera Miles, Gene Raymond, Robert Culp,

Edgar Bergen, and Norman Fell—all familiar movie or television personalities of the time—and had a large cast of extras. Our scene took place in a New Orleans club during Mardi Gras; we played while the principal characters plotted some gangland killing. In addition to the now-obligatory "Ipanema," we also did a new song commissioned for the movie, "Only Trust Your Heart," with music by Benny Carter and lyrics by Sammy Cahn. (In later years, I met both of them and was pleased to learn that each remembered me from the movie—quite unexpected, since at that stage in my career, I was just one of the guys in Stan's band.)

The second movie, very much a "B" flick, was an MGM production called *Get Yourself a College Girl,* starring Chad Everett and Mary Ann Mobley. It featured cameo appearances by about a dozen of MGM's recording artists, apparently to make up for the lack of a storyline. Our scene was filmed on a ski-lodge set left over from an Elvis Presley movie, complete with a machine blowing artificial snowflakes in the background. Once again, we performed "Ipanema," plus an original song titled "Sweet Rain" written by Michael Gibbs, a pal of mine from Berklee. That summer, we also did a couple of pop-music television shows, one called *Hootenanny* and another called *Shindig*. These were all unusual showcases for jazz, but it only went to prove how Stan's hit record had thrust him onto another level of fame.

Of course, jazz clubs remained our bread and butter. We played a week at the original Birdland in New York, just before its demise, and set the all-time attendance record for the club. (Astrud had to stay home that week because she had come down with chickenpox, and even that didn't hurt attendance.) The Birdland gig occasioned a strange incident involving John Coltrane, the legendary tenor saxophonist. One night, as we prepared to start the second set before a packed house, we noticed Coltrane sitting at a table right in front of Stan.

After the first song, Stan acknowledged Coltrane and made a very sincere introduction, calling Trane one of the giants of the instrument, and so on. Coltrane sat stone-faced. Then, as soon as we started the next song, he rather huffily got up and walked out. Whenever I tell this story to anyone who knew Coltrane, they can't believe it, because he was known as such a considerate and gracious guy. (A few years later, I would have a quite different but equally surprising encounter with Coltrane.)

While with Stan's band, I had the chance to at last record with another jazz icon, my idol Bill Evans. Bill and Stan were both signed to Verve Records, and the label thought it logical for them to record together. But the sessions didn't go well, despite some occasional good moments. Bill could hardly concentrate; he was going through another period of detoxing from his heroin habit, and it was hard for him to get all the way through a song. We recorded for a couple of frustrating days and still didn't have a single usable track. Bill would inevitably get lost somewhere about halfway through, playing the wrong chords or going to the wrong section of the tune. My first chance to play with my favorite pianist was a terrible letdown. (Those tracks were never released, though Stan went into the studio with Bill a couple months later, using a different group, and those tracks did come out a few years later.)

Stan roped me into another record that he made in collaboration with an old friend of his. He was doing a favor by lending the newfound Getz fame to a record by Bob Brookmeyer, a trombonist who later became known primarily as a composer and arranger. The musicians included the cream of the jazz scene: pianist Herbie Hancock and bassist Ron Carter from Miles Davis's band, and Elvin Jones, the drummer from Coltrane's band. But the first day of recording left Stan uncomfortable because of serious tension between Brookmeyer and producer Teo Macero, who thought the music wasn't commercial enough. Since this was the same guy who had produced all of Miles Davis' records at Columbia, his reluctance to just let the musicians "do their thing" came as something of a surprise.

That night, I got a frantic call from Stan instructing me, in no uncertain terms, to bring my vibes to the studio the next day. I was a little hesitant—and as I expected, I walked in to find that no one knew I was coming. Brookmeyer was especially gracious about it, however. It helped that he already knew me—we had met shortly after I arrived in New York, when he, Phil Woods, and Joe Morello helped me find my bearings—so at least, this wasn't a complete stranger crashing his record session. Of course, the arrangements had no parts for vibes, so Bob had to hurriedly rewrite the music, making room for me to play on the remainder of the tunes.

But the vitriol between Bob and Teo carried over from the previous day, with the two of them increasingly arguing and shouting at each other between takes. At the lunch break, Teo went to a local music store and returned with a stack of sheet music. He insisted that we play several standards from the music he had purchased, in addition to Brookmeyer's own songs. As a result, the sessions went longer than planned and the tension got so heavy that I retreated into my corner of the studio, next to Elvin Jones—who made fun of me when he saw me drinking a carton of milk with my sandwich. He said he had never before seen musicians drink milk. (You can take the boy out of Indiana, but....)

The record was released as *Bob Brookmeyer and Friends*, a title that hardly represented the mood in the studio. For years to come, whenever Herbie Hancock and I ran into each other, we would have a laugh about that title.

As Stan's new tour manager, I took on responsibility for getting the band from place to place, settling us into hotels, dealing with club owners and concert promoters, and collecting the money at the end of the night. I soon found myself taking care of Stan as well, whenever he drank too much to get home safely, and also had to intercede to quell arguments between him and the presenters. Stan would suspect them of trying to cheat him, at which point he would start to antagonize them, often threatening to walk out on the gig. It became routine for Stan to brew trouble and for me to smooth things over.

During a week in Seattle, Stan began obsessing over the time he had gotten arrested for trying to rob a drugstore there during his junkie years. He couldn't stop talking about it, and a few days into the gig, he walked around downtown and found the drugstore. He went in and saw, behind the counter, the same lady he had tried to hold up years before. He went up and asked if she remembered him, which she did. They had a short chat, and Stan invited her to come down to the club as his guest. He introduced her that night as an old friend, and asked her in front of the audience if she had any requests. In response, she asked if he knew any songs by Wayne King, a very commercial sax player popular with older listeners at the time. (We all got a laugh out of that.) The important thing for Stan was that he had somehow made amends for his youthful transgression, and I was happy for him.

But by the end of 1964, my first year with Stan, the daily turmoil had gotten so strenuous that I wondered if I could continue. On the other hand, this was a fantastic career opportunity and the chance to play with these great musicians. I just couldn't leave. And as it turned out, significant change was in the air after Astrud and Stan had a falling out, mostly over money.

Since Astrud's appearance on their hit record had not been planned, no one had provided for her to share in the royalties. In addition, Stan paid her only a small salary for our touring dates—even less than the musicians in the band. (Not that we were raking it in ourselves: that first year, the group members made $250 for a week in a club, or $75 for a single concert date, both less than I had made with Shearing. And of course, we had to pay our own hotel bills.)

Astrud got herself a manager, and they demanded a substantial increase in pay. They also instituted a suit against Stan and Verve Records for a share of the record royalties. Stan was livid at what he saw as ingratitude on Astrud's part, and that ended things between them—at least for the time being. Their messy affair might well have ended their professional partnership anyway, but money finally did it. We had a week of concerts in Mexico coming up just before Christmas, and that would be Astrud's last tour with us. Fittingly, it took the form of another poorly organized adventure.

One concert was scheduled about two hundred miles from Mexico City, in a town called Puebla. We waited in front of Mexico City's El Presidente Hotel—with our bass, drums and vibraphone all lined up—for the promoter to drive us to the concert. He arrived about an hour late in a Volkswagen beetle, and just then seemed to grasp that he couldn't get all of us, and our instruments, into the car. To my amazement, he began flagging down cars on the street and within ten minutes had found three drivers ready to drive us 200 miles to the gig. One of those cars broke down halfway, and that driver flagged down *another* car on the highway to finish the trip! I had never seen anything like it.

We made the promoter hire a bus for the return trip to Mexico City.

The holiday period also marked a watershed in my own recordings. I wanted to try a larger project of some kind. At the same time, RCA was looking for someone to create a jazz version of the hugely successful Broadway musical *The Sound of Music,* for which they had the recording rights. Jazz versions of musicals were fashionable at the time, and I figured it would give me the chance to experiment with larger instrumentation. I hired arranger Gary McFarland to write for a string section, and I planned to share the solo responsibilities with guitarist Jim Hall.

(Enlisting McFarland contained a bit of irony. Because we shared the same first name, and both played vibes after having attended at Berklee, people often got the two of us mixed up. In 1971, when McFarland died of a drug overdose at a club in New York, the rumors flew for weeks that it was actually me who had passed.)

Several disasters befell this project from the start. First, while the Getz band was still in Mexico, our plane tickets were stolen from my hotel room. It took an extra day to arrange another flight home, and I had to postpone the recording session. Next, Jim Hall canceled. His wife was about to have surgery, and at the last minute (and without telling me), he sent a sub. This meant a major revision of my plan for the record, since I had structured a lot of the music around Jim's unique musical personality. I ended up spreading the solo parts around to Phil Woods and Bob Brookmeyer, who were also on the session.

But the biggest problem lay in the arranging. I had always admired the fresh and original ideas in McFarland's writing. But it seemed like he must have cranked out these charts just a couple of days before the recording. Everything sounded very conventional and uninspiring. I was disappointed in every song.

One good thing did come out of this fiasco: my first chance to play with bassist Steve Swallow.

Jim Hall had taken me aside at some point earlier that year and told me, "Steve Swallow is the bass player for you." And boy, was he right about that. Despite my inauspicious attempt to jazz up *The Sound of Music*, Steve and I continued to play together for most of the next twenty years—mainly in my own bands, but occasionally on other projects since then, too. I've always remembered that Jim Hall has recommended people to me: first Astor Piazzolla and then Steve Swallow, two of the most important musicians in my life. Thanks, Jim.

That recording also marked a turning point in my relations with RCA. Once again, the label chose the cover art and the title without consulting me. They called it *The Groovy Sound of Music,* and it had a poorly done photo of a vibraphone and mallets. I later learned that the art department had forgotten the deadline and had to throw something together on one day's notice (and it looked it). But the title truly embarrassed me. "Groovy" was unhip the first time it was spoken, and for an emerging artist trying to establish his credibility, it was mortifying. Between the unsatisfactory music and this amateurish presentation, I wanted to buy up all the copies myself, just to keep people from seeing it. So, I threatened to quit the label. I demanded, and got, a promise that they would consult me on art and titles for all future records. And I felt vindicated when, a few records later, the cover for *A Genuine Tong Funeral*—a painting I had commissioned from an artist friend—received a GRAMMY nomination for album cover design.

CHAPTER 10

The Real Stan Getz Quartet

After Astrud left the band at the start of 1965, we reverted to a true jazz ensemble. But soon enough, bassist Gene Cherico told me he wanted to quit the band and spend some time in Mexico. I was astounded; I couldn't believe he would give up one of the best gigs in jazz and just take a vacation. But after I pressed him about it, he admitted that he had a heroin habit and couldn't control it anymore. He was going to Mexico to get straight. I didn't believe this either, because Gene was such a clean-cut guy, always on time, always taking care of business, always well dressed. I told Stan about it, and Stan said, "No way." Being a big time ex-junkie himself, he said he definitely could tell if Gene were using.

But then Gene told me something that convinced me. He reminded me about a gig in Vancouver (Canada) earlier that year, where he had behaved strangely during the entire week. I recalled that during those sets, he kept forgetting his place in the music and generally seemed out of it. He explained that he had been afraid to take his heroin supply across the border into Canada, and in order to deal with his craving, had drunk several bottles of cough syrup for the codeine. Unfortunately, this also made him sleepy, and he was barely able to function on the bandstand. (Gene did go to Mexico, and after a six-month stay, he made a comeback and spent the remaining years of his career playing for Frank Sinatra.)

After Gene bowed out, I recommended Steve Swallow as his replacement, and Stan gave me the go-ahead to hire him. Steve had an odd response. Instead of jumping at the opportunity, he said he considered playing with Getz a "commercial" gig, but that I had caught him at the right time because he needed the work. Our first concert was at Cornell University in upstate New York, and Swallow and I drove up together in a rented Dodge station wagon. We talked nonstop all the way there and back, about everything from music to drug addiction to the tragic death of bassist Scott LaFaro, who had died in a traffic accident on that same highway a few years earlier—also on his way to a gig with Getz's band.

Stan also decided to change drummers around this time. He had run into Roy Haynes on the street and asked him to join the group. Although Roy usually preferred to work with a band of his own, Stan caught him at the right time, too, and persuaded him to replace Joe Hunt. (Poor Joe drove up to Stan's house that very day to ask for a raise, only to get the news that he had lost the gig.) Roy had played with practically every important jazz artist from Charlie Parker and Lester Young to Miles and Coltrane, and had also toured for a decade with singer Sarah Vaughan. With Roy Haynes in the group, the "real" Getz quartet—for me, at any rate—at last took shape.

With Roy's arrival, we achieved a new level of group identity. The first rehearsal was a revelation. When Swallow and I walked out of the studio, we agreed we had just had a master class in drumming. Roy immediately took total charge of the music and made everything feel effortless. Swallow was a superb bassist on his own, and with Roy, we had a truly great rhythm section. Over the years, you keep trying new combinations of musicians, and every so often, a lineup will just click. It's happened for me just a handful of times, and this was the first.

Steve and I, in our twenties, represented the young lions. Stan and Roy, just entering their forties, were the established old hands. We each had things to offer and roles to play, on the bandstand and off. By virtue of their long careers, Stan and Roy provided the group's stylistic authority. I acted as the band's musical director, choosing our material and writing the arrangements (often with Steve's input). Steve and I handled the driving chores; I led with Stan in one car, and Steve followed with Roy in another. In those days, before GPS and Google Maps, I became known for both my ability to find the location of the gigs and, perhaps more notable, my ability to pretend I knew where I was going even when I didn't have a clue. This gave Roy unlimited pleasure, and he loved kidding me whenever I made a wrong turn trying to find a hotel or concert hall.

One day, in my capacity as music director, I received a lead sheet from composer Johnny Mandel, an old friend of Stan's from their early days in New York. I suspect Johnny sent the music to me because he guessed (correctly) that Stan would probably lose it before we ever got to try it out. I immediately liked the song and thought it would be perfect for Stan: it had a great melody that I knew he could work wonders with. I played it for Swallow, and he agreed, so I brought it to our next rehearsal. We ran it down several times, but in spite of my enthusiasm, Stan just didn't think much of it.

A few months later, the movie featuring that song came out, and "The Shadow of Your Smile" became a major hit, recorded by everybody and their cousins. Stan then started to play it as well, but it was really too late; had he recorded it first, I'm sure he would have scored yet another hit record.

During 1965, I became very close to the Getzes, who accepted me into their family with a lot of encouragement and warmth. This was partly because I spent so much time taking care of Stan when we toured, and partly because I was young enough to assume the role of an older son. And while Stan could fly into a rage at the slightest provocation, for some reason, he rarely lost his temper with me. Once, I arrived at his house to pick him up for a gig, and he was taking a nap. Monica asked me if I would go wake him, which I thought a bit strange. Monica explained that if she did it, he might have one of his tantrums, but that he probably wouldn't get mad if I woke him.

Stan was full of strange quirks. Benny Goodman once asked him to perform at a fundraiser for some Jewish charity near Benny's home in Westchester, NY. After the band had played our first song, Stan stepped up to the microphone and started in with, "Today I am a man," recounting the bar mitzvah speech from his youth; he ran out of words after a couple of sentences and then just stopped. It was a real "Springtime for Hitler" moment for the audience, and no one knew what to expect next. But after a moment of stunned silence, Stan simply turned around and counted off the next song. Whew! Just another night on the gig with the great Stan Getz.

But he could also be a lot of fun, when on the positive end of his mood swings. One year, we played quite a few dates with Tony Bennett, and we all got pretty chummy. Tony had recently gone through a divorce and was at loose ends in his personal life, so we sometimes had dinner with him. One night, Tony and I went to the Getz house for a pleasant home-cooked dinner. As we sat down, Monica set some artichokes before us, then returned to the kitchen to finish preparing the next course. None of us had ever seen an artichoke before. We tried to figure out how to eat them, poking at them with our forks. After about five minutes of us stabbing the vegetables and making no progress at all, Monica emerged from the kitchen and started laughing; she then showed us how to pull off the leaves and dine on artichoke, to the amusement of even Stan.

That same evening, I had the distinction of introducing Tony Bennett to hashish. In those days, I knew, Tony was a dedicated pot smoker; in fact, his road manager rolled almost perfect joints and carried around a little box of them for Tony. I presumed he had probably tried hash before, but after dinner, when I asked if he wanted some, he got excited and said he'd always wanted to see what it was like. I have no idea whether Tony still lights up on occasion, since it seems most people lose interest in pot as they get older; I know I did. In any case, the fact that Tony enjoyed an occasional joint doesn't seem to have diminished his talent or shortened his career.

I myself had discovered the fun of marijuana soon after moving to New York, and I smoked pretty regularly for about a decade. I maintained a policy of never going into a recording session high (though I certainly played quite a few gigs under the influence during that era). As for other drugs, although I knew a few people who used heroin or cocaine, I was scared of going near that junk. I never understood how someone as intelligent as Bill Evans, for instance, could become a serious addict. In the '40s and '50s, people almost expected that jazz musicians would use heroin, and many name players of those years were also well-known junkies. But by the time I came along, everyone knew that heroin could destroy lives as well as careers. Who in his right mind would touch the stuff? I wondered.

I also didn't drink alcohol during my twenties, so pot was my only vice—well, except for a couple of experiments with psilocybin mushrooms, and one afternoon when the whole Gary Burton Quartet tried LSD, which I found interesting but had no desire to repeat. (Hey, it was San Francisco. *In the '60s.*) I stopped smoking pot entirely when I learned I would become a father; I just couldn't imagine smoking around my little baby. That was thirty-some years ago, and I've never missed it for a moment.

Perhaps the pot helped me deal with the major crisis in my playing, at that point. I had crossed the threshold separating the youthful musician, who would play anything that popped into my mind, from the more discriminating and focused improviser I wanted to become. It was often frustrating: one night I could play exactly what I wanted, but the very next night the music would spill all over the place. Sometimes, I ended up furious at myself, literally in tears because I hated what I had played. I could imagine what it ought to sound like. But consistently achieving that ideal, on demand, did not come easily. I suppose it's something every improvising musician goes through, and looking back, I consider it just part of my musical maturation. At the time, however, it felt like I might never reach the level I wanted.

My first visit to Europe came when Stan played a jazz festival in Comblain-la-Tour, a little town in Belgium. The Comblain-la-Tour Jazz Festival was organized by an American Army veteran who had been sheltered by the local villagers during World War II after he found himself behind enemy lines. Out of gratitude, the guy returned year after year to stage a jazz festival there. (It recently celebrated its fiftieth anniversary.) We flew into Brussels Airport and were met by a festival staffer who had only one car. Not only was it too small for our group, but Anita O'Day had also arrived and needed a ride to the festival, too. So, the quartet decided to rent a car for the two-hour trip and set off, with me at the wheel following the festival vehicle.

About an hour into the trip, the lead car suddenly swerved to the side of the highway. There was a steady rain, cars were zipping by at high speed, and we couldn't figure out what was going on, but we pulled over, too. We sat there for a minute and could see the driver and Anita arguing. Then, she opened the door, got out, and right there in the rain, by the side of the car, she squatted down and took a pee. She didn't seem to care who noticed. We couldn't believe it.

At the end of 1965, Stan and Monica got the idea to bypass the promoters and put on a pair of major concerts themselves. They looked ahead to the holiday week and put holds on Symphony Hall in Boston for December 22 and Carnegie Hall in New York on December 24—Christmas Eve. Stan's popularity would guarantee ticket sales, they figured, and after decades of Stan playing gigs for others, how hard could it be to put on a concert themselves?

Thus began one of the great sagas of my tenure with the Getzes.

The plan called for the Getz Quartet to play the Boston date on our own, and then add the singer Dionne Warwick—only twenty-five years old and already a pop superstar—at Carnegie Hall. Preparations for the Carnegie concert took a major left turn when Joe Mooney, an old acquaintance of Stan's, entered the picture. Mooney was a blind jazz organist and singer whose career had faded some years earlier—and even in his heyday, he wasn't well known outside the New York area. But his manager had heard about the Carnegie gig and contacted Stan about adding Joe to the bill. Stan resisted but Mooney persisted, playing on their old friendship and begging for a small spot on the concert. And to my amazement, Stan caved in and agreed to let Mooney play at intermission.

Details for staging the production continued to take shape, and perhaps everything would have gone off fine had Stan not done something typically Getzian. The day before the Boston concert, he threw a tantrum over something or other and smashed his foot through a glass door, suffering serious cuts on his right leg and severing a major artery.

The band knew nothing about this, as we took off for Boston early the next morning, expecting Stan to meet us at Symphony Hall. When we arrived, we received a message to call Monica. She told us Stan couldn't make the trip to Boston, but at the last minute they had found that trumpeter Dizzy Gillespie was available, and in fact was already en route to Boston to fill in for Stan.

None of us had ever played with Dizzy before. I had, at least, met him a few times, but only because we shared the same accountant. And we had no idea what kind of material Dizzy would want to play. We briefly talked through the program as we set up for the concert. Dizzy wanted to play a lot of tunes we didn't know, and of course, *he* didn't know any of the stuff we'd been playing with Stan. Dizzy also had this disconcerting way of clowning around all the time, so you never knew if he was serious or putting you on. It all made for a strange night, but we got through it. And it didn't come close to the outrageous events that would follow at Carnegie Hall.

Stan was determined not to miss the Carnegie concert, especially after all the work that had gone into it. Tickets had sold out; it was unusual for a jazz icon like Stan to appear on the bill with a young pop star like Dionne, and this led to a lot of anticipation. So, Stan arranged with his doctor a way to sit in a wheelchair, with his injured leg braced out in front of him. He practiced all afternoon to get comfortable playing the horn at the odd angle necessitated by this weird posture.

Given this added wrinkle, I arrived at the hall early to check on things. Everything seemed in order. The organ was backstage, ready to be moved on for Joe Mooney, and Dionne's band had already started setting up. The first hint of trouble came when Dionne arrived from New Jersey at about 7, an hour before she would go on, and discovered she had left her silver lamé shoes at home; she had a silver gown but no shoes to go with it. There wasn't time for a trip back to New Jersey, and panic ensued as people rushed around trying to figure out what to do. She absolutely couldn't go on stage for her first Carnegie Hall appearance without the proper shoes.

By this time, people had begun filing into the hall to find their seats, and the word went out for the ushers to scan the audience for a pair of silver lamé shoes. And sure enough, about fifteen minutes later, one of them spotted a pair of silver lamé high heels. When told of the situation, the owner of the shoes graciously offered to sit barefoot for the concert so Dionne could use them. We were back in business.

Except for one problem: the shoes were a couple sizes too big. To solve this, someone stuffed the shoes with Kleenex to keep them on Dionne's feet, but this meant she had to walk in tiny, shuffling steps to keep from losing a shoe or toppling over. Carnegie Hall has a large stage, and when the announcer intoned, "Miss Dionne Warwick!" it seemed to take her hundreds of little steps to cross the divide to center stage. But once there, being a complete pro, she performed beautifully.

I can't say the same for the audience. Stan and Monica were a little ahead of their time with the concept of combining jazz and pop on the same bill—especially at hallowed Carnegie Hall—and the audience divided equally into two camps. Half had come to hear Dionne Warwick, their favorite singer, and couldn't have cared less about Stan Getz; the other half had come for Stan and were completely disinterested in Dionne, as I noticed from out front as I watched her sing. Of course, the situation would reverse itself for our part of the concert, but first, we had to get through Joe Mooney.

He had agreed to serve as a sort of intermission performer, playing a short set, maybe twenty minutes, between the headliners. The stagehands moved the organ to center stage, and Mooney was introduced. Since I already had experience guiding a blind musician (after touring with George Shearing), I was pressed into service to bring him on stage. As I got him seated at the organ, I could sense his excitement at playing Carnegie Hall—the big time at last.

Forty-five minutes later, we couldn't figure out how the

hell to get him to quit. Mooney, having the biggest night of his life, seemed on course to play every song he knew.

The evening was becoming a disaster.

The audience had shown its disinterest as soon as Mooney started playing and, perhaps realizing that he couldn't see them, freely got up and moved to the lobby. As the set wore on, the listeners dwindled to maybe a hundred diehards. I don't know whether Mooney noticed the applause shrinking as he went from tune to tune, and I don't know if he cared. When he eventually played a tune peppy enough to pass for a closer, the announcer was primed to jump in and talk him off the stage. Mooney clearly didn't want to stop, but I was already there to lead him off, at which point he gave in. If he hadn't stopped, I was prepared to wrest his hands from the keyboard and, if necessary, frog march him off.

At long last, the stagehands set up for Stan, and the audience returned to their seats. The main event was about to start—even though it was now 10 p.m., around the time the concert should be ending.

Swallow and Roy took their places at the bass and drums, the announcer called Stan's name, and I pushed his wheelchair onstage. With his horn in his hands, he couldn't maneuver the chair himself. Of course, the sight of Stan in a wheelchair caused a rumble of audience reaction. But given everything that had already transpired, they may have figured it was just part of the show.

Our set progressed normally—except for the fact that, as in the first set, half the audience really didn't listen—and then we headed into the grand finale. Since it was Christmas Eve, Stan and Monica had come up with the idea of getting everyone together for a rendition of "White Christmas." The quartet was already onstage, so Stan made his usual end-of-concert remarks to the audience, then introduced Dionne—who began another long trek from the wings in her Kleenex-stuffed shoes. I led the hapless Joe Mooney out to the organ and Stan counted off Irving Berlin's classic.

It was a bizarre scene: Dionne Warwick singing "White Christmas," Stan noodling along in the background from his wheelchair, with his leg straight out, Joe Mooney in his tux and ruffled shirt, plugging away on the organ. It got even more bizarre when the tune ended. As the applause rang through the hall, everyone on stage tried to exit as best they could. Swallow and Roy left as usual, Dionne started her endless shuffle to the wings, and my own dilemma suddenly became clear. Mooney had risen from the organ bench, his hands out in front of him, trying to find his way off the stage and getting tangled in the microphone cords. I hurried over to guide him when I heard Stan shouting, "Get me off the stage!" from center stage, in his wheelchair, trying to turn the wheels with his one free hand. But I couldn't leave a blind man stumbling around Carnegie Hall in front of two thousand people. I needed to guide Mooney off as quickly as possible and come back for the wheelchair. I led him to within ten feet of the wings and told him to just keep going straight, and then I hurried back for Stan. Amazingly, the audience had kept up the applause, but it had started to turn to laughter as Stan, red-faced and furious, jerked around in the wheelchair, all attempts at dignity discarded. I wheeled him off as the applause died out, and the lights came down on the wildest night in my career thus far.

CHAPTER 11

Trying Some New Things

When I wasn't on the road with Stan, I occasionally got to play in an orchestra organized by the eminent composer and conductor Gunther Schuller, in collaboration with the Modern Jazz Quartet. This project, called Orchestra U.S.A., combined jazz and classical music into the genre known as "Third Stream Music," a name coined by Schuller himself in the 1950s. The performances took place at a concert hall in Brooklyn. Each event featured different composers writing for the MJQ and the orchestra plus various guest players.

But despite their reputation for playing classical-style pieces and fairly intricate arrangements, the MJQ guys were not good at sight-reading. They learned their parts slowly, by rote and by ear, practicing them over and over till they had memorized them. Typically, as the orchestra rehearsals progressed, the members of the quartet would give up on the music, and Schuller would replace them with musicians more experienced at reading.

The first of the MJQ to bail out on new music was usually their vibist, Milt Jackson. As soon as he faced the prospect of tackling something he hadn't previously played, he told Schuller to get a sub. (That was me.) Bassist Richard Davis usually replaced the MJQ's bassist, Percy Heath. Dick Katz covered for John Lewis on piano. The quartet's drummer, Connie Kay, always seemed to hang in there on the concerts I participated in, but he was the only one.

On some concerts, though, John Lewis and Percy Heath would manage to play some of the material—with subs brought in for the more difficult passages—and on one occasion, I found myself playing vibes with the other three MJQ members. I was standing in Milt Jackson's shoes, as it were. Having heard the group so often over the years, both in person and on record, I was very excited by the idea of taking the quartet for a spin, to see how it would feel "being Milt Jackson" for a solo or two. But instead of the exhilarating breeze I had expected, I just couldn't get anything to work. I couldn't seem to find common ground with John for the time feel or the chord voicings. (I think I would handle it better now, simply because I've had a lot more experience adjusting to different styles.) Nonetheless, as far as I know, I am the only vibist to take Milt Jackson's place on stage with the MJQ—even if it was only for a couple of songs.

MILT JACKSON

I have always deemed Milt's contribution to the vibraphone as the greatest of all. The first generation of jazz mallet players, represented by Lionel Hampton and Red Norvo, employed hardly any phrasing or dynamics. They treated the vibraphone like a percussion instrument—a sort of metal xylophone—using hard mallets and a fast vibrato. (No wonder: Hamp started out as a drummer, and Red as a xylophone player.)

But Milt came from a different direction entirely. He was playing guitar and piano, and also singing in a vocal group, when his high school band director in Detroit introduced him to the vibes. It was extremely rare for a high school anywhere to have a vibraphone in the late 1930s, but Milt's did, and the bandleader needed someone to play it. Milt wanted to emulate the sounds from his guitar and achieve more of a vocal quality at the vibes. To that end, he chose softer mallets, giving the instrument a warm, mellow sound instead of the percussive clankiness of his predecessors. And he slowed down the fans in the resonator tubes to create a languid kind of vibrato, instead of the nervous flutter previously in use.

Milt came to New York with several other Detroit musicians at the request of Dizzy Gillespie, and by 1955, these players had spun off their own group, the Milt Jackson Quartet. The name didn't last long. They soon decided to make it a co-op effort and renamed themselves the Modern Jazz Quartet, keeping only the initials of the band's first iteration. They gained fame for eschewing the heated bebop and hard-bop styles of the era, carving their own niche by employing classical music themes and playing with a lighter (though bluesier) touch than most bands. The MJQ worked together on and off for over forty years, making them one of the longest-running jazz groups ever. Several times, Milt tried to start his own band, but it never seemed to work out, and he always returned to the original unit.

I got off to a bad start with Milt, even though he was my favorite vibes player while I was learning to play. The trouble stemmed from my first major interview in *Down Beat* magazine, in the early '60s. Asked about what I wanted to achieve on the vibraphone, I thought I gave a good answer, but I certainly didn't word it very diplomatically; I didn't yet understand that a comment could appear much harsher in print than in speech. I said that while there were major players on other instruments—like Miles Davis and John Coltrane, who had pioneered new directions for their instruments as well as jazz in general—I didn't think any vibes player had yet risen to that level. I explained that I aspired to expand the role of the instrument, and flippantly added that, "Up to now, vibes players have been like playing in a sandbox."

I discovered my mistake a couple months later at a jazz festival in Chicago. Milt was there too, playing with a local rhythm section, and his tour manager asked if Milt could use my vibraphone. Milt played first; I watched from the side of the stage, enjoying it all a great deal. As he came off stage, he turned to me and said, "Let's see what *you* can do, motherfucker!"

This clued me that I had hit a nerve.

I believe Milt hated my guts for the next several decades. Although I did become friendly with the other members of the MJQ, Milt steered clear whenever we saw each other backstage at jazz festivals. This continued until we both signed on as part of a "vibraphone summit" for a jazz cruise in the Caribbean, which meant me spending a week on a ship with Lionel Hampton, Red Norvo, Terry Gibbs—and Milt. I prepared to keep myself scarce when Milt was around to avoid any awkwardness. But the first night, as I walked through the ship's dining room looking for my assigned table, I happened to pass Milt and the musicians in his group, including pianist Cedar Walton—an old acquaintance of mine. I would have quietly glided past, but Cedar called to me, and I had to stop and chat for a few minutes, all the while noticing, out of the corner of my eye, that Milt was glaring daggers at me. As I walked away from the table, I overheard Cedar lace into Milt, saying something like, "What's the matter with you, anyway?" I gathered he gave Milt some feedback on his attitude, because the very next day, Milt walked up to me on the Promenade Deck and started chatting with me like we'd been friends forever.

That came as a great relief, and also provided an opportunity for us to get better acquainted. We even did some gigs together, where each of us played with his own group before joining up for a two-vibes finale. We took that act to Europe for a three-week tour, and as we traveled from city to city, I found it fascinating to hear how Milt had started in the business and about his other interests. (He was a talented cook, for one.)

The last time I saw Milt, we were both playing the Kennedy Center Honors in Washington, D.C. when they honored Lionel Hampton. I think Milt was kind of miffed that it was Hamp instead of him—Milt could carry a grudge, remember—and when they asked him to play one of Hamp's songs on the televised proceedings, he refused. He used his own song, "Bags' Groove," and left me to play Hamp's theme, "Flying Home."

Milt Jackson passed away in 1999 at the age of 76.

By the middle of 1965, my next RCA album was coming due, and I wanted to try something different. Bill Evans had just released a record, *Conversations with Myself*, that I found fascinating (though the critics didn't much go for it). On it, Bill played solo piano, but overdubbed two additional piano parts. It was like hearing three of him improvising with each other. Overdubbing had been used for decades—one of the first examples, from the 1920s, featured the New Orleans saxophonist Sidney Bechet—and had grown more sophisticated over the years. But it still used the same basic technology, which caused some loss of overall recording quality with each additional overdub. So for all practical purposes, the technique was limited to adding just one or two additional parts.

Then, the engineers at RCA invented a new process that allowed them to stack additional tracks on top of the originals, in perfect synchronization, and with no loss of quality. This gave birth to multitrack recording. Instead of just two tracks, we now had four, then eight, and sixteen; twenty-four-track machines soon followed and lasted quite a while, and even larger machines became common for bigger projects. (Of course, we now use computers instead of tape, making available a virtually unlimited number of separate tracks.)

Conversations with Myself was the first record to use this new multitracking technology, and it made me anxious to try it myself. And as it turned out, I soon became only the second jazz musician to use it, on my next album.

Larry Bunker came in from L.A. for the dates, and I asked Steve Swallow to play, too. We recorded a variety of music, ranging from a few originals to some standards (including a bossa nova I had learned with Stan), and even a Beatles tune. What made these unique was my addition, using the new syncing technology, of extra vibes, marimba, or piano tracks to each song, which I improvised on top of the initial parts. I called the record *The Time Machine,* and it was the first album for which I chose both the title and the cover photo. I enlisted a talented photographer, Tom Zimmerman, to shoot several multiple-exposure shots of me playing the vibes, giving us a dozen or more images of mallets flying all over the place. RCA liked it, and I got to pick my own covers from then on.

I often think of *The Time Machine* as the true genesis of my recording career, because with that record, I had found my own voice—and because at last, I had full control of the production end of things as well. I began working with Brad McCuen, an experienced executive at RCA, who had a special love for jazz and great respect for creative people. He was also a very capable producer, and the recordings we made together educated me about the role that a producer can play.

Most outsiders have only a vague idea of what a producer does. The musicians make the music; the engineer oversees the technical aspects of the recording. Sometimes, it seems, the producer mostly arranges for food deliveries and fills out paperwork. But a producer who has a high degree of rapport with the musicians can move the recording experience to a higher level. Brad and I continued to work together throughout my time at RCA, and we made some of my most important records, including those that launched my first band.

My final year with Stan Getz (1966) was filled with contradictions. On one hand, the music sounded better than ever. We had been playing together long enough to develop considerable affinity with each other, and the performances remain among the most memorable in my career. But Stan's drinking became an increasing problem, turning many of the gigs into damaged efforts.

Stan was in especially poor shape during an engagement at Basin Street West in San Francisco. The club kept late hours; they even had a 5 A.M. breakfast show scheduled for early Sunday morning. As ludicrous as that sounds today, it was fairly common then for the Saturday-night crowd to stay out all night, going first to the regular nightclubs, followed by after-hours clubs till early the next morning. The breakfast show gave the night owls a chance to come in for a last set of jazz and some bacon and eggs before they called it a night—or day, I suppose. As you can imagine, the folks that straggled in at 5 A.M. weren't too lively, but by then, Stan was even less functional than the audience. He had been drinking heavily all week (though he managed to get through each performance), and the club owner was furious. He sued Stan for breach of contract based on nonperformance; the proceedings dragged on for a year or two, eventually ending in favor of the club owner.

A similar scenario took place at the Newport Jazz Festival that summer, although it didn't result in a lawsuit. Stan had gotten so wasted before our set that he couldn't keep his place in the song—even though it was just a simple blues (ironically titled "Stan's Blues"). The rest of us followed him as best we could, and the song turned into a formless freestyle piece—another low point for Stan, and another sign to me that I needed to think about what to do next.

But there were times when Stan, sober if a little shaky, would play at his best. I looked forward to these nights and tended to let the bad ones slide. By now, Stan was spending the breaks between tours at various clinics, drying out, trying different diets, and so on. He would start each tour in pretty good shape, only to end up a mess within a few days. Oftentimes, it was comical, while still sad. Once, as we drove to a hotel in Akron, Ohio, Stan got sick from drinking too much and leaned out the passenger window to throw up—directly under the big hotel marquee reading "Welcome Stan Getz!" Swallow and Roy got to view this from the second car, and later wished they had a movie of it.

We tried to record the quartet several times during 1965–66, but it wasn't easy, given Stan's precarious state. When he got nervous or worried about something, he would either drink to excess or get angry and meanspirited—neither condition very conducive to a making an album. We tried recording "live" during a Japanese tour, and also at a club in Boston; neither attempt went well. To make matters worse, Stan felt a lot of pressure because of his recent hit records. He thought his next record had to be of great importance. We never did get a good recording with the group, and no one knows what became of the unreleased tapes. I think Stan kept them at home, and they were eventually discarded or lost.

By the summer of '66, I had my next record scheduled for RCA. I again wanted to try something novel, this time moving away from familiar jazz turf. My decision led to another of those crossroads at which I had to just trust my instincts and listen to my "inner player."

Bob Dylan had just released *Blonde on Blonde*, his first Nashville recording. It made me think of my own time in Nashville, which I remembered fondly. And the more I thought about it, the better I could picture a combination of jazz and country music. My idea was to bring a few New York musicians to Nashville and then surround us with the best country players. The material would focus on well-known country songs that I would arrange with jazz harmonies and styling. I proposed this to my Nashville mentor Chet Atkins, and he offered to help.

Chet found the right musicians for the sessions, and also proved invaluable when it came to choosing the songs. Over the next couple months, I made several trips to Nashville, and each time, he let me shadow him all day as he worked at his office. In addition to his own performance career, Chet was a top producer for RCA and spent most of his time meeting with prospective singers and producers, listening to their demo tapes. He was really the most casual and relaxed dude I've ever met. He didn't seem to mind me sitting there as people came and went, and I guess the visitors just assumed I belonged there. In between appointments, Chet and I talked music, until he would suddenly interrupt himself to say, "Here's one that Patsy Cline sang"—or Hank Williams, or some other country artist—and then start playing it on the guitar. Sometimes, he even sang me the melody. I wrote it all down on manuscript paper, and over the course of several days, Chet had taught me a dozen songs to work with.

Meanwhile, he was lining up Nashville's leading players for the session—several of the best guitarists, plus leading players on banjo, mandolin, steel guitar, and harmonica. From New York, I brought along my Getz rhythm section—bassist Steve Swallow and drummer Roy Haynes—and my Berklee pal, tenor saxophonist Steve Marcus. I had wanted something different, and I certainly got it, I can tell you that.

The country players didn't read music, so I had to spend an hour or two on each tune teaching them my new arrangements. Nor did they know the names of the chords, so I went from one player to the next, putting their fingers on the frets to show them each chord of each song. But they learned quickly, and within an hour or two, I could make it around the room, having taught each player his part for the next tune. It was a wild mix of opposing worlds, rural and urban, and in a way, it represented the essential duality of my own life to that point.

I loved the whole experience, as did the other musicians. But almost no one else did—at least not at the time. The record came out with little fanfare, and though I tried to promote it on country radio as well as jazz stations, people weren't yet ready for that kind of cross-pollination. For me, it made totally logical sense, because of my deep love for both jazz and country. But *Tennessee Firebird* ended up among my poorest-selling records ever. Risks don't always pay off as hoped.

Some thirty-odd years later, it was reissued on CD, and people started paying attention and offering compliments. And today, a combination of jazz and country shows up in the work of several established jazz artists. This wasn't the only occasion in which I was ahead of my time. And I never regretted making *Tennessee Firebird*.

I eventually got to know several musicians from Bob

Dylan's Nashville record, *Blonde on Blonde*—the one that inspired my "country-meets-jazz" project in the first place. They told me how Dylan had constructed one of the album's signature tunes. When he arrived at the studio at the usual 6 P.M. start time, he told the musicians that he just needed to finish writing one song, and they should hang around till he was ready. Then he sat down at the piano, and while a dozen or so musicians and engineers waited, on the payroll, he spent the next six hours writing! At midnight or so, Dylan got up from the piano and taught the musicians his new song, after which they spent the next six hours recording a final version. The song was "Sad-Eyed Lady of the Lowlands," a rambling narrative ballad that filled an entire side of one LP and became an instant classic.

I recognized that this was a guy who really understood how his creative processes worked and knew how to get the job done, no matter what was going on around him. It reminded me of what Hank Garland told me about recording with Elvis Presley. Elvis would go over a song with the musicians, then spend maybe a half-hour just hanging out, chatting with the sidemen, maybe banging on his guitar or the piano, to get himself psyched. Suddenly, he would say, "Let's do it," and they would record the song in one or two takes. Here was someone else who knew how the process worked for him. It's always intrigued me to learn how each musician functions creatively, partly because there are so many options. We all seem to find our separate paths for getting into the zone.

My one and only gig in Las Vegas came in September, when Stan played a three-week engagement at the Tropicana Hotel. Vegas isn't known for jazz, so this represented an experiment for the hotel, and they did the smart thing in hiring Stan, the most commercially popular jazz artist of the moment. The bill included an excellent big band led by the famed drummer Gene Krupa, featuring Anita O'Day. But even all that star power failed to attract much of an audience in Vegas—despite the fact that Vegas was, in many ways, Stan's kind of town. He had a good following among actors and show-biz folks, who considered him a celebrity on their own level, and many of them came to see us when we played clubs in California. Academy Award winner Donna Reed and her husband even stood witness at his wedding.

The Tropicana offered Stan a nice complimentary suite, but we sidemen were left to fend for ourselves. We found a cheap motel further down the strip and looked into getting a rental car. The motel owner suggested a local guy who rented old wrecks, for cash and without questions, and that afternoon, I picked up a '51 Pontiac from the Dunes Hotel parking lot—no names, no paperwork, just the instruction to leave it back at the parking lot, keys under the mat, the day we left Vegas. It cost only $25 a week. I was cautioned not to take it out of town. I spent the days driving past what seemed like hundreds of wedding chapels—Stan himself had gotten hitched in a Vegas wedding chapel—and everywhere, all the time, the spectacle of the casinos and neon lights. This was 1966, relatively early in Las Vegas's evolution, but it still posed quite a sight for a boy from rural Indiana.

The sparse audiences at the Tropicana had little interest in jazz, and our performances took on a somewhat surreal quality. The sets were rigidly timed by an automated system that triggered taped announcements for each act and opened and closed the curtains at precise intervals. You had to get on stage and in position at the right time—and you had to be certain to finish on time, too, because the curtain came down as scheduled, no matter what. Red Norvo told me that on one Vegas gig, the curtain caught the front of his vibraphone as it rose, lifting the instrument a few feet off the floor. The vibes fell apart and the pieces collapsed into a pile on stage, just as the recorded announcement proclaimed "Ladies and

Gentlemen, Red Norvo and his Quintet!" This didn't happen to us, but it would have at least made things a little livelier.

It seemed a waste that almost no one came to hear the music. Krupa had a great bunch of players, made up mostly of Los Angeles studio guys. Krupa himself played far better than I had expected. I previously knew him only from his early days with Benny Goodman, playing tom-toms on the classic hit "Sing, Sing, Sing." And the show offered a historic reunion of Krupa with O'Day, who in the '40s had sung in Gene's first band after he left Benny Goodman.

The highlight of our stay turned out to be our Monday nights off. Each week, Stan took us out to see some of the other shows on the strip. One Monday, we saw Victor Borge at Caesar's Palace, complete with half-naked Roman gladiators; Borge was hilarious in spite of the gaudy production. Comedian Buddy Hackett, a big Getz fan, entertained us another Monday night. Then Stan took me to see Lena Horne.

Lena's backing group included guitarist Gabor Szabo and bassist Albert Stinson, both first-rate players. I was frankly surprised to see some familiar jazz faces on the stage, and I looked forward to hearing the music. It was hardly what I expected. Lena sounded fantastic. She sang with grace and beauty, and she had flawless time and feel. But the musicians seemed to be off in some distant place, and Lena had to virtually pull them through each song. Their playing was so sloppy and lackluster, I couldn't tell whether they just didn't care about the gig, or they were high, or something else. But Lena made it unforgettable.

That experience opened my ears to what singers have to offer. My heroes had always been instrumentalists, the ones with total command of their instruments. But listening to Lena, I discovered what I could learn from singers—specifically, how to phrase melodies. I had already absorbed the influence of Stan's melodic expertise, but I still hadn't made the connection between how Stan played and how vocalists interpret a phrase. I'll always thank Stan for taking me to hear Lena that night. From then on, I heard singers from a whole new perspective.

Just before the trip to Vegas, I had received the rough mixes for *Tennessee Firebird,* and I spent a lot of time at the hotel listening, planning the song order, and deciding what tweaks we needed to make back in New York. Working on the project got me seriously thinking about when I should leave Stan's band and go out on my own.

Ever since I'd arrived in New York, RCA had hinted that I should start my own band, because record sales would remain somewhat limited as long as I remained a sideman. But up till then, I was still finding my own identity as a player. And I was still learning so much, both about music and the business, while playing with Stan. I kept asking myself: How can I leave Stan? And Roy and Swallow? They stood far above any musicians that I thought I could find for a group of my own.

But the bigger restraint on my leaving had to do with money. I hadn't managed to save any while working with Stan. He paid less than Shearing, even though Stan commanded higher fees because of his popularity. He handled money badly, and in addition to the cost of his fairly upscale lifestyle, Stan had endured two major financial crises. Most of the income from *Jazz Samba,* his first big record, had gone to the IRS to settle back taxes; then, a lawsuit regarding a personal management contract wiped out his royalties from "The Girl from Ipanema."

But Stan's financial woes alone may not explain the stingy pay. In the old days, leaders commonly paid their sidemen the bare minimum. Dizzy Gillespie and Lionel Hampton were also well known for paying their musicians poorly, and Dizzy even required them to pay their own local transportation to and from airports when they toured. Some leaders used an especially nasty tactic to string along their musicians, advancing them loans against future salary in lieu of giving them pay increases. The scam goes something like this: a musician tells the leader he's gotten behind in his bills and can't keep working for the current pay. Instead of offering a raise, the leader asks, "How much would it take to catch you up?" They arrive at a figure, maybe a couple thousand, and the leader advances it against future salary. This scenario repeats itself from time to time. Before long, the sideman owes the leader too much for him to repay from his meager salary, and now he *can't* quit because he owes all this money. (This was reputedly a trick Miles Davis used early in his career—although he did a U-turn in the '70s and began offering quite high salaries when it became fashionable to brag about how much you paid your sidemen.)

At least, I didn't owe Stan any money. But I didn't have any, either. And my modest earnings made me doubt I could finance a band of my own for the six or twelve months I would need to get established.

While Stan skimped on money, he was exceedingly generous on stage. He not only featured my unaccompanied solo pieces every performance; he also introduced the band members frequently, making sure the audience knew that he considered us exceptional. In some bands, the focus remains on the leader and the sidemen hardly get mentioned at all—as in George Shearing's band, for instance—but Stan took pains to let the audience know who we were. I'm quite sure that this helped me become sufficiently well known to start my own band after I left his group.

And Stan was especially protective of me. I think this had to do with my youth, and the fact that we had formed a strong bond. Whenever he sensed a threat of some sort, like a club owner getting angry, he would come to my defense.

One night at the Cellar Door in Washington, D.C., the time came for my solo piece. Typically, the crowd would go completely silent when I played alone, but this night, I could hear people continue to talk loudly at one table in the back. I played on, hoping they'd notice they were the only noisemakers in the room, but after another minute or two I was ready to stop mid-song and give them a piece of my mind. Standing a few feet away, Stan saw me on the verge of exploding and stepped closer to whisper, "Don't stop playing, it's Leonard Bernstein!"

Of course, I kept playing—and Lennie kept talking! I didn't quite forgive him until I saw him on television, conducting Mahler with the Vienna Philharmonic. I didn't talk through that.

CHAPTER 12

Going Out
with a Bang

The events that led to my final chapter with Stan Getz were set in motion almost a year earlier, in 1965, when we received our first invitation to play at the White House. President Lyndon Johnson's press secretary was a Getz fan, and we got an invitation to perform at a presidential function, along with comedian Bob Newhart and folk singers the Kingston Trio. That led to several more White House performances in 1965 and '66. At one White House dinner, I ended up sitting between television anchorman John Chancellor and U.S. Senator William Fulbright (two of the best-known men in the country). Afterwards, I thought of all the things I could have asked, but at the time I was too intimidated to say a word.

During our booking in Las Vegas, the White House called again, this time asking Stan to visit the Far East. The President had a goodwill tour to Asia coming up, and the government had asked the King of Thailand to choose an American entertainer that might accompany the President's visit. The King, a saxophone player himself, requested either Benny Goodman or Stan Getz, and Stan got the call.

The timing of the trip required us to go first to Bangkok, then directly to Europe, to begin a major tour that impresario

George Wein had already booked. I was really looking forward to this. I had visited Japan twice and South America twice, but had yet to really tour Europe. There was only one complication: the European promoters wanted Stan to team up with Astrud Gilberto for the concerts. By 1966, "The Girl from Ipanema" had receded into history in the U.S., but Stan hadn't played Europe since before his hit records. The European promoters wanted to present him in the setting that had brought his current success.

I told Stan this would be a big mistake, since he had never gotten over his anger with Astrud for quitting (and suing him for royalties) just two years earlier. There was also the little matter of their messy affair, which had ended badly. But Stan couldn't resist the fees under discussion, and he agreed to do the concerts with Astrud.

Meanwhile, it had become clear to the sidemen that this had developed into a major tour, and we would need more money. We were already underpaid, compared to other groups at Stan's level of fame, and the hotels and meals in Europe (which we had to pay for ourselves) cost a lot more than what we usually paid at home. It was decided that I should approach Stan about extra pay, even if just for this tour. Stan was outraged; he called us ungrateful, and told me that he had actually contracted the tour for *low* money, and had only agreed to do it because he felt a need to get back to his European fans. After my request, Stan called George Wein and threatened to cancel the entire tour unless *he* covered the band's hotel bills. Wein agreed, which made things a little better for us—and a lot better for Stan. He took to charging everything he could think of to his hotel room; he even made purchases from shops outside the hotels and charged those to the hotel accounts.

What a guy.

Before Europe, however, we had Thailand. Swallow came

down ill at the last minute, so Chuck Israels (who hadn't played with the quartet in several years) volunteered to make the Thailand trip. Monica came along, too, and Wein's office sent Charlie Bourgois, the most seasoned of his staff, to serve as our tour manager. A crusty Vermonter with a wry sense of humor, Charlie had a wealth of knowledge about the music business. He stayed with us in Thailand and went with us to Europe, assisting greatly when things got crazy. I've always felt indebted to Charlie for being one of my staunchest supporters, and also for serving as a valuable role model on how to work with musicians.

In an era before jumbo jets, the trip from New York to Bangkok (and back to Europe) included fueling or connection stops at an incredible array of exotic capitals: Cairo, Teheran, Karachi, Bombay, Rangoon, Baghdad, and Beirut, to name a few. Security was minimal in those days, so I got off at each stop and walked around, while the planes were cleaned and refueled—just to get a sense of each place. We arrived in Bangkok about a week before the presidential entourage.

The purpose of Johnson's Asian trip was to bolster support for U.S. involvement in Vietnam. Thailand had become an important ally, offering R&R for American soldiers but also hosting secret jungle bases just across the borders from Vietnam and Cambodia. None of us in the band liked the idea of having anything to do with the military or the war, and we made Stan promise that if he received any requests to play for the troops, he would decline. Officially, we were there to play just one formal event, hosted by President Johnson, to honor the King. We would receive no pay for this, since the request had come from the White House, but they did fly us first class.

Bangkok circa 1966 was a madhouse, swarming with American military. The hotels had filled to capacity, so we had to split up among several of them. At my hotel, I had a top-floor room, located off a patio, that I shared with about a half dozen lizards; each evening when I returned to the hotel, I spent twenty minutes or so scraping them onto a shirt cardboard and taking them outside. But by morning, several would have made their way back, hanging motionless on the ceiling or walls. I just found it hard to sleep with them lurking there in the dark.

My room had another quirk. Steaming hot water came out of all the faucets—but *only* steaming hot water, so taking a bath meant filling the tub and waiting half an hour till it cooled enough to step in. I had to brush my teeth immediately after turning the tap, before the water heated up to "scalding."

Our first day, word came that the King wanted us at the palace for lunch and a jam session. The King had taken up saxophone while a student at Harvard, and he still got together with some of the local musicians each week to play. Our jam sessions with the King may have lacked for great music, but our visits overflowed with respect and hospitality.

Thai kings are considered semi-deities, and as with most monarchs, hanging out with them involves a lot of dos-and-don'ts. For instance, it is impolite to be taller than the King, so in order for others to stand (rather than kneel) in his presence, he always stood on a raised platform, which made him slightly taller than the rest of us. It is also forbidden to speak too directly to the King, with certain topics—politics, family history, his personal life, and so on—strictly off limits. But he made exceptions for us Americans and told us to freely talk about anything we wanted. Naturally, Stan soon raised the most forbidden topic of all.

The King had originally been second in line for the throne, but while he was attending Harvard in the 1940s, a coup attempt resulted in his older brother's assassination. No official explanation has ever determined responsibility for either the attempt or the murder. The future King returned to Bangkok immediately and took the place of his brother, and to this day, it remains taboo to ask what exactly took place that fateful night. So, I cringed when Stan asked, point-blank: "What happened to your brother?" But the King graciously sidestepped the question, and the conversation went on to other things.

That first day set the pattern for the rest of the week. The palace would call and invite us over to either play music or share a meal, just so that the King could talk to Stan about jazz and saxophones. At the end of the week, the presidential entourage arrived for the formal dinner and concert, held in the historic (and non-air-conditioned) Royal Palace. Thailand has a very hot and humid climate—we had endured the jungle-like conditions all week, the only respite being our air-conditioned hotels—and the old palace dining room was sweltering even before the guests filed in for dinner.

I sat at a table with assorted government officials and visitors, resplendent in the white dinner jacket I had rented in New York, in accordance with the evening's dress code. The evening went smoothly, just small talk with the people seated next to me, until it was time for dessert, which turned out to be a less-than-wise menu decision on the part of the chef.

Waiters approached the tables with large tureens of what had started out as strawberry ice cream; by the time they arrived, though, it had melted into strawberry soup. One waiter leaned over to extend his ladle toward the lady next to me, and in the process tipped the bowl and spilled about a gallon of molten ice cream onto my rented white dinner jacket and into my lap. Before I could think what to do next, Monica appeared at my side to tell me it was time for us to play. Terrific.

Seated in the front row in living room-style chairs were the King and Queen of Thailand, President and Lady Bird Johnson, and the Secretary of State, Dean Rusk. We played for about a half hour. The King beamed—he loved it—and Rusk seemed to enjoy our set, too; Johnson sort of dozed off. My own attention was diverted by the picture I presented, with my jacket half pink and my pants sticky from the strawberry soup. I was not having a good night.

To top it off, after the set Stan called the band together to announce that at 5 the next morning, we would fly to some military bases to play for the troops.

We were stunned. When we protested, Stan got furious and launched into a spiel about patriotism, and that ended the discussion. He also called me a faggot (his usual insult). Mostly, I think he was embarrassed that he hadn't had the nerve to turn down the State Department request.

So, early the next day, our sullen group took off from a local air base in a rickety prop plane that had no seats, just those canvas slings to sort of lean on. The pilot warned that as we landed at some of the airstrips, we would hear shooting from the surrounding jungle, but that we shouldn't worry, since the plane would be out of range of the Viet Cong's rifles. Somehow, this information proved less than comforting.

Several of the bases were nothing more than a jungle clearing protected by cyclone fencing around the perimeter, with maybe a thousand soldiers inside. (These were the "secret air bases" whose existence our government denied till nearly the end of the war.) We would set up our instruments in the ever-present red dirt and play four or five songs as guys in their fatigues wandered up to check things out. They mostly looked dazed and frightened; I don't know what they thought. You can imagine how I felt, however: this civilian, about their age, flying in with a funny-looking instrument, playing some kind of music they probably didn't much understand, and then flying off without breaking a sweat, while they wondered if they would live through the week. We visited six remote bases on our "tour." I remained furious for days that Stan had gotten us into that.

Our week in Bangkok nonetheless ended on an upbeat. The King, delighted with our visit, arranged a large garden party at one of his country residences along a beautiful river, complete with royal court musicians performing Thai music. It was a lovely evening, and the King sat talking with us about music and American politics long into the night. (Bobby Kennedy had just started his presidential campaign, and I remember the King saying he was skeptical that Kennedy would make a good president.) Though I have returned to Bangkok a couple of times since then, that magical evening remains my most enduring memory of Thailand.

Back to reality.

We headed west to meet Astrud for the big European tour and to join up with the now-recovered Steve Swallow. The first few concerts were a little stiff, even prim. Astrud had brought her new husband, a tough-looking character who owned a Philadelphia nightclub, and I think his presence made Stan uncomfortable. I could sense the pressure building, and I knew that it pretty much had to blow.

The meltdown occurred the fourth night of our tour, in Rotterdam, Holland, when Astrud joined us on stage for her several numbers. Stan usually played softly in the background while Astrud sang the delicate bossa nova melodies. This night, however, he sort of strolled around as he played. Then, at a delicate moment in the song, he moved directly behind her, held the bell of his horn against her butt, and honked a loud low B-flat. It was as if a ship's horn had blasted into her behind. Astrud jumped; she immediately lost her place and kind of yelped the next lyric. She glanced around with a startled look at Stan, who just grinned and strutted, so proud of himself.

Stan carried things further on the next song. When it came time for his solo, he suddenly turned to me and called a different key, and we quickly modulated up about four steps. The obvious quickly dawned on me; at the end of Stan's solo, we would have to shift back to Astrud's key for her to sing the last chorus. But there was no way an inexperienced singer like Astrud would find her starting note with a substantial key change taking place at the same moment.

We lurched into the original key as her entrance came up, and just as I expected, Astrud had no clue what to do next. She began testing various pitches, hoping something would work; it took her about four bars to find her spot. Stan was beside himself with glee.

Astrud couldn't continue, and now in tears, she stalked off the stage. Her husband was livid and began to make threatening remarks to Stan. Understandably, Astrud refused to go on stage with Stan again (even though we still had about half the tour to get through). George Wein gave her the next night off, then flew a trio in from New York to accompany her for the rest of the dates. So much for the reunion of Getz and Gilberto, and for the next couple of years, whenever Stan played in Philadelphia, he hired a bodyguard to accompany him.

We got through the next few nights, and I thought we might finish the tour without any more shenanigans. But tension began to build when we hit London for a few days. Stan somehow connected with an old junkie acquaintance and starting getting high on heroin. This astounded me. I'd thought his junkie days were behind him; this was the only time he went near hard drugs in the years I knew him. Fortunately, we left London after a few days and headed for the tour's last gig, a double-concert in Belfast, Northern Ireland. Jazz concerts were few and far between in Ireland, and our two back-to-back performances had sold out early, with a large contingent of people even driving eight hours from Dublin to hear "the legendary Stan Getz." The promoter, a young man producing his first concert, was nervous about everything. Stan's dark mood, much in evidence as we went through the sound check, didn't help.

We returned to the hotel for a few hours rest, but as soon as the promoter dropped us off, Stan told me he was going back to London. He had convinced himself of some kind of deal going on between Astrud and Wein, which would somehow cheat him out of some money. It wasn't much of a story, and I think he just wanted to do something really mean as a parting shot at Astrud. I also suspected he wanted to meet up with his druggie pal in London. I didn't think he was serious, but a few minutes later I saw him coming out of his room with his bag and his saxophone. He had already booked a plane ticket and called a taxi for the airport.

Despite all my experiences with Stan, I still couldn't believe he would leave everyone in such a fix, let alone disappoint the audience. I told him that if he really did walk out, I was through. I hadn't planned to leave the group so soon, but this was the last straw. He never turned back. He just went out to the taxi while I yelled, "I quit!" from the top of the stairs.

When the promoter returned to take us to the gig, I told him and Charlie Bourgois what had happened. No one knew quite what to do. The promoter fretted about a rebellion at the theater, and I, anticipating the hostile crowd reaction, had no desire to play the concert without Stan. But the promoter, by now desperate, begged us to play anyway, and we reluctantly agreed. He decided to announce that Stan had taken ill, rather than say he had merely bolted, and that ruse worked, more or less, till we got out of town.

At first, the audience groaned with disappointment at the news, and I couldn't imagine this going well. People were offered refunds, but no one left. So Roy, Swallow, and I took the stage and started in. After the first couple tunes, people settled down, and by the time we finished, they loved us. Both concerts got standing ovations.

I was surprised and thrilled that we had managed to turn the situation around, and more than anything else, that night convinced me I could make it without Stan. Charlie Bourgois confirmed this and told me to come around to see George Wein as soon as I returned to New York. And I did exactly that—partly because, in my final capacity as tour manager, I had to pick up some paperwork to send to Stan's accountant. The papers included a copy of the contract with the fees, and I saw that they were probably the highest Stan had ever earned for a concert tour. He had lied to my face about working for short money when I'd asked him for a raise. Stan had caused a lot of pain and bother during my three years with him, but up till then he had never blatantly lied to me. That convinced me more than ever that I had made the right decision.

Monica called about two weeks later to discuss details for Stan's next tour, and I told her I had been serious that night in Belfast: I had definitely quit. They still didn't believe I would leave.

CHAPTER 13

The Gary Burton Quartet

In November 1966, I found myself back at my New York apartment, short on money and wondering what to do next. I hadn't expected my life to change so quickly. I needed to sit down and think things through. I didn't know what kind of group to form, or even what musical direction to choose.

There's a quote from the legendary dance teacher Agnes de Mille, stating that artists don't know where they are going; they just keep leaping, again and again, in the dark. I partly agree, but would add that artists don't leap randomly. We have instincts that give us some idea about what direction to try, even if we don't know precisely what we'll find once we get there.

As it turned out, I was about to make a very big leap.

Playing with George Shearing and Stan Getz had kept me in the jazz mainstream, where I estimated the average age of the audiences as forty and older. I was still in my mid-twenties and thought I needed to somehow connect with people my own age. So, I asked myself what music appealed to me, and surprisingly, I realized it was the newly arrived sound of '60s rock.

I loved the new freedom the rockers enjoyed, and my fascination with the Beatles and Bob Dylan had gotten pretty intense. Steve Marcus introduced me to the Beatles in 1964, and after the movie *A Hard Day's Night*, I was hooked. I owned every Beatles record. I loved the eclectic mix of styles they covered, ranging from shuffles to featuring Indian sitars or string quartet, etc. They were the first to use more sophisticated harmonies and song structures that went way past the stereotypical three-chord rock tunes, providing intellectual interest for musicians like me. They reached the epitome of their creative talents with *Sgt. Pepper's Lonely Hearts Club Band*, a record that influenced me greatly. My interest in the Beatles even led to the entire Stan Getz group, plus their families, attending the 1965 Beatles concert at Shea Stadium in New York. (It remains the most amazing live performance I have ever seen, even though the Beatles portion of the concert lasted only about twenty-five minutes.)

I couldn't see how to reconcile my jazz experience and my interest in rock, but I needed to get things rolling. So, even though I didn't have any musicians or material, I started looking for some gigs. I knew that if I committed to playing somewhere, anywhere at all, it would force me to find some musicians and choose some songs. After three years of nursing Stan through gigs at practically every jazz club in America, I knew most of the club owners on a first-name basis. I started by calling Lennie Sogoloff at Lennie's on the Turnpike, a friendly roadhouse-style club just north of Boston. The place had a lot of character, and Lennie always booked the best musicians. He offered me the first week of January, so now I had my first gig as a bandleader—and about a month to put together a group and a repertoire.

I called around and found out that Bill Evans had taken

another of his extended rehab breaks, which meant his sidemen (Eddie Gomez and Joe Hunt) were available. I thought I'd start out in a trio with those guys, both of whom I knew well. I still hoped to incorporate music that appealed to people my age. I just hadn't quite figured how to go about it.

Fate intervened when Marcus took me to a jam session in midtown Manhattan where I met guitarist Larry Coryell. Larry had come east from Seattle the previous year, looking for jazz work, but ended up mostly playing rock gigs. He even had formed an intriguing rock band called the Free Spirits, which was beginning to get some attention. I immediately liked his playing and asked him to join us for the week at Lennie's. We rehearsed for an afternoon and drove to Boston the next day, where the gig was a solid success—despite some perplexed audience reactions. People who knew my playing from Stan's band had to wonder what this new music was all about. But they still seemed to like it, and they gave us—and the music—a chance. Jazz-rock was born that week, though it took a few months before we had enough original music and gig experience to realize what we had.

With my Nashville album, I tried combining different genres, and it had bombed, making me a little wary of going down that path again. I knew I was taking a huge chance. If my concept of blending rock and jazz didn't gain acceptance, I would likely blow my chance to establish myself as a bandleader. But by this time, I had spent a lot of time in heart-to-heart talks with my "inner player," and in the end, we both were convinced this would work.

After the week in Boston, the Gary Burton Quartet returned home, and I got on the phone to call more club owners. I scored our first New York booking at a familiar haunt: the Cafe Au Go Go, where I had recorded with Stan a few years earlier.

Howie Solomon, the owner of the Go Go, had an instinct for new trends, and over the years, he introduced a lot of young performers in both music and comedy. At the time we launched our new brand of jazz, several important rock and blues groups came on the scene and also found their way to the Go Go: Paul Butterfield's Blues Band, the Blues Project, Mike Bloomfield, and Frank Zappa's new band, the Mothers of Invention. Howie owned a theater upstairs from the club, where the Mothers played while we were at the Go Go. Frank worked steadily in the theater for several months at a time during that year; whenever we returned to play the Go Go, the Mothers were in residence. Their band seemed to hang around all day, holding long drawn-out rehearsals of Frank's very complicated music. He was a stickler for perfection, and he terrorized his musicians, always threatening them with dire consequences if they didn't play a certain piece better, or memorize all their parts by the next day, or something of that sort. Frank absolutely shunned drug use of any kind, so the band took care not to smoke pot anywhere in his presence. If he caught them, he would fire them instantly. Ironically, he was such an "out" character that fans kept coming up and handing him joints or packets of mystery pills. Frank would glare at them and angrily stalk away, leaving them thoroughly confused.

One night, at a jazz festival in Florida, he invited me and Roland Kirk, the blind saxophonist, to join the Mothers for some on-stage jamming. Frank had high aspirations for what we could accomplish without any rehearsal. He had some complicated music on hand, which I looked at but knew I couldn't sight-read. Roland, of course, couldn't use written music at all. In addition, Frank had worked out an elaborate system of cues and hand signals, letting him direct his band to do things that didn't appear in the written parts, such as changing time signatures or tempos or keys; of course, these signals wouldn't mean anything to Roland either. So, in spite of almost an hour's discussion about the two pieces we would play, it all turned to chaos as soon as we got under way. Frank was constantly signaling to the band and to me, but I couldn't keep up with whatever he intended, and Roland was just in his own world. All this took place in a jai-alai palace, with acoustics resembling the Grand Canyon, somewhere in the Miami suburbs. I've always wondered what people must have thought that night. I certainly never understood any of it, but I suspect Zappa probably did; he was a kind of genius.

The first time my group came into the Go Go, we played opposite George Carlin, one of several comedians who got their start at the club. Howie also often paired us with a rock or blues band. Word must have gotten out that we had something new going on, because for that first engagement, a number of important music-industry people stopped in to catch a set. Among them were Quincy Jones and my new mentor George Wein, who wanted to see what I'd put together. The group had begun to cohere stylistically and build an original repertoire, and I was especially pleased by George Wein's reaction. He said he always liked to see someone come up with a new direction, and then he offered to book us on all his festivals and tours for the coming season! By itself, that covered about half my schedule for 1967.

I wanted to release a new record so the group would have something for promotion, but I wasn't sure how to approach the recording. Once again, fate took care of this. Joe Hunt and Eddie Gomez informed me that Bill Evans had ended his self-imposed rehab, and that they would be going back on tour with him. I wanted Swallow to leave Getz's band and join mine, but I doubted I could offer enough work for him to leave Stan. Enter fate, part 2.

One afternoon, during rehearsal at the Go Go, someone called me looking for Swallow. Steve's wife had just gone into labor, and no one could find him. I found out that Stan had refused to let him hire a sub for a gig in Detroit, so Swallow had traveled west, hoping the birth would wait until he got home. Knowing he'd gone to Detroit, I also knew he would be at the Wolverine (the musicians' hotel), and I passed along that information. Swallow caught the first plane back to New York, but he was quite angry about what had gone down and was ready to quit. He joined my group the next week.

Roy Haynes remained with Stan, but he also remained my all-time favorite drummer, so I asked him to at least play on the album. We went into the studio a few weeks later to record *Duster*, the first album by my new quartet, and the very first to blend jazz and rock—although these days, compared to subsequent recordings, it sounds awfully tame.

For the gigs coming up, I hired Bob Moses, a friend of Larry Coryell's from the Free Spirits, to play drums. Only nineteen, he was (and is) extremely talented. He would join and leave my group three times over the next decade, always making creative musical contributions before he left.

As my first year as a bandleader progressed, a lot of good things came my way. I managed to hustle up quite a number of bookings because of my contacts from the Getz years; those club owners who remembered me helping Stan through difficult nights really came through. I didn't yet have an agent or a manager, but informally, George Wein was helping me out in both those capacities. When I needed advice on anything, George was always available. He even cosigned a loan so I could buy a van for the band. And for the time being, I could handle the details of club bookings myself. We spent the spring of 1967 on the East Coast, then played up and down the West Coast all summer. Our reputation for new and different music had started to spread. After the first few months, Larry, Swallow, and Moses settled in, and we really committed ourselves to the idea of fusing jazz with rock—even though many jazz mainstreamers saw rock as the enemy, stealing fans and jobs away from jazz musicians.

As we embarked on the first road trip in our new van, we

decided we should also emulate the look of rock musicians. This bordered on heresy for a jazz group in the '60s. The jazz musician's dress code then called for suits and ties, occasionally even extending to tuxedos (at least on weekends). Hard to believe now, but back then, even the biggest names, like Getz and Miles Davis, still performed in business attire, even when they played the dingiest jazz clubs. At first, we abided by the dress code and wore jackets and ties; the jackets just happened to be purple velvet, or gold lamé, or buckskin. We also let our hair grow longer, like the rockers. I suppose the club owners went along with it because our outfits qualified as stage costumes. (At least, we didn't show up in torn Levis and T-shirts.) It also helped that we were doing good business.

In the fall, Wein arranged for us to play throughout Europe. Having made only one European tour with Stan—an especially difficult one at that—I could hardly wait to play there with my new band. We began with two weeks at Ronnie Scott's Club, the main jazz venue in London, right after they had expanded the club to double its size. Of course, we shocked them completely. Even though the Beatles and other British bands had made "rock" and "England" interchangeable, Ronnie Scott's had doggedly stuck to straight-ahead jazz.

We were an instant sensation. Word quickly got out, audiences packed the place every night, and we reveled in the attention. Lots of major performers were in town for the London BBC Jazz Festival at the same time, and almost every night, we would spot important musicians in the house, from Count Basie and Joe Williams to Sarah Vaughan to Gerry Mulligan. Even Marlon Brando came in one night. (He was a pretty serious jazz fan.)

During our engagement, Philip Larkin reviewed the band and gave us a favorable write-up. Larkin was Britain's leading poet—and also a lifelong jazz fan and reviewer, having gravitated to swing-era bands as a youth. But he really didn't like modern jazz at all. In the preface of his early '70s book *All What Jazz*, he wrote eloquently about how art in general, and jazz in particular, had been mangled by modernism. He wrote so persuasively that he almost had me agreeing with him. So, it comes as a real surprise that I was one of only a few modern jazz musicians to gain his approval. That's one review I will always treasure.

One night in London, in front of the visiting celebrities, Moses invented air drumming. I regularly featured his drum solos in our performances, but this time, he simply went through the motions, stopping just short of actually hitting anything. The effect was electrifying. As you watched his sticks almost striking the drums and cymbals, you couldn't help imagining, in the total silence, what sounds he might have played, had he in fact made any sounds at all. It left the audience spellbound, along with those of us in the band, and air drum solos became a standard part of our sets for the next few months.

We had gone shopping for clothes as soon as we arrived in London. Prices were dirt-cheap by American standards, and Carnaby Street, the Mod fashion headquarters, had just the styles we wanted for our rock-band look. We created such a buzz in London that by the time we moved on, we began to feel like rock stars, and now we looked the part, too. We expected to take the continent by storm.

It was definitely stormy. Our first concert, part of the Paris Jazz Festival, took place at the historic Salle Pleyel—the same concert hall where, decades earlier, the audience had booed Igor Stravinsky when he premiered *The Rite of Spring* (an odd coincidence, in retrospect). We shared the bill with the Stars of Faith, a female gospel group who led off the night, and my all-time favorite singer, Sarah Vaughan, who followed us to close the show.

After our hearty reception in London, we took the Paris

audience for granted. But our music wasn't at all what they expected. Just seeing us walk on stage, sporting gold brocade jackets and buckskin fringe, the crowd began to stir. We started the set and at first, I thought it was going okay. But as each tune ended, I felt the crowd getting more agitated. I couldn't see them very well because of the spotlights, but I sensed something going on. On one song, Larry used some feedback effects on his guitar; that resulted in a major crowd eruption, and when we finished that tune, there was hardly any applause. Instead, we heard shouting and arguing. Half the audience wanted to throw us out, while the other half was defending us. They were fighting with each other over our music!

The yelling grew almost as loud as our playing, but we pressed on to our next tune—a drum feature—and as Moses started his solo, one of the tom-toms came loose, hitting the floor with a bang before it rolled a few feet. That brought an instant hush to the crowd. "What next?" they must have thought. Never one to pass up an opportunity, Moses figured he might as well work with this new development, and as he soloed, he proceeded to knock over his drum kit piece by piece. He ended up lying on the floor, still playing the drums that he had by then scattered all around him.

The audience went berserk, and that was the end of the set. We couldn't have continued anyway, since the drum set now littered the stage, but it didn't matter; the audience was in complete riot. We escaped to the wings, and the police came in to clear the hall. It took about an hour before they let people back in and Sarah could finish the evening. For years after, whenever I ran into her, she would tell me that was the most amazing thing she had ever seen.

About fifteen years later, as I boarded a plane somewhere in Europe, I noticed an elderly black woman staring at me. Later, I saw her talking with another woman and pointing at me. Finally, they came up the aisle to my seat and tentatively asked, "Are you Gary?" Somewhat surprised, I said yes, wondering how this grandmotherly woman knew my name. It turned out they were from the Stars of Faith, the gospel group from that unforgettable night in Paris. One of them reached into her purse and pulled out a faded newspaper clipping from that night, with a picture of me on stage. She called it the most exciting night of their lives and said they would never forget it. Me neither.

I crossed paths with Sarah Vaughan many times over the years, along with many other legendary musicians, but no one meant as much to me as Duke Ellington.

My first encounter came backstage at the Pittsburgh Jazz Festival in 1965, while I was working with Stan Getz. As usual, Stan featured my solo vibraphone piece during our performance. When we finished the set, Duke was waiting for me backstage; he took me aside and told me he was really impressed with my number. He said he always liked to see a musician who had found a new way to play his instrument. During the late '60s, I found myself on concerts and tours with the Ellington band pretty often, and whenever our paths crossed, Duke went out of his way to express interest in whatever I was doing and to always offer encouragement.

Many people consider Duke the most important jazz musician of them all. He pushed the jazz world into new territory for most of his seventy-five years, and his influence remains omnipresent, through his huge catalog of songs, his enduring classic recordings, and his revolutionary orchestration techniques. I was very fortunate to make his acquaintance and to benefit from his support as I embarked on my career as a bandleader.

Duke's sister Ruth, who oversaw his considerable publishing interests, once told me that her brother was a product of the jazz century. He had grown up with it: born at the beginning (1899), he entered his twenties in the 1920s, his thirties in the 1930s, and so on. At least through the '60s, Ellington's timeless innovations kept him at the forefront of jazz. And throughout his lifetime, he ably captured the social climate and cultural experience of American society as well.

THE DUKE AND I

Edward Kennedy Ellington enjoyed a reasonably privileged life for a young black man growing up in turn-of-the-century Washington, D.C.—which, for all practical purposes, was really a Southern town with a high degree of segregation. His father worked as a blueprint maker for the Navy, as well as a butler for a prominent white physician. Both his parents played piano, and young Edward received a good music education, instead of having to learn on the fly like many early jazz artists.

Ellington led his own band from 1923 (when he was twenty-four) until his death in 1974. I think he got such an early start as a leader because of his training. Because he read and wrote music, he got to skip the usual route of apprenticing as a sideman. He could already compose and arrange, and he could instruct the musicians on how to play what he wrote. He also had a personality that destined him for leadership. Even as a youth, he dressed flamboyantly, which led one friend to nickname him "the Duke."

It's the source of his inspiration that mystifies me. Duke had no obvious precedents; he had to almost invent modern jazz. He seemed to just "hear" what this music should sound like, and his unique big-band compositions practically defined jazz for everyone else. He started with medium-size ensembles that predated the big bands of the '30s, and his music reflected the job opportunities of the time. At first, he composed primarily for dancing, doing most of his writing on buses and trains or in hotel rooms on the road. But while the circumstances required commercialism, Duke nonetheless strived to rise above the conventional.

By the 1930s, Duke had moved his band to Harlem's famous Cotton Club, which brought him widespread recognition. He eventually enlarged his orchestra to the now typical 18-piece instrumentation and began to forge lifelong relationships with the players who helped build his legacy. Among the band's most notable characteristics was the enduring loyalty between musicians and leader. Behind his back, they called him "the baggy-eyed bastard," but they stayed in the band for decades—in part, because Duke recognized and celebrated their individuality. While most bandleaders looked for homogeneity in their brass or reed sections, Duke reveled in the *lack* of uniformity among his musicians. Listening to his sax section, you didn't just hear five saxes; you heard the specific voices of each individual player.

Like many of my generation, I knew Ellington's music not just from records, but as something I often experienced in person. His band worked continually for over fifty years—and by "continually," I mean "every night." George Wein, who became his primary agent in the '60s, told me that even in Duke's later years, Duke wanted the band to play seven nights a week. He told George that if the guys had a night off, they just got into trouble; at the time, he was describing a busload of seventy-year-olds. One summer in Europe, George had trouble filling an open date. He waited to break the news, hoping that something would turn up, but finally went to Duke's hotel and said, "Hey Duke, I have a surprise. We're here in Nice, on the Riviera, and we've arranged for you to have a day off tomorrow, to relax and enjoy yourself." Duke pondered a minute and replied, "We better go on to Hamburg for the next gig, George. I wouldn't want people to think we're having trouble getting work."

The band's nonstop schedule astounded me. Often, when promoters could easily sell out a concert, they would book the band to play a second show at midnight. A tour manager told me that once, after playing these double-concerts every night for a week, they finally had a night without the midnight show. So what did Duke do? He called a midnight rehearsal to work on new music, until 5 A.M. Unbelievable. I found it significant that within a few months of Duke's death, several longtime band members also passed away. It was as if they had been carried along by the momentum of the band, and without it, they just faded away.

Duke and I both recorded for RCA during the '60s, and I often found myself attending events with him. He sometimes brought his sister Ruth, a lovely, friendly woman who shared his house and idolized her older brother. On one such occasion, the 1968 GRAMMY Awards ceremony in New York, I was asked to present Duke with a Lifetime Achievement Award. As always, he was impeccably but creatively dressed. Long before anyone else thought of it, he wore a black tuxedo shirt instead of white, along with a kind of Colonel Sanders bow tie that looked very, very cool. And as usual, he was the center of attention, telling stories and keeping everyone entertained. I was a little nervous for the presentation, but it went fine, until I ended with "...the great Duke Ellington!" The audience gave him a standing ovation, the spotlight began circling the room looking for him—and Duke wasn't there. He had gone to the men's room; when he returned a few minutes later, he got a second standing ovation.

I continued to see Duke from time to time in our travels, and he always had something gracious to say; he was famous for his outlandish flattery to everyone. If he spotted me at some event, he would make his way across the room and say, "Now I know this is a class affair, I see you're here." At after-parties, he could be persuaded to sit down at the piano and play. At one such soiree, I saw a middle-aged woman lean in and ask him for "Twelfth Street Rag," a hack novelty song from around 1915. Several people gasped; after all, this was a guy who wrote some two thousand songs, many of them well-known standards. But Duke just smiled broadly and launched into "Twelfth Street Rag." What a gracious man.

I idolized Duke, which explains why the audience behavior at one year's Berlin Jazz Festival infuriated me. First, I noticed some people in the audience reading newspapers instead of paying attention to the band. A few songs later, some started booing. I had heard this could happen with Berlin audiences, but I had never seen it myself—and directed at Duke Ellington, of all people! I never forgot that, and I didn't forgive it, either. I've played Berlin only a few times since that incident, and I never look forward to going there. I can't erase what happened that night.

I'd have loved to play with Duke, even just once. I never got the chance; as far as I know, he never played with a vibist. But I did get invited to one of his recording sessions. One night, he told me the band would be making a new record the following week and asked me to drop by the studio. I considered this a great honor, picturing myself and the engineer in the booth, with maybe just a few other invitees. Wow.

My excitement built as I got off the subway and turned the corner onto 23rd Street, the address of RCA's studio. It was 10 at night, when normally there'd be no sign of activity in that neighborhood. But I spotted five or six limos lined up in front of the building, and when I got inside, I saw the band all set up in Studio A—and maybe a hundred other people decked out in tuxedos and gowns and fur coats! It looked like a grand Harlem ball had moved downtown. The engineer's booth was already jammed, and people spilled into the studio, facing the band on folding chairs to form an impromptu audience. I was the only white guy in the place.

I grabbed a chair and watched in awe. On one take, they played without the great alto man Johnny Hodges, who hadn't returned from a break. On another, Duke stopped the band because something didn't sound right. Someone was playing the previous piece; when asked about it, he said, "Well, nobody told me we were changing songs." For this jaded bunch of guys, it was just another gig.

In this chaotic spectacle, I couldn't imagine how Duke could focus on the music. But some months later the recording—the *Far East Suite*, considered by many the best work of his career—arrived to critical raves. Even now, as I listen to the album, I can hardly believe I was there in person. Perhaps in tribute, I've recorded three songs from the suite myself over the years.

Ellington had a reputation for creative business methods. My old Berklee pal Herb Pomeroy told me Duke supposedly established a sort of retirement program for his long-term sidemen, way before anyone thought of an IRA and/or a 401(k). I also love the story I heard about Duke's contract negotiations with Columbia Records in the '50s. Paisley neckties were all the rage with corporate types at that time, so Duke, always a flamboyant dresser, showed up to sign his new contract wearing a paisley suit.

Ellington's innovations in jazz composition continue to influence us as players and writers to this day. But I have another, quite personal reason for admiring him.

If Duke wasn't gay, he was uncommonly gay-friendly, a rare attribute during his era. He also maintained a highly unusual relationship with Billy Strayhorn, his long-time writing partner who was openly gay: very prominent in Harlem society as well as the gay community, and unabashed about his two long-term relationships. (All of this was quite uncommon at the time, too.) Their arrangement was both mysterious and very personal; for instance,

Strayhorn didn't draw a salary like the other musicians, but simply sent the bills for whatever he needed to Duke.

And I've always wondered why Duke, with so many others always occupying his attention, went out of his way to befriend a young jazz/rock musician, even to the point of inviting me to an important recording session. Maybe he saw something in my orientation that I didn't yet recognize in myself. It's too bad he didn't live to see all the changes that have come about in the music world as well as society at large.

I'm proud to have known him even in a casual way, and his music will always influence me. I didn't attend the birth of jazz, but I was lucky enough to know quite a few of the pioneers (such as Duke) first-hand. I think I came along at just the right time to connect with those who invented the music, as well as take part in the transition to follow, when my generation came into its own.

When I assess that first year with my band, I have to consider it awfully successful. We had played across the U.S. and toured Europe, and I had provided enough work to keep the musicians solvent. We had recorded two records for RCA, the second of which, *Lofty Fake Anagram*, for release in early 1968. Yet, I myself could barely make ends meet. I had always worked for someone else; now on the other side of the coin, I discovered that with all the expenses of a bandleader, I was ending up with less than I had made as a sideman.

But that's to be expected in the start-up phase of most new bands, and I tried not to let it distract me. And the work was going far too well for me to look back.

1933 TO 1975

Mom and Grandpa.
Odon, IN, 1933.

2207 Delaware Street, Anderson, IN, 1943.

With Dad.
Anderson, IN,
1943.

With Dad and Ann. Anderson, IN, 1944.

With Grandpa Aishe. Odon, IN, 1944.

With Burton
Grandparents,
Ann and Phil.
1945.

The Burton Family. Anderson, IN, 1946.

With Claire Musser. DuQuoin, IL, 1951.

Evelyn Tucker Recital. Evelyn is third from Left; I am fifth from left.
Anderson, IN, 1952.

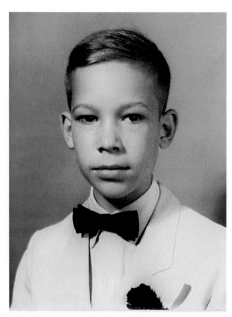

Publicity Photo.
Anderson, IN, 1952.

Left: Publicity
Photo. Chicago,
IL, 1952.

Following:
Publicity Photo.
Anderson, IN,
1952.

WESTERN UNION

1201

W. P. MARSHALL, PRESIDENT

The filing time shown in the date line on telegrams and day letters is STANDARD TIME at point of origin. Time of receipt is STANDARD TIME at point of destination

DEA030 DE•CA508 PD=CHICAGO ILL 18 200P= 1952 JUL 18 PM 2 15

GARY BURTON=

421 W EMERSON ST PRINCETON IND=

WE ARE HAPPY TO INFORM YOU THAT YOU ARE A PRIZE WINNER ON B SACHS AMATEUR HOUR. PLEASE REPORT BACKSTAGE AT ABC CIV SUNDAY — JULY 20 — 11:45 AM ASK FOR MISS WENTSEL=

MORRIS B SACHS AMATEUR HOUR=

:ABC CIV 20 11:45 AM=

THE COMPANY WILL APPRECIATE SUGGESTIONS FROM ITS PATRONS CONCERNING ITS SERVICE

AVAILABLE FOR SPECIAL ENTERTAINMENT

GARY BURTON

Marimba and Vibraharp Artist

421 W. EMERSON ST.

PHONE 1322   PRINCETON, INDIANA

Piano Tuning and Repair

PROFESSIONALLY TRAINED

GARY BURTON

421 W. EMERSON ST.

PHONE
FU 5-5112   PRINCETON, IND.

Top: Telegram, 1952.

Middle: Business Card, 1952.

Bottom: Business Card, 1958.

P8

The Burton Family. Chicago, IL, 1955.

With Hank Garland. Nashville, TN, 1960.

Preceding: Nashville, TN, 1960.

Above: With Chris Swansen, Dan Martin, and Don Jones (Left to Right), Berklee Student Band, 1961.

Left: 34 West 73rd Street, New York City, 1962.

With Evelyn Tucker, George Shearing, and Lee (Left to Right).
Indianapolis, IN, 1963.

With Stan Getz.
Boston, MA, 1965.
Photo by Lee Tanner.

With Steve Marcus (Left), Steve Swallow (Back Center), Helen Swallow (Bottom Center), and Hannah Swallow (Bottom Right). Nashville, TN, 1966.
Photo by Tom Zimmerman.

With Larry Coryell, Bob Moses, and Steve Swallow (Left to Right). New York, 1967.

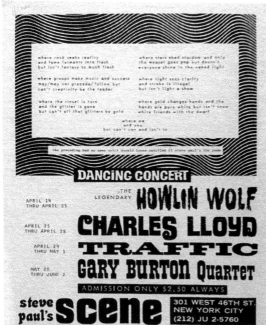

Preceding: Boston, MA. 1967.
Photo by Lee Tanner.

Above: Newport Jazz Festival, 1968.

Left: Poster for The Scene. New York, 1968.

With Oliver.
New York, 1969.

With Mick Goodrick, Steve Swallow, Bob Moses, and Pat Metheny
(Left to Right): The Gary Burton Quintet, 1973.

P16

1975 TO 2012

With Ted Kurland and Chick Corea. Moscow, 1982.

With Chick Corea, composer Rodion Shchedrin, Prima Ballerina Maya Pletzkaya, and Poet/Novelist Yevgeny Yevtuschenko (Left to Right). Moscow, 1982.

With Makoto Ozone (Left) and Steve Swallow (Right), 1984.

With Terry Gibbs, Lionel Hampton, and Red Norvo (Left to Right). S.S. Norway, 1987.

Teaching at Berklee. Boston, MA, 1975.

Receiving
an Honorary
Doctorate
Degree from
Berklee.
Boston, MA,
1985.

Berklee in Japan. Hammamatsu, Japan, 1989.

Above: With Lionel Hampton. New York, 1986.

Following: With Roy Haynes at GRAMMY Telecast. Los Angeles, CA, 1999.

With Red Norvo. Los Angeles, CA, 1988.

Awarding "Gary Burton Chair in Jazz Performance" to Joe Lovano. Boston, MA, 2001.

With Makoto Ozone at a Recording Session of *Virtuosi*. Boston, MA, 2002.

Berklee Commencement with Producer Arif Mardin, Singers Diane Reeves and Steven Tyler, Susan Berk, and Lee Berk (Left to Right). Boston, MA, 2003.

With Chick Corea, 2007.

With Julian Lage, James Williams, Luques Curtis, and Vadim Neselovskyi.
(Left to Right): Next Generations Band. Boston, MA, 2008. *Photo by Bill Gallery.*

With Pat Metheny. New York, 2009.

With Chick Corea. Vienna, Austria, 2012.

With Julian Lage, Antonio Sanchez, and Scott Colley (Left to Right):
New Gary Burton Quartet, 2012.

FAMILY PHOTOS 1975 TO 2012

With Dad, Catherine Goldwyn, Mom, and Tony Goldwyn (Left to Right)
at Our Wedding in Los Angeles, CA, 1975.

Stephanie and Sam Burton. Stonington, CT, 1982.

With Sam Burton. Stonington, CT, 1982.

Sailing "Fatcat." Boston Harbor, 1985.

Preceding: Stephanie and Sam Burton. Princeton, IN, 1984.

Above: With Earl Dimaculangan. Provincetown, MA, 1988.

With Sam Burton in Italy, 1997.

Stephanie Burton's Wedding Day. Los Angeles, CA, 2010.

With Catherine Goldwyn and Tommy Scordino: Grandparents and Grandson.
Los Angeles, CA, 2012.

With Jonathan Chong and Tommy Scordino (Left to Right). Los Angeles, CA, 2012.

With Jonathan Chong. Boston, MA, 2012.

CHAPTER 14

Life in the Big Time

In 1967 and '68, we played several times at the Trident, a restaurant and club in the San Francisco Bay area, and it became a comfortable home base for us on the West Coast. It was also the setting for a couple of memorable events. One afternoon, as I watched television, "The Dating Game" came on, and when they announced the prize, I could hardly believe what I heard: the couple had won a trip to San Francisco to hear the Gary Burton Quartet at that famous jazz spot, the Trident! The next time we played the club, I asked about it and sure enough, the winning couple was expected that very week. You couldn't miss them: her, obviously a professional model; him, a geeky character with an ill-fitting suit and white socks. They sat, stiff and awkward, at a table for two, with a chaperone and photographer at the next table snapping pictures of their "dream date." Clearly, she had done the whole thing to promote her show business career, but then she had to actually go through with the date. They both looked like this was the last place on earth they wanted to be.

Also at the Trident, I had a scary encounter with Miles Davis. Actually, I didn't encounter him directly, but it was still frightening. Miles had come into the club to have lunch with the manager, Lou Ganapolar, an old friend from when Lou used to manage the Village Vanguard in New York. Miles casually asked about the club, and Lou raved about my new group. As Lou described it to me that evening, Miles's mood immediately darkened when my name came up, and in his raspy voice he said, "Tell him if he ever mentions my name again, I'll kill him!"

Lou asked me what could possibly have gotten Miles that upset, but I knew immediately what it was about. A week or so earlier, Leonard Feather, the well-known jazz writer for the *Los Angeles Times,* had interviewed me for his column. Leonard asked lots of questions about my new band and the jazz/rock phenomenon. Mainly, he wanted to know why we dressed so differently, and why we'd chosen such a radical musical direction. I told him that as young musicians, we were seeking our own identity, and went on to say that every trumpet player can't play like Miles and every tenor player can't play like Coltrane—an answer I considered pretty reasonable.

The next day, the headline for the article read, "Burton Claims Miles and Trane Are Old Hat." Mortally embarrassed, I called Leonard immediately to complain. He insisted that this was how he had understood my meaning, and he refused to correct it. I just hoped that since it appeared in a local newspaper rather than a national magazine, it might blow over in a couple of days; it never occurred to me that Miles himself would also be in L.A. when the article appeared. At Lou's suggestion, I sent a short note to Miles at his hotel, explaining that I had been misquoted and apologizing for the misunderstanding. I never learned whether he received it or not.

MILES DAVIS

I mostly crossed paths with Miles on George Wein's tours, but we never spoke to each other. He pretended not to know me, and I never felt bold enough to approach him. He was one of the few people that instantly intimidated me whenever I saw him. (Having someone threaten to kill you tends to have that effect.) Of course, I greatly admired him and his music—as did every musician I knew—and many of his group members over the years have become friends of mine. But Miles himself often seemed insecure and lonely, despite his swagger as a player and bandleader. Back when a lengthy transatlantic telephone call could cost hundreds of dollars, he would spend two or three hours each night calling from gigs in Europe to New York, just to hang out with friends back home.

For a while, he traveled with a sparring partner. In spite of his small stature, or maybe because of it, Miles loved boxing and would ask concert promoters to arrange gym time for him each morning. (This was years before hotels had fitness centers or anyone gave much thought to working out.) Because of his early sparring sessions, he insisted on playing first each night; normally, a headliner like Miles performs last on the bill, sometimes starting past midnight at summer festivals. Many times, I saw him open to a half-empty hall as audience members moseyed in to discover they had missed most of his set.

On one European tour, Miles' band flew into Barcelona and was detained by Spanish customs officials. His tour manager told me later all the band's luggage had been piled together, and the Spanish customs police wanted to inspect each individual piece. The tour manager knew that Miles had a stash of cocaine in a small Pan Am Airlines shoulder bag. As he watched the customs agents closing in on the bag with the coke, he offered to assist them by handing the bags to the inspectors, speeding up the process and hoping to cause a diversion. In the process, he succeeded in subtly moving the Pan Am bag onto the pile of luggage that had already been searched, thereby saving everyone a lot of trouble. He then announced he was flying home the next day; he said his nerves couldn't take any more episodes like that.

Throughout his career Miles made music that changed forever the way people thought about jazz. Most of his breakthroughs occurred on the cusp of a new decade. In 1949, he worked with some of the best jazz arrangers of the day to pioneer new writing styles with his *Birth of the Cool,* which shaped jazz in the '50s. In 1959, he released *Kind of Blue*, the record that signaled the end of bebop in the '60s. And in 1969 it was *Bitches Brew*, his entry into the fusion jazz of the '70s, which I and a few other early adopters had introduced in 1967.

Like many of Miles' fans, I was dismayed when he went electric. His fantastic groups of the '50s and '60s, and especially his collaborations with arranger Gil Evans, represent the best jazz anyone recorded in that era; he could have kept to that style for the rest of his career and easily remained the number-one jazz artist. But he had an insatiable need to keep changing, challenging his fans, as well as his fellow musicians. It took me years to sort out my own feelings about the later Miles. Not long before he died, my band shared a concert with his at the Tanglewood Festival in Massachusetts, and I stayed after our set to hear him. Along with the five thousand people who filled the amphitheater that night, I heard some great trumpet playing, and some songs that I didn't quite get. But instead of rejecting what I heard, I felt impelled to understand it. And I gained an appreciation of his drive to keep growing, even if he ran the risk of losing audience in the process. Miles' music inspired me when I was younger; his commitment to music's future inspires me to this day.

In the summer of 1968, with my career as a bandleader taking off, I got called in to talk with Roger Hall, the head of RCA's Classical Division. He wanted to find a project that would expand the range of their offerings, and he wondered if there were any classical musicians with whom I might like to collaborate. I was taken by surprise and at a loss for suggestions. I knew that the Guarneri String Quartet recorded for RCA, and I certainly admired their work, so I mentioned them. Hall asked about composers and the only name that came to mind—other than old dead guys—was Samuel Barber, whose music I found enthralling. I had seen his Pulitzer Prize-winning opera *Vanessa* at the Metropolitan Opera in New York, in the early '60s, and I owned several recordings of his orchestral music.

Hall immediately said, "I'll give Sam a call and see if he's interested." Just like that. I was stunned that he actually knew Barber personally, and even more so that he planned to propose we work together.

A week or two later, I met Barber at his New York apartment.

(He mostly lived in a country house an hour north of New York, but he maintained a quite nice apartment in the city as well.) Barber wanted to know about my music: he hadn't heard any of my records and didn't know much about jazz. He wanted to hear some things on the piano, so I played a couple of my compositions—including one inspired by something I had heard in *Vanessa*. He didn't have much interest in that one, but he was very complimentary about one of my other pieces. That first day, we spent a couple hours together, and as I walked back to my apartment, I thought we just might hit it off.

Next, he invited me to his Mt. Kisco home. This initiated a series of visits filled with rambling discussions, about music and the music business, as we narrowed down a concept to work on. We settled on the idea of a piece for two quartets: the Gary Burton Quartet and the Guarneri String Quartet. Reflecting on this now, I was seriously naïve to expect this composer and these musicians to mesh with my little band. But in those heady days, I was kind of fearless.

SAMUEL BARBER

Sam had a lot of misgivings about the music business by the time I met him. After having achieved early success, he had fallen out of favor as atonal music and other developments came into vogue during the '60s. Around this time, I mentioned to a music critic that Sam and I were discussing a collaboration, and he laughed at me, making some remark about Barber's old, dated music. That surprised me, but it soon became evident that this issue weighed heavily on Sam. At the time, his most recent work was *Antony and Cleopatra*, his second opera, commissioned in 1966 to celebrate the opening of the new Metropolitan Opera at Lincoln Center—a lavish production that was not particularly well received. (To complete the score in time for the opening, he had worked virtually seven days a week for nine months, standing at the large easel where he did his writing. He explained that if he sat down to write, his back would give out within a few hours, but if he stood, he could write all day.)

Sam had a piano in his music room, and I asked if he used it in composing; most jazz musicians use a piano or guitar when they write, testing out melodies, chord voicings, etc. Sam said he never did this, because as soon as he heard the notes on the piano, he could no longer imagine how they would sound on other instruments, a real problem for someone so well known for his orchestration abilities. But he was very proud of his piano, a Steinway that had belonged to the iconic Russian pianist and composer Sergei Rachmaninoff. Rachmaninoff had promised Sam he could have the instrument upon his death, though it had taken many years for Sergei's widow to finally give it up.

Sam was fairly bitter about his treatment at the hands of the classical community. There he was, arguably, the greatest living American composer, but virtually exiled by the critics and his peers. A lot of our conversations centered on the fallout from him tackling a project with a jazz musician. On one visit, he said he had called his nephew, a jazz fan in Chicago, to ask about me. He was concerned about my reputation, not knowing anything about my music other than the recommendation from Roger Hall at RCA. But his nephew, whose opinions he valued, had spoken highly about my band. If not for that, he would most likely have called the project off.

Our visits became a mix of music and personal sharing. I sensed almost immediately that Sam was gay, and in time, he talked a little about that part of his life, even though we hadn't addressed my orientation. I think he just assumed I was gay. If he had asked me at the time, I'm not sure what I would have said, because I hadn't yet figured that out.

His longtime partner was the Italian composer Gian Carlo Menotti, though I gathered they no longer had an active physical relationship. Once, as we were walking through the house, he opened the door to a darkened room and, with some reverence in his voice, said, "That's Menotti's room." (They also owned a house together in northern Italy, where they spent about four months each year.) Sam took great pride in his residences. When he showed me his swimming pool one balmy day, he explained that Schirmer's, his music publisher, had commissioned him to compose something in honor of the company's one-hundredth anniversary; when they asked what he wanted for a fee, he told them he had always wanted a swimming pool with lights in it. "So," he said pointing, "There's my Schirmer's swimming pool."

Sam had some favorite musicians, including the pianist John Browning, who recorded his piano sonata, and Thomas Schippers, his favorite conductor. There was a scintillating gay connection that involved the exceedingly handsome Schippers; apparently, both Barber and Menotti had affairs with him at one time or another. (I later learned that in his early life, Sam had a reputation for hosting celebrity-studded parties, and that he was quite the gay lothario.)

Sam talked about how the recorded performances of his works usually disappointed him. In most cases, he was never consulted about the interpretations of his music, and one conductor in particular—Howard Hansen, who built his reputation recording many of Barber's works—especially left him cold. But he glowed when he spoke about working with Schippers. Together, they recorded a collection of Sam's most popular orchestral works, and he expressed his pleasure at having been there at the recording to give input. I've always considered their RCA recording, *Samuel Barber/Thomas Schippers*, the best recorded example of Sam's music.

As we began to focus on our project, two things became important to Sam. First, he knew nothing about improvisation but wanted to understand how we did it, so he could incorporate it into the composition. I spent a lot of time trying to explain and demonstrate how we use harmonic progressions to create spontaneous melodies, until one day, he asked me to invite my band to his house to play for him. So, a few weeks later, I brought the guys up for a Sunday afternoon spaghetti feast and jam session with Samuel Barber. We socialized as his Italian cook served lunch, then brought in our instruments and played a couple of pieces for him. And then, he asked if he could try playing piano with us. I sketched out the chord progression for a 12-bar blues, and showed him the chord scales involved, and away we went. It was fascinating to watch him improvise.

Typically, when someone tries improvising for the first time, he quickly runs afoul of the song structure as he concentrates on making up a melody. But Sam was daring. He would create a theme and keep extending it, attaining some complex variations, before finally losing track of the chord progressions, forcing us to stop. We went at it for a while, and as we drove home, I analyzed what had just taken place: I had tried to teach Samuel Barber how to improvise, and he had sat in with my band. Pretty amazing. (Before we left Mt. Kisco, Sam told me somewhat conspiratorially that he found Larry really attractive. I figured it best not to pass that compliment along.)

The bigger concern looming over Sam was the whole idea of writing something new. He hadn't taken on a project for some time, other than the opera *Antony and Cleopatra* (completed more than a year earlier), and he shied away from starting anything that would bring out the critics' barbs. He told me he considered the string-quartet format the most challenging instrumentation of all, simply because there were so many perfect examples already in existence, and reminded me he had written a grand total of one string quartet in his career—and that was back in his student days. (The Adagio movement of that piece, standing alone, became known as "Adagio for Strings"—ironically, his most famous work.) So, he had a major case of nerves about writing again for a string quartet, not to mention throwing our jazz group into the mix as well.

One day, when he stepped out of the room, one of his servants came over and urged me to strongly encourage Sam to take the job: "He really needs this, he's just sitting around all the time, and it isn't good for him." Sometime later, Sam called me to come up to the house, and I could tell from his voice that something had changed; I guessed he had decided against the project. So, imagine my surprise when he told me he had decided to go ahead with it. But then he explained that when he'd called RCA to discuss payment, their small offer struck him as insulting, and now he just couldn't possibly do it.

Maybe, that was an easy out for him; I don't know. In one way, it probably came as a relief, not having to confront the critics with something as radical as a jazz project. I understood. We said we would stay in touch, but we never spoke again. After a time, Sam resumed writing, though he often suffered from clinical depression through the remainder of his life. He continued working until he turned seventy, the year before his death in 1981.

CHAPTER 15

Flower Power

Meanwhile, three thousand miles away, an amazing transformation was taking place in San Francisco. In late 1967 and '68, rock music and hippie culture all but took over the city. When we played in the Bay area, we met new musicians almost every day, and soon enough became part of that scene ourselves (even though we were really outsiders from New York).

Bill Graham had opened the Fillmore Ballroom, a major rock venue, and he called about booking my group; he remembered me from when I played with Shearing for him in 1963. Bill loved jazz and wanted to include it on the Fillmore lineup whenever he could. But he needed a group that could fit into the Fillmore scene—not a likely fit for most jazz bands at the time. He needed a group like mine. While the audience in Paris hadn't known what to make of our new look, we were right at home at the Fillmore.

Our favorite Fillmore engagement was the week we played opposite Mike Bloomfield's Electric Flag and the first "supergroup," Cream (with Eric Clapton). All the performers belonged to the new movement, each in our own niche, and we all had heard each others' music. The Cream guys were staying at a small inn-style hotel in Sausalito, across the Golden Gate bridge from San Francisco. We also stayed in Sausalito, in several rented houseboats. And the guys in the Electric Flag actually lived near there, in Mill Valley, the next town over. So, sometimes during the day, all of us got together to hang out.

The saga of Bloomfield's band typified the era and would have been comical, if it weren't also so tragic. Seriously into drugs, Bloomfield and the rest of the Electric Flag barely dealt with reality. Of the six nights we all played the Fillmore, their entire band showed up just twice. Some nights only half the group made it, playing whatever songs they could handle.

One night, none of them could get it together and another band showed up to sub for them. As the story goes, Bloomfield's wife was driving on the expressway and noticed a psychedelic-painted van stalled on the shoulder. She pulled over to check it out and discovered a band from Ohio, just arriving in town to seek their fortune, so she asked, "You guys want to play the Fillmore tonight?" Can you imagine the excitement this elicited? Not to mention panic? These poor bastards—"The Flaming Groovies" (honestly)—struggled their way through an amateurish set, with almost zero response from the audience. When the time came for them to play again, Bill Graham polled our band and Cream on what to do; we all thought it best they skip their second set. Somehow, the "Groovies" remained together until the early '90s; they even put out a record or two, so they must have improved along the way.

The Fillmore was a huge, wood-floored ballroom without any chairs. The crowds of two-thousand or so people milled around throughout the music. The bands played super loud, and the sound was heavy with reverb, rendering the lyrics mostly indistinguishable. That, along with the continuous light shows throwing shadows and colors across the walls, created a swimmy, drifting atmosphere. And the Fillmore audience was unlike any other. They packed the place every night, all those stoned people wandering around, mesmerized by the high-volume music and the oozing, shadowy images on the walls. (The wall projections looked like bacteria under a microscope—perfect for all the acidheads on hand.) In fact, most of the audience didn't pay much attention to the music at all.

The first time we played there, we noticed maybe a hundred people clustered in front of the bandstand. We quickly identified this group, with whom we actually had eye contact, as our "audience," opposed to the rest of the zombies milling around the darkened ballroom. As we proceeded through our set, all I could think was, "My god, we're bombing." Our volume level was minuscule compared to the rock bands, but we poured ourselves into each number, trying like crazy to reach out and generate some response. When the set ended, I felt totally defeated and slunk off the stage.

But Bill Graham, standing offstage, started raving: "Great set! Wow, that's the best reaction I've ever seen from our audience. Those people were really listening!" I couldn't believe it! Apparently, what I considered a minimal response completely outstripped what other groups usually generated, so we were a success.

We played the Fillmore several more times, and also the Fillmore East when it opened in New York a year later. Graham had a different setup in New York. The theater had seating and more conventional acoustics, and the bands were more New York in style. A couple times, we played opposite the Fugs, a very innovative, politically outspoken band. We almost got to share a Fillmore East weekend with the Band, Bob Dylan's backup group, and one of my favorites at the time. But they vetoed the idea of sharing a gig with a jazz group. Quite disappointing; I would have really enjoyed that.

Encountering the rock world opened the door to several projects outside jazz. Through the years, I have played on records with Kenny Rankin, Bruce Cockburn, k.d. lang, Howard Jones, Eric Clapton, and most recently the Eagles' Timothy B. Schmit, giving me a glimpse of how things are done in another part of the music world.

The first rock musician I got to play with was Tim Hardin, who I met at an odd little club on West 45th Street. Its full name was "Steve Paul's the Scene," and it had started as a late-night hangout for show people, from stars to stagehands. In 1967, my band used to play there semi-regularly. Steve was something of a character, and he liked us; other than us, he booked only rock or blues groups.

Jimi Hendrix's first New York gig came at the Scene, with Larry Coryell and I sitting right in front of Hendrix. It was deafening—I've never heard anything that loud in my life—and while this may be heresy, the music didn't impress me all that much. The set had a lot of show business going on (a Hendrix trademark), like when Hendrix broke a guitar string but continued to play while his road manager reached around him and put on a new string.

A lot of up-and-coming as well as established musicians dropped by the Scene in the late hours. The club didn't even open till midnight, and we usually played from about 1 A.M. until 3:30 or 4. Paul Simon was a regular, and Tim Hardin came in almost every night. A hard-living folk-rocker, weighed down by the burden of drugs and alcohol, he would go on and on about the record he would make someday. I didn't take him too seriously; he just seemed like a good soul doing his best to get by. But about a year later, a producer called asking me to play on a Tim Hardin session, released under the title *Reason to Believe*. It turned out pretty successful, especially a tune I played on called "Misty Roses." After that, Tim hit the big time with "If I Were a Carpenter." His career bubbled along for a while, but his life was unsteady, and he eventually died of a heroin overdose in 1980.

Later on, I got invited to an Eric Clapton session. I was recording in the same building, in a studio adjacent to his, and we ran into each other in the hallway. I knew Eric slightly from the week we had shared with Cream at the Fillmore Ballroom.

After we chatted for a while, Eric's producer suggested adding vibes to one of their tracks, so after my own session finished, I rolled my vibes over to their studio, and they played the track for me. As I listened, I immediately noticed that the form of the piece was a bit complex, although it had familiar harmonies. I grabbed a pad of manuscript paper from my bag and jotted down the chord changes and the form of the arrangement so I could play it without stumbling into any wrong notes. Clapton's producer asked what I was doing. When I said I was just writing down the song so I could read along as I played, he shook his head. "Interesting," he said. Apparently, the others were so used to playing by ear that it never occurred to them to construct a lead sheet.

I've actually "played" on many records by people I've never met. Modern pop has seen the rise of digital sampling, where an artist "borrows" a few seconds of a recording—often from some historic album—and loops it to play continuously in the background while a rapper does his thing. At this writing, some of my early records have been sampled, by various rap artists, a total of nineteen times!

NEIGHBORS TO THE NORTH

My two most memorable collaborations with popular singers have involved Canadians: k.d. lang and Bruce Cockburn, both artists I greatly admire. I met k.d. through an old Nashville connection, the legendary country producer Owen Bradley (who owned the studio where I first recorded with Hank Garland). k.d. was bringing her band to play Berklee's Performance Center, and Owen sent word that I should meet her. I was surprised to learn she knew some of my records. And I loved her concert, where I discovered her incredible gifts as a singer no matter the genre. (She straddles the lines between country and pop and even jazz.)

A couple years later, out of the blue, k.d. called and invited me to Vancouver to play on her next record. Usually, when I get asked to play on a non-jazz record, they only want me for one song, but k.d. wanted me to play on half the record. She modestly explained that she wasn't a trained musician. In reply, I suggested they roll the tracks, and I would offer different types of fills and solos, and maybe she could say what sounded good to her. On the first song, after I played a few versions, she came out from the booth and said something along the lines of, "I like the single-note lines you played in the first part, but when you come to the A chord, use that phrase you played when you went from the F# to the A; then leave a space." She knew exactly what she wanted musically—and for someone "untrained," she was pretty good at explaining it, too. We got along just great.

Our collaboration had a subtext. At the time, k.d. was generally assumed to be lesbian, although she had not yet gone public about her personal life. By then, I had come out to friends and my Berklee colleagues, but there was no reason for k.d. to know this. As we finished work the first day, she asked me if I liked martinis, and I said "Definitely!" so she suggested we go to her favorite restaurant.

No sooner had we gotten into our spaghetti than she asked, "Do the people at Berklee know about your preference?" During one day of working in the studio, she had concluded I was gay; I never thought of myself as that obvious, but she quickly figured it out. As we recorded the rest of the songs over the next few days, we talked a lot about coming out, explanations to family, and so on. I learned the main thing holding her back from going public was that she didn't want to cause her mother, home in Edmonton, any awkwardness among her friends.

k.d. released her record *Ingénue* the next year, and she won the GRAMMY for Female Vocalist of the Year. At the telecast, I saw she had brought her mother. By then, she had been interviewed for a cover story in *The Advocate* and spoken publicly about her personal life. I was extremely happy for her, and also very proud to have played on *Ingénue.* The hit single, "Constant Craving," continues to get played on radio and in malls and restaurants, and every time I hear it, I'm transported back to the good times we shared in Vancouver.

Toronto-based guitarist and singer Bruce Cockburn has a long list of records to his credit. Bruce had attended Berklee some years earlier, and he got in touch with me in 1997 about an upcoming record. While the music remained solidly folk and rock, I was very pleased to see the craftsmanship in his writing. He even provided me with written parts, knowing that as a jazz guy, I would prefer having something on paper to guide my playing. *Ingénue* and Bruce's record *Charity of Night* are my favorite popular-music collaborations among those I have recorded.

During that first Fillmore gig in San Francisco, composer Carla Bley flew out from New York to work on a record we were planning. RCA had suggested I do some kind of larger project, and when I mentioned this to Steve Swallow, he told me Carla had a larger work she'd been trying to get recorded for a while. We'd already had success playing some of her songs, so we agreed for her to rearrange this new piece to feature our quartet plus a half dozen additional players.

The piece was *A Genuine Tong Funeral*. Carla conceived it as a sort of opera without words. It had a story line symbolizing the death of old art and birth of the new, the art in this case being jazz. Once back in New York, we went into RCA's Studio B with a high-profile cast of cutting-edge guests: saxophonists Gato Barbieri and Steve Lacy; Howard Johnson, playing bari sax and tuba; trombonist Jimmy Knepper and trumpeter Mike Mantler (then Carla's husband); and Carla herself on piano and organ. Carla had precise ideas of how the music should sound; she even insisted on describing to each player how he should play his solo. Telling a soloist how or what to play is blasphemous for some musicians, but it seemed right given the nature of the project. Overall, Carla did a wonderful job of communicating her vision, and I consider *A Genuine Tong Funeral* one of my most important recordings.

In fact, only one musician objected to Carla's direction—Bob Moses, who resented this intrusion into his artistic freedom. He felt so strongly about this, he asked that his name not appear on the record cover; hence the credit for a drummer named "Lonesome Dragon" on the album. (Carla came up with the name.) Actually, Moses was becoming increasingly restless in the band. Although only twenty years old, he felt the clock ticking. He desperately wanted to play more avant-garde music before the opportunity disappeared. He talked to me about leaving my band, and I reluctantly accepted.

And now, I had to find a new drummer who could fit into the unique musical niche we had created. But before looking far afield, I decided to take a long shot and see if I could interest Roy Haynes, who was still with Stan Getz. I went down to catch Stan's band at the Village Gate in New York. On the first break, I started my conversation with Roy, saying, "I'll just throw this at you, and you can respond any way you want. My group is working steadily now, and we're doing pretty well. Is there any way I can talk you into joining the band?" Roy hesitated a minute, but then he mentioned he was getting near the end of his time with Stan. And then he brightened and said, "Look, if I don't have to carry the drums, you've got a deal." No problem, I told him, and from then on, Swallow and I carried Roy's drums whenever we went on tour—a small price to pay for such a great artist.

Today, I marvel at Roy's willingness to join the Gary Burton Quartet. He was a jazz star in his own right and, then in his mid-forties, a generation older than this bunch of kids with long hair playing some pretty different music. I don't know if he caught any flak about joining our band, but I sure did appreciate his presence. He not only played marvelously (as always); he also brought a lot of status to our group. It thrilled George Wein to hear that Roy had come aboard, and I think our standing in the jazz community took a big leap just because of his presence.

YOU'RE PLAYING WHERE?

If you thought the Fillmore sounded like a strange place to play, you have no idea what kinds of venues jazz musicians can find themselves in. I don't know what it is about New York's northern regions, but some of the quirkiest gigs I've ever played took place upstate. At one club in Rochester, we walked in to see what looked like any ordinary, well-worn jazz room. Showtime arrived, and we played the first set to only a handful of people. It was a Tuesday night, unlikely to have much business; but during our set I noticed people coming in and walking through the club, past the bandstand and into the kitchen. At first, I took them for employees, but this kept happening; eventually I counted twenty or thirty people who had gone back there. I was curious about all these people, so when we finished the set, we walked back into the kitchen ourselves, and found it empty. Very strange. Then, someone appeared and asked if we had gone downstairs yet, telling us the musicians' dressing room was there, and people hung out there. So we went down some stairs and found a whole other space, almost the size of the club upstairs—along with the missing people! Instead of listening to the music, they were downstairs smoking pot, drinking beer, playing cards, and hanging out. This went on every night. The place had an upstairs audience listening to the music, and even on the weekend, almost as many people downstairs drinking, getting high, and having their alternative version of a wonderful evening. The club itself probably lost money that week; it was among the most unusual gigs I have ever played.

Another time, for a concert at a summer resort upstate, we found the address and were stopped at a security gate by some husky guards. Once we identified ourselves, they told us to drive in and meet the entertainment director. Dinner was scheduled a couple hours later, and after we set up our instruments, we were invited to the dining hall, where they had reserved a table for us. The people at the other tables looked like they had just come from filming *The Godfather*: large Italian families, the men dressed in black suits and ties, the ladies in black dresses, lots of children—and each table had its own bodyguard keeping an eye on the family while they ate. We were at a Mafia vacation resort, and as out of place as possible. Our after-dinner concert didn't go too well; they had expected some kind of Dixieland band, and what's more, there was some big soccer match on television that night. About twenty people attended the first half of the concert, and they all left at intermission. The entertainment director told us to just call it a night, but we did get paid, and without any questions.

I've had a fair number of experiences working for "the boys" over the years, starting with Rocky at the 1233 Lounge in Boston during my student days. I also played quite a few clubs with Getz that were obviously Mafia-owned. But never did I feel threatened or uncomfortable in those circumstances. On the contrary, they were always absolutely honorable businessmen when it came to dealing with us. They always paid well, and what's more, they almost always liked the music.

One other memorable concert took place in Germany in the '70s, when we arrived at the site and discovered that we'd be playing in a cave. Literally, a cave. Balver Höhle was a cavern large enough to hold about a thousand people attending a weekend jazz festival, and we performed last on the program. We played our usual set, plus several encores; the audience was wildly enthusiastic (and really drunk). After about the fifth encore, I decided we'd done enough, even though the crowd had fallen into the rhythmic clapping typical of European audiences. We waited a while, then returned to the stage and packed up our instruments. All the while, the audience continued to applaud; by now, they had become entranced by the sound of their own clapping as it echoed through the cave, and didn't really care whether we played or not. This being a cave, it had only one entrance, and we had to make several trips with our equipment walking straight through the crowd to our van parked outside. After we were all packed, I sat down with the promoter for about ten minutes to complete the necessary paperwork and get paid. But even after that, as we drove off we could still hear the sound of clapping coming from the cave.

At about this time, a second on-and-off California romance—with another musician friend's wife, no less—was fizzling out, making me wonder if I was destined to end up in relationships with musicians' wives. I also continued confronting my sexual identity issues in therapy. I absolutely didn't want to be gay, for all the obvious reasons. I still felt attraction to men; I felt attraction to some women as well, which left me pretty confused. But then, I found myself in a situation I couldn't turn away from. I had developed strong feelings for a guy in New York, although I never expected to do anything about it because I assumed he was straight. (For one thing, he usually had a girlfriend with him.) But one day, as the two of us talked about music, he just blurted out that he knew it was a mistake to become my friend because he found me so attractive. Thus began an awkward affair, kept secret from everyone, of course, since neither of us considered ourselves really "gay." It sounds so foolish now, but at the time, I still believed I was primarily straight. I just thought I had this additional ability to appreciate men—an "artistic" kind of thing. He and I spent nights together whenever the opportunity presented itself, between tours and so on, but it always felt incomplete. Keeping it secret, we couldn't really have a meaningful relationship. Neither of us knew much about gay sex, either, so there was a lot of fumbling around. This went on for nearly a year, before a weeklong engagement in Boston changed the picture.

The club had an attractive young woman named Donna Hanley as its cashier, and during the course of the week, we got pretty friendly. I didn't really expect to see her once we left town, but a month later, she surprised me by walking into a club we were playing in Washington, D.C. As it turned out, she had a long flight layover in Washington. Noticing in the local paper that we had an afternoon show, she decided to come hear the band and say hello. Afterward, I suggested we get some dinner before her flight to Boston, and we got better acquainted. Later she would tell me she had originally fancied Larry Coryell—the girls were always drawn to Larry, and he was never without a girlfriend—so I guess I was second choice. But that didn't really discourage me. After I got home, we stayed in touch, and soon, I was traveling back and forth to spend time with Donna in Boston.

And after six years living on West 73rd Street, I also decided I wanted to move to the suburbs. By sheer luck, I stumbled onto a great house, through my therapist. I mentioned to him that I felt the time had come to move out of the city, but I needed to find something fairly reasonable. (My rent in town was $175 a month; I figured I could afford $300, tops, for a new place.) He called me later to say he knew some friends who owned a house they wanted to rent, because they were moving to Rhode Island.

I drove out to the address in Douglaston, a lovely spot on Long Island—the only house on a short street called Gary Place, coincidentally. As I pulled into the driveway, I saw an impressive structure with a lot of property and gardens around it, and knew I couldn't possibly afford this. I started quietly backing out of the driveway, planning to call later and apologize for canceling, when the lady of the house came out on the porch and waved at me. I had to be polite, so I went inside, where she and her husband, a charming couple, showed me the whole house and explained all kinds of details (like how to run the furnace)—as if I had already agreed to move in. This made me more and more uncomfortable, knowing I wouldn't be able to take it.

The awkward moment arrived when we sat down to discuss finances. After a short pause, the husband said, "We were wondering if you could manage $100 a month?" I struggled to keep a passive look on my face. I lived there four years, after which my brother moved in and stayed for several years after that. What a deal!

In addition to the house in Douglaston, Donna and I set up an apartment in Boston. She was finishing her degree at Boston University, and we planned to divide our time between New York and Boston until her graduation, when we could live full-time in New York. We also agreed that once she finished school, we would get married.

So, on a summer weekend in 1969, we drove to the eastern end of Long Island, found a justice of the peace, and made it official. Three days later my next tour started; that became our honeymoon, and throughout our marriage, Donna toured with me whenever possible.

CHAPTER 16

Finally Part of the New York Scene

In 1968, the second year of the Gary Burton Quartet, I got a big break courtesy of George Shearing's longtime tour manager, Ed Fuerst. Ed loved the music and the jazz scene, and he would invite me over to his rather lavish Park Avenue apartment to catch up on musician gossip, and to play me tapes of well-known musicians he had recorded during private parties at his place. (He came from a wealthy family, and he lived well.) Ed had taken great interest in my career as it evolved during the Stan Getz years, and when he learned I had started my own band, he insisted on taking me down to meet Max Gordon at the Village Vanguard.

The Vanguard was then (and possibly still is) the most prestigious place to play in New York, mostly because Max was so selective about the bands he brought in. He had an ear for quality musicianship and couldn't bear to hire musicians who didn't meet his standards. The room itself, one flight down, looked like nothing had been replaced, or maybe even cleaned, since it opened. On New York visits in my student days, I always felt a little intimidated going there, mainly because as a customer, I had to deal with Mike, the seemingly gruff bartender. (In those days, if you stood at the bar instead of sitting at a table, you'd only have to buy one drink; Mike was the one who intimidated you into ordering the next one.) A funky kitchen at the back of the club served as the dressing room and hangout for the musicians. I think the club had to have a kitchen to qualify for its license (or something like that), but it never saw action in terms of actual food preparation. Thank goodness for that.

Ed took me down and introduced me to Max—a slightly built older guy with a fringe of gray hair around his bald head—and we chatted for a bit. Max had spent decades in the New York nightclub business. At one time, he owned not only the Village Vanguard, but also the Blue Angel, a more upscale supper club in midtown. Max proceeded to give me a lecture on the kinds of bands he would hire and the kinds he wouldn't. I didn't know where this was leading, since he had never even heard me or my band. With my long hair and hippy clothes, I figured he was building up to tell me I didn't belong there. But probably because Ed had vouched for me, Max ended up offering me a weeklong booking opposite Thelonious Monk's band the following month.

Thus began a wonderful experience that lasted a couple years. We soon became the Vanguard "house band," in a way; we had an open invitation to play there whenever we liked (often sharing the bill with Monk—a singular thrill). I quickly learned that Max was an old softie who loved the music and the scene and everything about his little run-down club. He would arrive every day around 1 P.M., sitting in the darkened club all day, signing for deliveries in the afternoon, occasionally going out for a cigar or a paper; he would then stay until the club closed around 2 A.M. Night after night, he heard every set from a table at the back of the club, and he knew the music as well as anyone.

I have some strong recollections from the Vanguard. My final encounter with Coltrane took place there. I had first crossed paths with Trane at Birdland, the night he'd treated Stan Getz rudely, and because of that, I always kept my distance if we found ourselves playing at the same festival. So one night at the end of our set, when I noticed Trane standing near the door, wearing some kind of African shirt, I decided to avoid him. I didn't figure him for a likely fan of our new jazz. But as I was trying to keep my distance, he continued moving toward me until he met me halfway. To my surprise, he was beaming; he said he loved the music, and he had many compliments for the guys in my group. He was so different from that earlier incident at Birdland. A few months later, at the Quartet's next Vanguard engagement, Max walked in while we were setting up and told us Coltrane had died; almost no one even knew he'd been ill. I'm glad I had that last opportunity to speak with him, if only to revise my first impression of him.

Another poignant experience came during the week we shared with the legendary tenor saxophonist Coleman Hawkins. Getting up in years and in poor health, Hawkins could no longer play well. He was also in bad financial shape, so his friends implored Max to offer him a week at the club, if only to help cover his rent. At the end of one night, as Swallow and I started up the flight of stairs to the street, we discovered Hawkins in front of us, struggling to climb the steps. Even though we could have passed around him, it seemed more respectable to let him go at his own pace—a laborious effort that took several minutes, before he made it to street level and got into a cab. Swallow and I looked at each other and agreed that we must never let that happen to us. To be that ill and in such suffering, and still have to work gigs to pay the rent—a terrible way to end a great career.

The real treat at the Vanguard came from hearing Thelonious Monk's longtime quartet, and Monk in particular; they played so well together, and Monk was such a warm and inspiring person, despite his public persona as an unpredictable oddball. He rarely spoke, and even when he did, it often wasn't clear what he meant. But he genuinely liked our band and always commended us when we added new tunes to our repertoire. (Because of our departure from traditional jazz, I usually didn't expect established musicians to like our music, but we were steadily winning people over. It would take another two years before Miles Davis, John McLaughlin, and others started playing our kind of music—what eventually became known as "fusion jazz.")

During the time we played regularly at the Vanguard, Max couldn't always pay me our full salary. Struggling with back taxes, trying to just keep the place open, he would come up maybe $500 or a $1000 short. This went on for a couple years, and while he always acknowledged the fact, it got to the point where he owed me many thousands of dollars, and I reluctantly realized I had to find another New York "home." After that, I was never comfortable going into the Vanguard, for fear of an awkward encounter with Max. About five years later, I did run into him, at an Italian restaurant in the Village. He smiled and said, "I haven't forgotten that I owe you that money." He even remembered the exact amount.

Of course, I never got any of it. Max passed away in 1989, beloved by everyone in the jazz community, me included.

THELONIOUS MONK

Jazz fans know of Monk as a quite unusual character, but those who met him knew the kindness and gentleness he communicated. His career had a tragic underside. Monk was among the pioneers of bebop, but because he behaved oddly and people considered him unreliable, the spotlight shone mostly on others (especially Dizzy Gillespie and Charlie Parker). According to Robin D.G. Kelley's excellent biography of Monk, he was bothered most of his life by what he considered a lack of credit for his jazz contributions. He had a point. It's hard enough to make a successful career in jazz; it augments the challenge if you don't show up on time (or sometimes at all), and if you're too eccentric for people to understand you. With Monk, you never knew what to expect. And it seemed to me that the family and friends protecting him may have actually helped encourage his behavior.

One night at the Vanguard, Monk's band began their set with one of his familiar compositions. But instead of playing the melody once or twice, then opening it up for improvised solos (as you'd expect), Monk just kept repeating the written melody. After several minutes, the other band members gradually quit playing and left the bandstand, but Monk just kept going, endlessly rehashing the melody. Monk's guys and my band were now all standing at the back of the half-empty club wondering what to do. His drummer, Ben Riley, tried yelling at him from the side, but Monk just kept going. Max Gordon thought that he might stop if we all applauded, so we spurred the audience into a round of clapping, but Monk continued to play. After fifteen minutes or so, the audience started to show signs of bewilderment. At last, Ben went up to the piano and just lifted Monk off the bench, then firmly walked him to the kitchen, put his coat on him, and led him out the back door, obviously disoriented. But the next night, Monk was back again and playing wonderfully. I guess that kind of thing just befell him now and then.

The Monk band played on a summer festival tour organized by George Wein in 1968, so in addition to our evenings at the Vanguard, we also saw a lot of their group as we toured from city to city. Monk seemed in good form; some of his best records came from that time. The next time I saw him, on another Wein tour about four years later, it was a different story altogether. He was part of The Giants of Jazz, touring Europe with Dizzy Gillespie, saxophonist Sonny Stitt, trombonist Kai Winding, bassist Al McKibbon, and drummer Art Blakey: a genuine all-star group of bebop survivors. Wein had put me on the bill to play a solo set before the beboppers came on. As usual, Monk's wife Nellie came along on the tour to assist, but in fact, Monk was barely there himself. He didn't seem to recognize people much of the time. I recall him staring into my face intently, somewhat puzzled, as Nellie kept saying, "Come on T, that's Gary, Gary from the Vanguard. You remember, don't you?" He looked physically ill, too, and his skin was kind of gray. His playing had little energy—hardly the Monk I had heard at the Vanguard.

Monk and Nellie were both eccentric. For one thing, they never discarded anything on tour. They kept every magazine, every empty pop bottle—whatever they acquired each day of their travels became part of their luggage. And they also liked to buy little souvenir items wherever they stopped. So as the tour progressed, the Monks' luggage grew incredibly overstuffed. On top of that, they insisted on unpacking everything when they arrived at each hotel; soon, they needed an adjoining room just to handle their collection. By tour's end, their tour manager had to help them pack and unpack each day so they could show up on time for gigs and planes.

Monk pretty much stopped playing after that, though he lived almost another decade, spending most of his time sleeping or lounging around the New Jersey apartment of the Baroness Nica de Koenigswarter, his longtime friend and supporter and a well-known jazz patron. Reportedly, he would put on a suit and tie and then lie in bed all day, fully dressed, in a state of some confusion, possibly exacerbated by the medications prescribed for his mental state.

I had once pointed out to George Wein that, since the vibraphone was such a young instrument (invented in 1929), most all of the famous vibes players were still alive and performing. This gave him the idea to organize a Vibraphone Summit at the Newport Jazz Festival in the summer of '68. He didn't specifically ask my advice, but he chose the players I would have picked: Lionel Hampton, Red Norvo, Milt Jackson, and Bobby Hutcherson (and me, of course). The concept called for us each to play a couple of tunes with a rhythm section (in this case, the Billy Taylor Trio); then, we would all do a concluding jam session at the end. The day of the Summit, Mother Nature stepped in to complicate things. A light rain began falling just as the outdoor concert got underway. We had a fair-sized crowd, considering this was an afternoon concert in the rain, and the people seemed determined to tough it out. As we continued, the rain got heavier and the audience got out their ponchos and umbrellas and pressed forward to get closer to the stage.

Time came for the group jam session, which we hadn't yet discussed. The stage crew lined up our five vibraphones, and we all took our places, unsure of what to do next. We needn't have worried, though, because this was exactly the kind of situation where Hamp always took charge. He immediately counted off one of his favorites, "Hamp's Blues," and directed the order of the solos; then he segued us into "Flying Home," his theme song, and we were grooving. It made no musical sense whatsoever, the five vibraphones all ringing together, but as a spectacle, it hit the jackpot. The audience, which had persevered through the rain, went crazy, and for years after, people have come up to me saying that they were there that wet afternoon and will never forget it.

Following Newport, we embarked on a Wein tour of U.S. festivals, with concerts in practically every major city. For these events, we always had a minimum of six bands: us, Monk's quartet, saxophonist Cannonball Adderley's quintet, singer Dionne Warwick, flutist Herbie Mann, and some-times pianist Ramsey Lewis or saxophonist Gerry Mulligan. My band loved traveling around with such illustrious musi-cians. We already knew Monk's group, and we quickly got to know Cannonball's guys too. In San Francisco, I invited Victor Gaskin (Cannonball's bassist) and Joe Zawinul (his pianist and later co-founder of the fusion band Weather Report) to go sailing. I had learned to sail during my extended stays in San Francisco, and whenever I returned, I made sure to get out on the water. Victor, Joe, and I had a great time bouncing around San Francisco Bay on our day off.

The tour started with a major setback: the great guitarist Wes Montgomery was scheduled to play, but he died, suddenly and far too young, the week before we started. George Wein had to book substitute groups along the way; on the tour's very first concert, in Charlotte, N.C., Art Blakey's Jazz Messengers covered Wes's spot on the bill. Then George landed an extra booking the next afternoon, just for my band and the Messengers, at a college a couple of hours away—a booking that gave me personal (and painful) insight into Blakey's legendary reputation for disorganization.

Our band left the hotel in midmorning to drive to the college. When we arrived, we received a shock, as did our college hosts. It was an all-black college holding their annual Mother's Day celebration. Standing there in our rock 'n' roll outfits, we looked as if we could have just arrived from Mars. The auditorium brimmed with families dressed in their best church clothes to honor their mothers, waiting for the afternoon entertainment to begin. At this point, a call back to Charlotte revealed that Blakey and his band were just now getting out of bed, with several hours driving ahead of them.

We delayed as much as possible and then began one of the longest sets I've ever played, as we tried to fill the time till Blakey's band arrived. We went over moderately well given the circumstances, but the crowd had to be wondering what the heck was up with these hippies playing at their Mother's Day celebration. The Jazz Messengers showed up an hour or so later. We didn't even stay to hear them; we just drove back to Charlotte to rejoin the main tour.

The Gary Burton Quartet had some big changes in store, as summer came to an end.

I loved our lineup. As three-fourths of the old Getz quartet, Roy Haynes, Steve Swallow, and I were quite familiar with each other's playing, and Larry Coryell's rock-influenced presence supplied an element of "newness." During his eighteen months or so in the band, we had established a good (if occasionally tense) rapport in the front line. We had a very successful combination of players, and I hated to see things change; but I also knew Larry was close to going out on his own, even if he didn't fully realize this himself. I recognized all the signs. They reminded me of my departure from Getz's band, only now, the shoe was on the other foot. It's a fairly common pattern for sidemen. You feel yourself pulled in two directions: to either maintain the security of a job in a successful band, or to risk it all and try to make it on your own.

There always existed a degree of competition between Larry and me: both the same age, both featured soloists in the group, both on the leading edge of a new jazz style—frankly, I think we were occasionally jealous of each other. I believe he resented me as the leader, further along in my career. I simmered over the ease with which he, as the guitar player, seemed to draw attention. I've never been quite at ease in social situations, and I envied Larry's ability to easily talk it up with anyone and everyone. Things could get tense sometimes.

All this took its toll on me, and Larry had started to behave strangely, too. He showed up at the last possible minute for gigs, sometimes drunk; I discovered he had also begun to use cocaine. (He even showed me how to prepare it for shooting up.) This made me increasingly uncomfortable. He was now trouble looking for a place to happen. When Roy and Swallow told me I had to do something about him, I knew I couldn't put it off any longer. But I worried about breaking up the group so soon after we had gotten established.

By then, Larry had grown so unpredictable that I hesitated telling him I planned to let him go. If it went badly, he might leave in the middle of the tour. We had some time off in the fall, and I decided to wait till then. Meanwhile, I quietly looked around for someone to replace him. Both Swallow and Roy suggested pianist Chick Corea. I'd never played with him but had heard one of his records, and thought he would be perfect for our group.

I called Chick, who was accompanying Sarah Vaughan but ready to leave; as much as he liked Sarah, he didn't have much chance to solo or play any of his own music in her group. This put the plan in motion. When our tour ended, I intended to give Larry the customary two weeks notice; a month or so after that, when Chick had left Sarah, we would relaunch the band.

But Larry somehow heard rumors, and in the car on our way to San Diego for the last summer gig, he turned to me and said he'd heard Chick was going to replace him. I was momentarily shocked that he knew, but recovered and explained that in order to avoid any awkwardness on the last few gigs, I was waiting till we finished the tour to tell him—but yes, that was my intention. I told him I believed it best for him, too, and everything went fine that night, except for a bit more tension than usual. Larry joined Herbie Mann's band for a while before going on to lead his own groups, and I have always wished him well. (In his own 2007 autobiography, Larry wrote at length about his early struggle with drugs, something he eventually conquered.)

CHAPTER 17

"There'll Be Some Changes Made"

Chick Corea came aboard in the fall of '68, and I anticipated a true dream band. We were all strong players; even better, Chick had already made recordings with Roy and Swallow separately. At Chick's house in a section of Queens not far from my house, we rehearsed and chose some new songs while his kids played in the next room. That first get-together went all right, and we started touring; we played a handful of dates, including jazz festivals in St. Louis and Buffalo, then returned to New York for a week at the Village Gate. By then we had played enough gigs to judge that this wasn't really working out as we expected.

For some reason, Chick and I just couldn't mesh our musical styles. If we relaxed, we seemed to clash and bump into each other. We could avoid this if we restrained ourselves, but that wasn't much fun, and it didn't bring out our best playing. On our last night at the Gate, we sat down to talk and both agreed that this just didn't click. I'd thought this would be another of those magical band combinations that come along every so often. As it turned out later, I was only half wrong.

I decided to go back to guitar in my group, and Chick

started looking for a new gig; happily, he called me a week or two later with the news that Miles had just hired him (for what evolved into the historic album *Bitches Brew*). Meanwhile, I needed a guitar player.

That week, late one night, I heard a track on the radio featuring a guitarist who sounded just right. I didn't recognize his playing, but I tracked down the record and found it was a San Francisco guitarist named Jerry Hahn. After I persuaded Jerry to take some time off from home life with his family, he toured with us through most of 1969, and played on two of my records.

Around that time, I received a pleasant surprise that helped compensate for my ups and downs with the band's personnel. *Down Beat* magazine's annual Readers Poll for 1968 came out, and not only was I voted the number-one vibes player for the first time; I also received the award for "Jazzman of the Year." Both of these honors had great significance for me. As my visibility increased during my tenures with Shearing and Getz, I thought I would steadily move up in the poll rankings. That didn't happen, but now, it seemed, I had suddenly arrived as a vibist. As for "Jazzman of the Year," that honor had always gone to an established star, and an elder statesman of jazz. I was the first (and to this date, one of only three) to win this honor at the age of twenty-five or younger, and I saw it as recognition of the band's breakthroughs and our new approach to jazz.

I can't say enough about the bond I've shared with Steve Swallow. He is a unique bass player, a brilliant composer, and he also became my closest confidant and advisor. I talked everything over with him: every personnel change, every record project, the long-term future of our band, the music itself—everything. A keen judge of character and events, he always helped me stay on course. As the years progressed, his role in the group became even more important. Other musicians came and went as the band evolved, and we made many different kinds of records, but Swallow remained right there with me for more than two decades. A lot of critics at the time misread the dynamic of my first groups; they assumed the important connection was between me and the guitar players. But it was Swallow on whom I depended every step of the way.

STEVE SWALLOW

Steve Swallow truly exemplifies the tale of the academic who ventured outside the ivory tower and promptly got lost. He grew up a single child in New Jersey, attending the Choate School, one of the country's best prep academies (the Kennedys went there), and spending summers at Camp Half Moon, also in Massachusetts. To this day, he can still sing the camp song, which always breaks me up. His parents ardently wanted him to succeed in a distinguished professional field, so he headed for Yale and spent a couple years majoring in Latin Languages. On the side, he played bass, which his parents hoped would remain a hobby, but in his sophomore year, he got a call from pianist Paul Bley, who in not so many words said, "Come down to New York and play jazz."

Early on, Steve played with such disparate musicians as swing giant Benny Goodman and modernists like Bley; he had a knack for fitting into any kind of music. But leaving Yale for New York ushered in a period of estrangement with Steve's family, which lasted until he got married and started a family of his own. (There's nothing like grandchildren to bring parents back into the picture.) I always thought Steve might have developed his sense of rebellion as a result of his family experience. He delighted in tweaking the nose of convention and authority, though he always did it subtly and with great wit. He has a natural warmth—tenderness, even—that outweighs his moments of cynicism.

I view Steve as a holdover from the beat generation, reading William Burroughs and Allen Ginsberg and questioning society's norms. He was the first person I knew to speak out against the Vietnam War. In our early years, George Wein would greet him with, "Hey, Steve, how goes the revolution?"

Steve was also among the first of my highly educated friends, and we had long conversations about politics, literature, and just about everything else, as we spent hours together on the road.

Along with a few others, Steve garnered praise as one of the young bassists carrying on Scott LaFaro's innovations at the bass, specifically the use of more soloistic lines (rather than a steady walking beat) when comping. Actually, though, Steve didn't play much like LaFaro at all. His influences were more traditional—the tremendous bop-era bassists Oscar Pettiford and Percy Heath, for instance—and his solos epitomize melodic construction as opposed to dazzling dexterity.

Never afraid to pursue his instincts, Steve surprised everyone when he gave up the acoustic bass in the late '60s and switched to electric bass guitar. That instrument had been around for some years, popularized by rock bands, but the jazz world had not yet welcomed it in. Steve started experimenting with electric bass in 1968, after trying one at a music convention. At first, he used it on maybe two songs per concert, playing acoustic the rest of the set. But within six months, that had reversed, and we were carrying around the acoustic bass for just a couple songs per night. At that point, Steve decided to fully commit to the new instrument. He left behind his traditional bass technique and learned an entirely different fingering system, similar to that used for guitar, and also started playing with a guitar pick. It was like starting over, but it resulted in a method that serves him extremely well. Today, he plays a custom-made five-string bass guitar, with a style so unique that you need hear only a few notes to recognize his playing.

Because of his established reputation, Steve's move to electric opened the door for other jazz bassists to switch. A few years later, players such as Jaco Pastorius were choosing the bass guitar as their primary instrument, ensuring the electric instrument its place in jazz. (In fact, Steve's own electric bass style is often cited as the only precedent for Jaco's innovations.)

By 1969, the Quartet had plenty of work, and could command high enough fees to not only cover expenses but also provide something for me to save. Just in time, too; I had kept things together by not paying my taxes, a time-honored tactic when operating on the edge. But you can't stay on that edge too long, and I had reached the point where I had to get caught up (or get caught). Within the year, I managed to pull even. Meanwhile, Donna and I had established a nice rapport with my parents back in Indiana, where property was quite inexpensive, and we found a house on seven acres of woods, with a lake, in the picturesque village of Nashville, Indiana. That's about twenty miles from Bloomington, home of Indiana University, where I attended my first jazz camp. The property cost $21,000, and I paid for it in installments over the next five years, thinking Donna and I would divide our time between the house in New York and our rural retreat in Indiana.

I had a working band; I had been recording on a major label for the past eight years; I had a new wife, and we had started buying our first home. I was twenty-six and felt like I had it made. I wrapped up 1969 with a quartet record called *Country Roads and Other Places*—which turned out to be my last for RCA.

In 1970, the music business entered a slow period. The economy went into recession, and many club owners and concert promoters cut back on bookings or went out of business altogether. I started the year with a full calendar but lost half the dates as the year wore on. And then, I canceled some more when, out of the blue, Hollywood beckoned.

George Wein called to say that MGM wanted me in a movie. Wow! I thought; what are the details? I assumed they wanted me to either compose and perform the movie's score, or maybe have the band play on screen, as I had done with Getz back in 1964. I found out the movie would star Ava Gardner, with Roddy McDowell directing—both huge names at the time—and would film in London. MGM would cover the expenses for me and Donna and put us up in an apartment. They told me to be available for ten to twelve weeks at

$1,000 per week. That was decent money in 1970 (when you could buy a good new car for under $4,000), so it all sounded pretty good. But I still didn't know exactly what they wanted me to do.

George went back for more information, and incredibly, they didn't want me to play or write or do anything at all musical. They wanted me to act! They must be kidding, I thought; I had no acting experience. But Hollywood was calling, and I had no intention of missing the opportunity.

The script concerned a hip older woman (Ava Gardner) in swinging London, surrounded by musicians and artists, and the various adventures she would get into. I would play one of the musician/artist types hanging around the scene. They were going for realism, apparently. I assume that someone, maybe a casting director or maybe Roddy McDowell himself, had seen me playing in L.A., or owned one of my records, and thought, Hey! This guy would be perfect for the movie!

Problem was, they wanted us in London in a few weeks. I frantically canceled the next two months of gigs, renewed my passport, and started making all the arrangements needed for an extended absence. But a few days later, the news arrived that because of Britain's strict union rules, only so many Americans could work on a movie in the U.K., and it came down to a choice between Ava Gardner's hair stylist and me. (Guess who won?) I pleaded and begged, but it was over. I went from budding movie star to out-of-work jazz musician overnight.

I took some solace months later when I heard that the production company ran out of money and ended up mired in lawsuits. Apparently, no one got paid—a real fiasco. Still, I'd have liked the chance to at least give the movies a try.

In the summer of '69, my contract at RCA had come to an end. They offered to renew it for several years. My records didn't cost much to make, and they wanted to keep at least some jazz on the label. So as long as I didn't cost too much or make any big demands, they would happily keep me on as their token jazz artist. But I didn't want that. In a situation like this, a label likely won't try too hard to sell records or build one's career. What's more, all the people I knew at RCA had by now left the company. I went to the office on 23rd Street to meet with some of the new staff and the guy they proposed as my new producer. His big idea was to make a record with pianist Billy Taylor, which they would market as "Burton and Taylor." He figured people would think of the movie stars Richard Burton and Elizabeth Taylor and buy the record by the thousands, only to discover it was just us jazz musicians instead.

I definitely had to leave RCA.

George Wein came through for me again. He set up a meeting with Nesuhi Ertegun, who along with his brother Ahmet, had founded Atlantic Records. It had a long jazz history (courtesy of Nesuhi) and a very successful R&B catalog (thanks to Ahmet and his collaborator Jerry Wexler). After our meeting, Nesuhi invited me to join the label.

Atlantic differed greatly from RCA, a corporate behemoth with lots of structure and process. Atlantic was a family company where decisions were made on a fast and personal basis. They assigned me to work with Joel Dorn, a former Philadelphia disk jockey. On the radio, he had helped propel several Atlantic records onto the charts, so they brought him in to produce some of their artists. Joel was blustery and at times insensitive, but I enjoyed working with him. He could rub some people the wrong way, but I understood him. He had lots of ideas, many of them off the wall, but he would occasionally hit on things that were golden, and that I'd never have thought of myself.

One of my first projects for Atlantic came out of left field but became one of my favorites. The Gary Burton Quartet played the Newport Jazz Festival in 1969, and among our listeners was the venerable violinist Stephane Grappelli. Jazz fans and historians know that Stephane came to prominence in the 1930s as a member of the Hot Club of France, where he partnered with legendary gypsy guitarist Django Reinhardt. George Wein brought Stephane over to perform at Newport and arranged for him to play with a group of older musicians. But while listening to my band, Stephane complained to George that he always got stuck with the old guys. When George asked what younger musicians he preferred, he answered, "Well, I like Gary's band." Given our jazz-rock set and our Carnaby Street regalia, that certainly surprised George. But after we finished, he introduced me to Stephane and suggested we consider recording together. Nesuhi Ertegun was there, too, and he loved the idea. Growing up in Paris, he had followed Stephane for many years. I knew very little about his music, so I wasn't sure what to say. But since everyone else seemed so positive about the idea, I decided we'd give it a try. We had a tour in Europe coming up a few months later, so we set a plan to meet and play together one afternoon in Paris. If that went well, we would proceed to a recording studio the next day.

I did some research on Stephane, which did not encourage me. His career had been slowing down as he got older (he was then sixty-two), and at the time, he played mostly in the lounge of the Paris Hilton Hotel—not very auspicious. He had few recent recordings to go by, and I worried that as an older musician, he would have trouble playing tunes with more complex harmonies. In the weeks leading up to the session, Swallow and I fussed over the material, finally deciding to divide the material between songs Stephane knew and songs from our repertoire that we hoped he would find comfortable.

We worried for nothing. The rehearsal went very smoothly. Stephane had no trouble digging into the new songs we threw at him, and after just a few hours, we agreed to record the next day.

The studio was, putting it mildly, low-budget. The only heat in the place came from a potbellied wood stove in the middle of the studio. It was a chilly day, and the engineer had to come out periodically to throw more logs on the fire. None of this mattered, though. The music was fun, and we were having a great time with Stephane—a really charming guy who, I only found out later, also happened to be gay. He wrote a song for me titled "Gary," and sent me a handwritten copy that I framed and kept on my office wall for years, until the ink had faded away completely and it was just a yellowed piece of paper. Meanwhile, Stephane continued to play well into his eighties, enjoying every minute of his rebounding career. I love that the lead sheet he gave me faded out long before he did.

Some years later, Swallow told me a story he heard from a French bass player. After our recording session, Stephane had dropped by a Paris musicians' bar, boasting about the great record session he had just done, as he put it: ". . . with that American vibes player, Gary, uh, Gary... Gary Cooper!"

But then, Atlantic Records lost enthusiasm for the project. It was so different from my other records, they feared it would confuse my growing fanbase before I could establish myself on the label. I kept asking them to release it, and they kept putting it off. A couple years went by before they quietly slipped *Paris Encounter* into the release schedule. Of the six records I made for Atlantic, this remains a favorite.

Around that same time, I at last got to know one of Stephane's contemporaries and a true pioneer on my instrument: Red Norvo. George Wein booked a European tour for us, and I had a terrific time listening to Red's stories about his early days in vaudeville and jazz.

RED NORVO

We think of Lionel Hampton as the "father of the vibes," and for good reason: Hamp made the first vibraphone recording in the early '30s, and by the end of that decade, had become a household name. But there's another side to this story—the history of jazz mallet playing, which actually began with xylophone players in the '20s, before the vibraphone had even been invented. The first popular xylophonists (such as George Hamilton Greene) were not exactly jazzers. They mostly performed ragtime-style pieces patterned after the early piano compositions of George Gershwin and the novelty composer Zez Confrey, and they didn't improvise. (As a kid, I would mail-order sheet music for G.H. Greene's songs, and play them on marimba.) Red Norvo was the first significant jazz improviser on mallet instruments, gaining fame for his innovative recordings on xylophone and marimba.

He first studied piano and switched to xylophone in his mid-teens. Red began his professional career in vaudeville, occasionally leading his own marimba ensembles, and then joined the renowned Paul Whiteman Orchestra, the jazz-flavored commercial band that famously premiered George Gershwin's *Rhapsody in Blue* in 1924. (When Whiteman performed in large ballrooms, it was Red's job to entertain during the band's intermissions; he did this by rolling his xylophone around the dance floor and stopping at patrons' tables to play short solo pieces.) When he married the band's singer, Mildred Bailey, they worked together as "Mr. and Mrs. Swing" until they divorced in the early '40s.

Red was always breaking new ground. He had no qualms when it came to the winds of change. In 1933, he recorded two commercial hits, "Knockin' on Wood" and "Hole in the Wall." After the label owner left, he returned to the studio and recorded two more tracks that stood for years among the most innovative recordings in jazz: an arrangement of Bix Biederbecke's "In a Mist," and Red's own composition, "Dance of the Octopus." (On that session, Benny Goodman played bass clarinet, somewhat unusual for the time.) Listening to these early recordings now, I can hardly imagine what the musicians thought of Red's new music. Red told me the label owner, furious that he had recorded something so unsalable, didn't even want to release the songs. It's said the owner literally tore up Red's contract. But the tracks did become available, thank goodness, and are now considered true classics.

Although Red belonged to the previous jazz era, he was nonetheless interested in bebop, which came onto the scene in the '40s. In 1945 he organized the first swing-bebop collaboration. The historically significant "Congo Blues" session brought the best-known beboppers (Charlie Parker and Dizzy Gillespie) together with several leading swing musicians (including pianist Teddy Wilson from Goodman's group). By then, Red was playing vibraphone—he made the switch from xylophone in 1943 (coincidentally, the year I was born)—and he stuck to vibes for the rest of his career. When he switched, he also stopped using four mallets, despite having demonstrated considerable facility with them on his early recordings. In 1995, after watching me play a couple of solo pieces, he told me he regretted having given up on four-mallet technique. He had done so because the other vibes players in the '40s all played with just two, and he decided to go with the trend.

Red continued to lead a variety of groups based in New York throughout the decade, but by the '50s, he had tired of running a larger group, and was also entertaining the idea of relocating to the West Coast. One night, Red played a New York gig with a new guitarist, Tal Farlow. Red was so impressed that after the set, he told Tal, "Look, I don't have any jobs yet, but I want to move to Los Angeles and start a new band, and I would like you to be in it." Tal said yes, and without anything more than the promise of work to come, he followed Red out west.

Wanting to keep expenses down, Red hit on the idea of a trio, with vibes, guitar, and bass. In L.A., someone recommended bassist Charles Mingus— and therein lies the tale of how Red resurrected Mingus's career. The bassist had grown discouraged with the music business and was working at the post office. Red told me he called all over town, checking with different branches of the post office, till he found the one where Mingus worked, and then had to go find him in person, since Mingus didn't have a phone. Red offered him the job while they stood in the street outside the post office. Mingus said yes, and just like that, he was back into the music biz.

When you look at Mingus's subsequent legacy of aggressive post-bop compositions, it seems incongruous that he would be in a band with Red and

Tal. But for the year and a half they played together, the Red Norvo Trio was the hottest band around. They were known for fast tunes and exceptionally tight ensemble playing, but Red told me they used no written music. They came up with all their arrangements during rehearsals. Their brief partnership did wonders for all three, especially Mingus and Farlow. Based on the trio's success, each could proceed to leading his own band. (Years later, Red and Tal occasionally reunited; I got to see them a couple of times in the '80s, though musically, it didn't rise to the level of their first work together.)

I think any musician would envy Red's legacy. He was a pioneer of mallet instruments, a swing-era innovator and a bridge to bebop, and he had played with most of the big names in the business before he passed away in 1999, at age ninety-one. I paid my own heartfelt tribute to Red's legacy when I recorded some of his songs in 2001, on my album *For Hamp, Red, Bags, and Cal.* I recreated Red's famous trio records, using guitarist Russell Malone and bassist Christian McBride. I even borrowed a marimba and xylophone and tried my best to replicate "Dance of the Octopus" and "Hole in the Wall," accompanied by pianist Makoto Ozone.

I toured with Red in Europe for several weeks in the fall of 1970. We planned the usual sort of thing: Red would play a few songs with my rhythm section, then my band would play a set, and finally he would join me for a big two-vibes finale. The first date took place at a resort hotel in the British countryside, a few hours outside London. We hadn't yet rehearsed, so as the start time approached, we sat in the dressing room talking over what to play. I asked Red his choice for the finale, and he suggested "Tea for Two." Then he said no, he wanted to play that in his own part of the program, and named "Back Home Again in Indiana." The dressing room had a piano, and I thought we should go over the harmonies. I sat down and started playing the tune, and Red immediately went to the piano's upper register and began playing along (using two fingers like little mallets); however, he was playing "Tea for Two." Since both start in the same key, nothing clashed at first, and since the two songs seemed to be working together, I thought maybe he knew some clever way of altering the chord sequence so the two songs could continue simultaneously. But after eight bars, "Tea for Two" actually changes its key—at which point, our little duet sounded drastically wrong.

I stopped and Red gave me a puzzled look. He said, "Weren't you playing 'Tea for Two'?" And that's when he explained that he couldn't hear what I was playing; he had become almost deaf. He told me he had to stand quite close to the other musicians on stage, and that for the most part, he could only hear the bass consistently, so that was the instrument he homed in on to avoid getting separated from the band.

Red's hearing problems resulted partly from an ear infection and partly from a gun being discharged close to his right ear. (He said he couldn't even hear a dial tone on that side.) He was an avid shooter with an extensive gun collection, something he talked about often; it caused him great remorse later on when his son used one of Red's guns to take his own life. After his wife passed away, Red retired to Colorado, where an old clarinetist friend lived. He lasted about a year before realizing he was bored to death. He got his hearing treated and managed to return to playing for a few more years, until he suffered a stroke that rendered his left arm immobile. He spent his remaining years in frustration. He told me his only interest was music, and now, he could no longer play. I'd visit him occasionally when I passed through L.A., and he called me in 1992 after I recorded "Knockin' on Wood," to thank me for playing his tune.

Even though the stroke prevented him from playing, Red was invited on that Caribbean cruise celebrating the vibraphone in the '90s. One afternoon, with Lionel Hampton, Milt Jackson, and myself already on stage, Terry Gibbs coaxed Red to (somewhat reluctantly) sit in on one song. With just his right hand, Red played the melody to "When You're Smiling," and then stole the show by improvising a simple one-handed chorus that was as sweet as the man himself.

In 1970, I made an important record with Keith Jarrett. I had known Keith on a casual basis for some time. When I first toured with my own band, Keith was on the road with saxophonist Charles Lloyd's group, and we often crossed paths. Although he was a couple years younger than me, we had attended the same jazz band camp in Indiana, and he had even gone to Berklee for a short time before turning professional—a history similar to my own.

During a tour in France, we heard that Keith was booked with a trio in a small club nearby. We had a night off, so Swallow and I went to check them out. As expected, I enjoyed the music very much, and especially several of Keith's new tunes; I just knew they would make a great fit for our band. I talked to him afterward and asked if I could record some, and after a minute, Keith said, "How about if we record them together?" It helped that we both recorded for Atlantic Records; that made it easy to work out the business arrangements.

Keith joined my quartet for a few summer concerts to settle on the material before going into the studio. But when it came time to record, I ran into some resistance from Atlantic. They opposed the idea of me collaborating with him. They said they found it difficult working with Keith, that he was too demanding and inflexible, and they advised me to steer clear of him for my own good.

I insisted on going ahead with the project anyway, and reserved several days at a New York recording studio. Along with Swallow, my band at this time included drummer Bill Goodwin and guitarist Sam Brown (an inventive player who tragically committed suicide the following year). Sam had a serious dependency on prescription drugs, enabled by a doctor who liberally prescribed for him. At the session, Sam brought some of his pills, which combined an upper and a downer, and between takes, he used a nail file to scrape away the downer half so that he could take the uppers and get a lift during the session. But the session went remarkably smoothly—mostly first takes on every song, since we had already been performing the pieces on tour. In fact, we finished in about three hours— by which time Sam had just finished filing down his pills. We recorded the whole record before he had a chance to take any of them.

In the cover photo for the record, *Gary Burton and Keith Jarrett,* it looks like we're at the ruins of some European castle. In fact, it was the foundation of an old farmhouse a few miles from where Keith lived in New Jersey. By the time we finished the record, Keith and I and our wives had become friends, visiting each other occasionally at either their place or our house on Long Island. Keith and I went on to share the billing on quite a lot of concerts in the next few years: the Keith Jarrett Quartet (with Dewey Redman, Charlie Haden, and Paul Motian) and the Gary Burton Quartet.

Both our groups were more-or-less equally well-known, so we took turns opening and closing the concerts. We alternated from night to night, and most nights when we opened the show, my musicians would hang around to hear Keith's band play the second set, just to catch their latest tunes. We were two bands, each at the top of our game.

CHAPTER 18

Working Two Jobs

The '70s presented a paradox. I was with an excellent record company—fortunately, throughout my career, I have never been without a record contract—but I still struggled to find gigs. The recession had decimated my work schedule, and now I had a new house to pay for. I needed another source of income.

Through my affiliation with the Musser Company (manufacturer of the instruments I play), I sometimes got hired to give presentations, about the vibraphone and about improvisation, at music stores, schools, and music conferences. These clinics, workshops, and master classes—they take various forms and names—then constituted a new job category for jazz musicians in general, and a welcome source of income for me in particular. And as I conducted these, I discovered that explaining music came naturally to me. What's more, I genuinely enjoyed interacting with students. So, I started to consider teaching more.

I was even offered a faculty position at that time, although I didn't see it as a realistic possibility. I had twice visited the University of Illinois to lead workshops with their excellent jazz orchestra, and the director, John Garvey—a very likeable guy, who had started out as a classical musician—asked if I would like to teach at the university. But since I toured regularly and mostly lived in New York, how could I teach in Champaign, Illinois? The job sounded good, but I just couldn't imagine being so far away from the music scene. To my knowledge, no prominent jazz musician had ever taught full-time while still maintaining a tour schedule. I worried that if I wasn't readily available for gigs, I would lose my audience. Though it has become increasingly common for established musicians to balance performance and education, no one was doing this in 1971. The only musicians who taught had taken themselves off the road entirely.

But if Illinois wouldn't work, Boston just might. I called Berklee and asked if they might have any interest in me coming back to teach, and a week later, I was sitting in the office of Lawrence Berk, the college's founder and president. The school had grown incredibly since I had left in 1962, from perhaps 150 students to over 1,000, and had moved to a new building that formerly housed a six-story hotel. Larry and his second-in-command, Bob Share, welcomed me into the faculty. Donna and I started planning our move to Boston later that summer, in time for the start of the 1971–72 school year.

First, though, I actually had some road work, for a change, beginning with a quartet tour to Japan. After that, I was scheduled to fly directly to the Montreux Jazz Festival in Switzerland, to play as a guest soloist with John Garvey and his U of I jazz band. But just before I left for Japan, I learned that the Illinoisans had failed to raise the money for their trip, and had to cancel. Claude Nobs, the director of the Montreux Festival, called and asked me to come to the festival anyway, since they had already advertised my presence. He offered to find some other musicians on the program for me to play with, and I said okay. But as I thought more about it, I became less comfortable with the idea of playing a major festival with a pickup group, and I worried about this for most of our time in Japan. As we wrapped up in Tokyo, though, I suddenly hit on what to do.

Ever since joining Stan Getz's band, I had included one or more unaccompanied vibraphone pieces on almost every set. I always imagined that someday I would play an entire concert of solo pieces. Now, Montreux would provide the opportunity.

In Switzerland, I told Claude my idea. He encouraged it strongly—Montreux is famous for unexpected and one-of-a-kind performances—but I didn't get the same support from everyone. Atlantic Records was sponsoring that day at the festival; the program consisted entirely of the label's artists, and they planned to record the whole night. The schedule had me playing first, followed by Latin bandleader Mongo Santamaría, and finally vocalist Roberta Flack to close the concert. Nesuhi Ertegun himself was there, and he firmly opposed the idea of me performing alone; he said that recording a set of solo vibes would be a waste of time, because a record without a rhythm section would never sell. George Wein was there as well, and he took me aside to say that although he admired my solo pieces, this probably wasn't the right occasion for such a radical idea, and that maybe I should follow the label's advice.

But by then, I had my mind set. My "inner player" was saying "Do it," and with Claude's encouragement, I prepared for the performance, running through my repertoire of unac-companied pieces in a room backstage. When I came out on stage, the hall looked immense. People were still finding their seats and getting settled (which, as the opening artist, I had expected). I wondered how the audience would react when they realized it would be me and me alone for the first set.

As I began to play, I noticed the audience start to quiet down. I moved on to my second number before I stopped to make any announcements, and by then I knew I had them. You really could hear a pin drop. When I finished, fifty minutes later, the crowd jumped to their feet. I later heard that I had received the best audience response of that year's entire festival. I had played Montreux before, but it had never occasioned a turning point in my career—which was certainly the case this time.

The recording, *Alone at Last* (from the 1971 Montreux Jazz Festival), was a great success. The title has a double meaning. It of course refers to the fact that after years of playing solo pieces on my concerts, I finally got to record a solo album. But I also meant the title to describe the feeling I get after a long day of traveling, doing interviews, and playing a gig, when I finally return to my hotel, walk into my room, close the door behind me and think, "Alone at last"—my introvert side, expressed in an album title.

My solo concert garnered a lot of attention, and it helped launch a new wave of jazz performances. We've always had solo piano records, but once I started performing concerts unaccompanied, players of various other instruments—guitar, saxophone, bass—followed suit. I had pictured my Montreux experiment as a one-time thing, but it led to a fair amount of solo bookings, particularly in Europe, where the trend proved especially popular.

There would come another important Montreux performance in 1985. Montreux has been a very lucky place for me.

After finishing my European dates, I flew directly to Boston to see the house Donna had found for us in the suburb of Stoughton. I began teaching at Berklee a week later, with a mixture of anticipation and confusion. I genuinely liked the idea of teaching, since I had enjoyed presenting workshops, but I didn't know what was expected in a college curriculum— especially at the world's leading jazz college, which had gotten so much bigger and more fast-paced since my student days.

At first, they assigned me to teach a range of courses: improvisation, small-group arranging, ensembles, and, of course, vibraphone. I grouped all my teaching hours into three days, and I brought lunch from home to eat during one of the private lesson periods; this allowed me to skip breaks throughout the day. It sounds extreme, but I needed to arrange the schedule so I could travel on weekends to play gigs with my band. And I needed to play; I worried that people would think my performance career was kaput. ("He's a teacher now. Don't bother calling him for gigs.") So, at first, I took every gig I could, just to maintain my visibility as a player. I filled the school's vacation breaks with longer tours, to Europe and Asia, and packed gigs into every weekend when school was in session. Fortunately, the academic calendar has some flexibility, and I managed to get in plenty of work. I just didn't have any free time to myself.

I totally misread my first student ensemble. Because I was an established jazz artist, Berklee assigned me the top students for a small group ensemble, and I thought long and hard about what song to bring for that first rehearsal. I wanted something they would enjoy playing, but not so simple or familiar that the students might feel, "Hey, we already know this one. We're not impressed." I felt I needed to challenge them, but not with something too hard for them to get through. I decided on Steve Swallow's clever and catchy "Falling Grace." Every musician I know has admired and enjoyed that song, and I pegged it as the perfect choice.

Boy, was I off base.

I showed up with copies for everyone, chalked it up on the board, gave some explanation of its structure, and counted it off. None of the students came close to covering it! I hadn't realized that the jazz style then popular at Berklee was modal jazz, a style with very little harmonic movement. This makes it fairly easy for beginning improvisers (though actually quite a challenge for advanced players, since such simple structures make it harder to play something interesting). "Falling Grace" had too many chords, moving at too rapid a pace, for students weaned on the modal style. That first meeting of the ensemble was a disaster—and a warning. These students definitely lacked exposure to the kind of music they needed to master in order to compete in the professional world. The next week, I brought in something much easier, and then set out to slowly introduce more challenging music to Berklee students. I wanted to provide them the kind of practical advice that only an established musician can offer, using my own student experiences as a guide.

From that time on, my teaching philosophy became clear: find out what the students know and what they need, and start from there. It's not about the teacher or his personal musical interests.

SCHOOL DAYS

I did the greatest amount of practicing during my own Berklee years, but once I left school and went on the road, everything changed. When you travel, you can't carry the vibes under your arm—as you would do with a trumpet or sax—and in my first year of touring, I found that my instrument was always either at the club, or still on the truck, or en route to somewhere else. Playing gigs almost every night and traveling by day, I didn't have the chance to practice exercises or scales, and because I toured steadily in the decades that followed, I got used to not practicing on any regular basis. I've also never had an official "music room" in any house I've owned. Even today, I only bring the vibraphone in from the garage when I have new music to prepare.

Why does this work? How did I continue to grow and develop as a player, both technically and creatively? I have some theories about this. I firmly believe that mastering music is mostly a mental rather than physical experience. We don't have to repeat things on our instruments, over and over in real time, to evolve as players. I develop my skills and abilities "on the job"— probably the most natural way to grow as a player.

In any case, this whole idea of practice—learning to play by hammering away at scales and exercises—is a relatively recent phenomenon. When Bach wanted to teach his children to play keyboard instruments, he wrote his "Inventions." I guess you could call them exercises, but that would do them a great disservice. They are wonderful, illuminating creations that for more than two centuries have provided fulfilling musical experiences for pianists at all levels of ability. In Bach's time, music lessons were only available to those youngsters who showed a high aptitude for music, and these students almost always came from well-to-do families that could afford both instruments and training. But by the 19th century, a middle class had taken root in Europe, and more and more families included music in their everyday lives.

This meant that more students of varying abilities (not just the prodigies) wanted to study music, and this created a need for more teachers beyond the highly-paid professional tutors. These new teachers themselves had varying levels of skill. Now, there were more teachers of mediocre abilities teaching more students of average (or limited) talent. And this in turn led to the creation of mid-level exercises and method books—aimed primarily at the *average* student—to replace the former system of private apprenticeship to master musicians.

Today, you can find exercise books for every instrument, revered by many and treated as bibles: the Arban's book for trumpet, the Hanon and Czerny books for piano, the George Stone book for drummers, and the Goldenberg book for mallet players. Unfortunately, the exercises in these kinds of books lack musical expression. They contain no story, no meaning to the notes; they're simply calisthenics that develop the physical manipulations of an instrument, while ignoring the most important part—getting the music to say something. Many students rely too heavily on this type of practicing, short-changing the development of their musicianship. Exercises should never be more than just a part of one's practice routine.

I dug into my first semester of teaching at Berklee and enjoyed it immensely. I liked exploring how music takes shape, and I liked explaining the workings of intricate processes. And now, more gigs were coming in, too—more than enough to keep me busy—as the music business began to recover along with the economy. I had jumped into teaching because I fretted about not having enough work, but by the end of my first year at Berklee, I had as many gigs as I could handle. I no longer needed the Berklee job for financial reasons after all. And yet, I had discovered how much I enjoyed teaching, and I didn't want to give it up. In fact, I couldn't wait to get started on my second year, and already had some ideas for creating new courses.

One day in the spring of '72, a recent graduate from Brandeis University named Ted Kurland made an appointment to see me. He needed a haircut, and he dressed kind of sloppily; all in all, he looked to be about twenty. He was casting about for a career and thought he might want to become a booking agent—a pretty unusual career choice. I was intrigued. From outward appearances, he didn't seem cut out for the booking business, but I filled him in on the kind of gigs I did, my typical fees, and so on, and told him to call me if he got any offers—and before I knew it, Ted Kurland Associates opened shop. That first year, he came up with two college dates in New England for my band; the second year, his new office generated about thirty gigs for me. As we went into Year 3 of working together, he was doing so well for me that I made him my exclusive agent and manager, and we've worked together now for four decades. Ted came into a field that cried out for innovation, and he practically reinvented the booking business. I can truly say that one of my greatest strokes of good fortune occurred when I met up with that scruffy Brandeis student in 1972. Today, Ted Kurland Associates is the leading booking and management firm in jazz, and I can't even count all the opportunities he has brought my way. But I *can* count him among my closest friends. And I am exceedingly proud of everything he has accomplished.

CHAPTER 19

Going Solo

The success of *Alone at Last* sparked a string of offers for me to perform solo in Europe. One of the concerts—a large festival in Munich, coinciding with the 1972 Olympics—presented an entire evening devoted to solo jazz: Chick Corea, guitarist John McLaughlin, French violinist Jean-Luc Ponty, and German trombonist Albert Mangelsdorf.

We were each slated to play about twenty minutes, but the promoter didn't think that would make for a full concert, so he asked each of us if we would join in a jam session for the finale. No one wanted to do it, which was understandable. Our assemblage of instruments didn't comprise a logical band. We had no bass or drums, and thus no real rhythm section. Only Chick and I volunteered, so we decided we would play a duet; after all, we had worked together for some gigs in 1968. At the sound check, Chick quickly taught me one of his new compositions, "La Fiesta."

After the last solo performance, we came on stage and tore into our tune. The audience went wild. We probably didn't sound all that great, but the duo came as something unexpected after an hour and a half of unaccompanied solos. As we left the stage (following several bows), Manfred Eicher, the founder of ECM Records—Chick's label at the time—walked up to us and said we absolutely had to record a duet album. I thought he had just gotten caught up in the excitement of the concert, because I couldn't imagine anyone wanting to listen to a whole record of piano and vibes—even though I had just released a solo vibes record myself.

In 1972, I also won my first GRAMMY award, although I hadn't even known I was up for one. I got a call one day from guitarist George Benson, who was playing that week at Boston's leading club, the Jazz Workshop. George told me he had gotten a GRAMMY nomination, and since the awards would be announced on Wednesday night—and he thought he had a good chance of winning—he wanted to fly down to New York to accept in person. First, though, he needed someone to fill in for him at the club. I confirmed the availability of my band and told him sure, we would cover for him. (Since moving to Boston, I often played at the Jazz Workshop anyway.)

About a month later, Ted Kurland called and suggested I drop by his office. When I walked in, he handed me a box; inside was a GRAMMY for *Alone at Last*. Truthfully, I hadn't paid much attention to the GRAMMYs since I left New York, so I didn't even know about the nomination. This was long before the Recording Academy (the GRAMMY folks) made so much hoopla about announcing the nominees. Later, I recalled George Benson going to New York to attend the ceremony. I checked; he didn't win that year, but he must have heard them announce that the guy covering his gig in Boston had won instead.

THE GRAMMY

Most musicians consider the GRAMMY the ultimate award. If you remain in the business a long time, many kinds of recognition come your way, but getting a GRAMMY is unique, because your peers in the music business choose the winners, in much the same way that the Oscars honor moviemaking.

The Recording Academy came into existence in 1959, but without the fanfare of today's awards industry. It took over a decade for them to even make it onto live television. When Stan Getz won "Record of the Year" in 1965, the Academy presented the awards at simultaneous ceremonies in Los Angeles and New York. Sometime later, footage of these events was cobbled into a one-hour television special showcasing some of that year's winners. I attended several GRAMMY ceremonies in the late '60s, just as my career as a bandleader was taking off, even though I wasn't yet winning any awards myself. I remember going one year to the L.A. ceremony and seeing Paul McCartney wearing a tuxedo and tennis shoes, which I thought was just the hippest thing ever. I also saw Linda Ronstadt napping on a couch in the lobby of the Hollywood Palladium, while her manager stood guard so no one would bother her. That's show biz—and show biz loves the GRAMMYs.

In 1968, the GRAMMYs afforded me a proud moment having nothing to do with my own records, and I never pass up the chance to brag about it. Stan Getz was supposed to present one of the major awards at the New York event, but he didn't show up. I was there to present the "Lifetime Achievement Award" to Duke Ellington, and as I left the stage, someone said, "Here, Stan didn't make it, go back and announce this award, too." I returned to the microphone, opened the envelope and nearly fainted. It was the "Album of the Year" GRAMMY for the Beatles' groundbreaking *Sgt. Pepper's Lonely Hearts Club Band,* one of my favorite records, and it marked the first time that a rock band won the GRAMMYs' top prize. Producer George Martin came up to accept, and I handed him the statuette—yet another reason to thank Stan Getz. Many years later, I visited George at his Air Studio in London and asked if he remembered that night. To my surprise he said absolutely, that it had been a very important recognition for the Beatles then. What's more, he told me he had already been a Gary Burton fan at the time, which made me prouder still.

I became disillusioned with the GRAMMYs the following year when a poorly chosen presenter disrespected Duke Ellington. In 1969, Duke's album titled *And His Mother Called Him Bill*—honoring his longtime collaborator Billy Strayhorn, who had recently died—won for Best Jazz Performance. But the jerk announcing the award started making fun of the record, something along the lines of why would anyone choose such a stupid album title, who would do this, and so on. A lot of us winced when this went down. Obviously, this was someone unfamiliar with jazz, but even so—it had just won a GRAMMY. And it was *Duke Ellington*. I stopped going to the GRAMMY events after that, and I let my membership lapse. But a few years later, after *Alone at Last* won for Best Instrumental Solo in 1972—an award created only the previous year and won then by Bill Evans—I decided maybe I should get involved again.

The Recording Academy has changed immensely over the past five decades, and since 1971, when they began broadcasting the award ceremonies live around the world, it has evolved into one of the most-watched television events each year. While a jazz performance rarely makes it onto the show, I've been fortunate to play on two of the telecasts, in 1988 and 1992. And as of this writing, I'm honored to have received twenty-one nominations and seven GRAMMY awards spanning five decades.

As time went on, I found a good balance between teaching and touring. I also managed to complete a record project each year for Atlantic. All aspects of my career were on the rise and about to get even better—but not before my personal life took a stumble.

The move to Boston had not worked out as well for Donna as it had for me. She missed life in New York. Moreover, she had embarked on a career of her own, designing knitwear for a company in Connecticut. We grew further and further apart, and eventually I knew the time had come for us to go our separate ways. Our marriage didn't really work. We certainly didn't hate each other, but we had become just roommates. At our young age, the idea of spending the rest of our lives in a dysfunctional relationship really didn't make sense.

I was the one who at last brought this into the open, insisting that we make a decision about the future. We agreed to get a divorce. This struck me as doubly troubling. First, there was disappointment. I viewed the divorce as a colossal failure, and I wasn't used to failing, at anything. Straight-A student, youthful bandleader, *Down Beat's* "Musician of the Year," you name it: I was the poster child for success in everything I did—except marriage, apparently. But more than disappointment, I also felt fear. In the back of my mind, I wondered if the marriage had failed because I might be gay. That was one reason I desperately wanted things to succeed. It would allow me to keep avoiding any doubts about my orientation.

Donna and I parted amicably. I pulled together as much money as I could and did my best to set her up in a new home, with a car, furniture, and enough to live on for the next year—whatever she needed. I drove with her to Connecticut so she could start her new job. But when I returned to the empty house in Boston, burdened by the weight of total failure, I knew I couldn't stay there. I found another house nearby and moved as soon as I could. And then, I did what many people do in similar situations: I escaped my depressed state by immersing myself in work, day and night, to avoid thinking about being alone.

Yes, yes—it all seems like a contradiction, since I've never felt all that comfortable dealing with other people. But I still hate being completely on my own. I had always had people around me: first my family, then other students when I went to college, and certainly my fellow musicians when traveling on the road. I was used to plenty of company. I still had my band and my students at Berklee, and I kept myself as busy as possible. That got me through the adjustment period after the divorce. But for quite a while, home was a very lonely place.

CHAPTER 20

New Duet, New Label, New Band

Manfred Eicher, the German record producer who had so enthusiastically lauded my duet performance with Chick Corea in Munich that summer, can be quite persistent. He kept calling and writing to us both about making a duo record, and he eventually talked us into it. He arranged for us to play together at the Berlin Jazz Festival, which takes place in the fall, after which we flew to a studio in Norway that Manfred often used for his records.

We set aside three days for the recording. Except for that one tune in Munich, Chick and I hadn't worked together before Berlin, so we figured we would need a fair amount of time to choose the songs and finalize the arrangements. But to our amazement, it all went incredibly fast. We would spend maybe twenty minutes creating an arrangement, and then record. We did every song in just one take, except that we required a second spin through "Señor Mouse." Just as when I had recorded with Keith Jarrett, we finished the whole record in a few hours.

That was when I first realized I had such a unique rapport with Chick—a musical chemistry that had somehow eluded us four years earlier, when Chick played briefly in my quartet.

The situation was now exactly opposite. It was as if we could read each other's minds.

I've often wondered why Chick and I have this ability to anticipate each other's improvisational ideas. It's true that we both came of age musically in Boston (where Chick grew up and I went to school), and thus had many of the same teachers and early influences. And it's true that we belong to the same post-bop generation of jazz musicians, and that, since we both play keyboard instruments, we probably think a lot alike as we improvise. But those factors also hold true for many people I have worked with, and while I often attain a good rapport with others, the interaction between Chick and me is at another level entirely.

After we finished in the Oslo studio, we listened to the playbacks for a while and decided we had nailed it. Since we didn't need the additional studio time, we changed our flights and headed back home the very next day. The album, titled *Crystal Silence* (after one of Chick's tunes), came out around the middle of 1973, released at first only in Germany. I didn't expect it to get much notice, and I don't think Chick did, either. After all, Manfred's ECM label was then quite small, with no U.S. distribution, and the music veered sharply from any of the jazz styles typical in the early '70s.

Wrong, wrong, and wrong.

Crystal Silence started to build a following, and before long, we received a request for a duet concert from the University of Michigan in Ann Arbor. (Pat Metheny, who had just recently joined my band, said he wanted to go. The duo record was a favorite of his. Figuring this might be his only chance to hear the music in concert, he joked he would do whatever necessary—even carry my vibraphone—to attend.) When I saw the auditorium in Ann Arbor, I got quite concerned. It had a capacity of four thousand seats, and since our little project strayed so far off the beaten path, I thought we might draw only a few hundred (if we got lucky). I dreaded playing a concert in a mostly empty hall.

Just before the curtain went up, I stuck my head out for a look. I almost fell over to see the hall completely full! So then I redirected my concern; I worried about how to hold the attention of that many people with just two lonely instruments on stage. But the audience was entranced from the very first song. I think only then did I fully realize what Chick and I had. Since that night in Michigan, we have played a few thousand concerts, over four decades, in all kinds of places and for all sizes of audiences (some of the largest crowds have numbered as many as thirty thousand), and the music has never failed to connect with the listeners.

Meanwhile, the Gary Burton Quartet evolved to incorporate the inevitable lineup changes. When Swallow decided to move his growing family from New York to the San Francisco area, I had as of then replaced all the original group members. When I first moved to Boston, I didn't know if I could find musicians I liked in Boston. But a month or so after I started teaching at Berklee, I got invited to stay late one day for a jam session. The players included a faculty member, guitarist Mick Goodrick, and a student, drummer Harry Blazer. The session went so well, and Mick and Harry impressed me so, that I immediately started to build a group around them. I needed a local bass player to complete the package—preferably one who played electric bass, since Steve Swallow had made that such an important part of my band—and Harry and Mick recommended Abe Laboriel, a Berklee student from Mexico. From the first rehearsal, I knew this would work. I especially liked that Abe and Harry were new young players, and that Mick—a contemporary of mine who few people outside Boston had heard—could bring an equally fresh sound to the mix.

After we gigged for a few months, I wanted to record this new quartet, but first I had to decide where. My five-year contract with Atlantic had run its course. They offered me a new deal, but I now had the same misgivings about Atlantic that had prompted me to leave RCA. I felt the label was mostly ignoring my music while they lavished attention on Aretha Franklin and their other highly popular R&B artists. And Nesuhi Ertegun, who first signed me to the company, had moved from day-to-day operations to become the international representative for the newly merged conglomerate Warner/Elektra/Atlantic.

Instead of renewing my contract with Atlantic, I did have one alternative: I could sign with ECM, a fledging German record company that didn't even have distribution in the U.S. I had really enjoyed working with Manfred on *Crystal Silence,* and based solely on artistic consideration, I would have made ECM my first choice. But in the music business, at least in those days, a major label had a lot of cachet. Artists would struggle for years to reach that level, and most jazz musicians never made it beyond the small independents. And while the big labels had some distinct negatives (less personal, more corporate), the advantages outweighed them, starting with the all-important matter of general visibility. I had been fortunate to start my recording career with RCA Victor and then continue to Atlantic, both major companies. I wasn't ready to just casually give that up. And I already had lucked out on a couple of risky ventures, first in launching a band that combined jazz and rock, second in leaving New York to undertake a teaching career. Now, I was mulling yet another counter-intuitive move: leaving a major label for a startup company that had so far released a mere handful of records.

This time, I decided to postpone making a commitment until I could be more certain about how to proceed. Then, I used some of my savings to pay for the next record myself. I asked Manfred if he would have any interest in producing it for me, and offered him this deal: If at the end of the session I felt comfortable leaving Atlantic for ECM, he could release the new record on his label. If not, I would pay him a producer's fee and re-sign with Atlantic.

We recorded the new group at a small studio in the Boston suburbs. By the time we finished, I was really proud of my new band. I also knew I wanted to continue working with Manfred. Although my ECM experience had begun with *Crystal Silence*, my relationship with ECM became official with the album *New Quartet*.

Going with ECM remains among the best decisions I ever made. I got on board the company just as it started to build a worldwide fan base, and I also learned a lot working with Manfred. In the '70s, he almost single-handedly raised the technical standards of jazz recording to new heights. He found top-notch European studios and the best engineers, and he put more effort and time into each project than most producers had ever envisioned for jazz records. He also got quite personally involved in the music itself. As Chick once described it, "Manfred falls in love with every record he makes."

When you make a record, the biggest hurdle involves maintaining two different perspectives at once. In the studio, you concentrate on getting everything just right (from the ensembles to your own solos). You then need to step back and imagine the whole, from the viewpoint of someone listening to an hour-long record. But with Manfred, I could stop at any moment to ask him things—"Is the introduction too short?" for instance, or "Are the drums too busy?"—and he would immediately give me the right feedback to help shape the performance. That saved me from having to stop and listen to playbacks all the time, and it allowed me to play without losing my focus. Of course, Manfred had his own opinions, too, and sometimes we argued over a point of music or methodology. In those discussions, he would try his best to convince me. But if he couldn't win me over, he would let me do it my way. And many times, his challenges convinced me that my approach wasn't as solid as I had first thought. Over the course of recording with Manfred for sixteen years, we developed a tremendously effective working relationship that resulted in eighteen records—a body of work that many people consider my most accomplished.

The new band sounded great, and I hoped it could continue for a while. But late in 1973, Abe informed me that his wife was graduating from medical school, and they would have to move to Cleveland for a year (and then on to L.A.) for her to complete her internship and residency. He would have to leave the band.

Luckily, at that exact time Steve Swallow informed me that he was moving back east, after living for a while in California, and that he was available to rejoin the band. I loved Abe's playing, and it didn't surprise me at all that he went on to a major career in the Los Angeles studio scene. But Swallow's return to the band, after those couple years' absence, was an absolute joy, because we already had so much history together.

Meanwhile, I had another invitation to take part in a concert featuring solo performers. George Wein, who had witnessed my unaccompanied Montreux concert in '71, wanted to produce an evening of solos at Carnegie Hall. His concept echoed the concert I had played in Munich, with one difference: George picked six players who could compose a plausible group for the final jam session. Besides myself, the lineup included pianist John Lewis, violinist Joe Venuti, guitarist Joe Pass, and a rhythm section of bassist Charles Mingus and drummer Art Blakey.

At the sound check, George asked us to choose a song we could play together for the finale. A long pause ensued, because no one wanted to take charge. (Not yet thirty and surrounded by these legendary musicians, I certainly wasn't going to step up; I just hoped that whatever they chose would be something

I knew.) When no one spoke up, George said, "Play anything, just play a blues," to which Mingus responded, in a low growl, "Not everyone can play the blues, George."

I froze, assuming that he had aimed this at me, the young white kid. But when I looked over I saw that it wasn't me who had inspired Mingus's comment; instead, he was glaring at John Lewis, who took a far more genteel approach to the blues than did Mingus. This was going to be some gig.

As I waited backstage for the concert to begin, Mingus waved me over. Now what? I thought. It turned out, he had heard a recent record of mine on which I recorded one of his songs, "Goodbye Pork Pie Hat"—and he loved it. What a relief! At least for that night, I could do no wrong, as far as Mingus was concerned.

The solo portions of the concert proceeded as expected, and eventually we all trooped onto the Carnegie stage for the finale. Tension flared immediately, this time between Mingus and Blakey. Each was a giant on his instrument, and each was used to leading his own band. Not surprisingly, they had different concepts of the time feel. At the drums, Blakey kicked the time forward, playing on top of the beat, almost rushing the tempo; at the bass, Mingus wanted the rhythm to lay back, somewhat behind the beat. The battle was underway, Blakey pushing the time as much as possible and Mingus lagging way behind, pulling the strings of the bass harder and harder and shooting nasty looks in Blakey's direction.

With all this going on, I started wondering just what would happen when it came my turn to solo. I tried to tune out the scuffle behind me and just play, but I had a more immediate distraction to contend with. Joe Venuti, who I had met just that night, was next to me making quite a bit of noise. Joe had a legendary reputation for his comic antics, on stage and off. That night, I discovered that he also tended to yell encouragement while other players soloed. He stood there shouting things like, "Go Gary, you got it," and just as I wound up my last chorus, he whacked me on the butt with his violin bow! I'm on stage at Carnegie Hall with five jazz legends, two of them itching to drop their instruments and start punching each other, and then the guy on my other side hits me with his bow—definitely a night to remember. A few months later, someone sent me a photo of the whole bunch of us on stage at Carnegie, and I still have it hanging on my wall. At this writing, I'm the only one still around, and whenever I stop to look at it, the nostalgia takes over.

My encounters with Mingus always seemed to involve controversy. (Of course, it wasn't just me; no one in jazz got into more confrontations than Mingus.) Twice, I found myself with him on festival jam sessions where he spent the time swearing and glaring at the other musicians. My final Mingus memory takes place in a restaurant late one night after a concert at the Nice Jazz Festival in southern France. The place was crowded with musicians stopping off to eat after their sets, and Mingus had ordered a large salad to take back to the hotel. By then, he had been diagnosed with ALS—Lou Gehrig's Disease—and he was on a complicated diet, part of a New-Age healing regimen he had started. He had specifically ordered the salad without dressing, but when he opened the take-out box, he saw the salad drenched in oil, and he flew into a rage. He threw the salad at the waiter, covering him in lettuce and salad dressing, and then I watched him stride to the door in a huff, with the waiter chasing after him. Mingus was a big guy with a quick temper, and I couldn't tell what would happen next. But the last thing I expected was to see the waiter pull out a marker pen, and a piece of paper, and ask Mingus for his autograph! Only in France, I thought. And only with Mingus.

CHAPTER 21

Discovering New Talent

I have a knack for spotting talented players before anyone else hears them, and I must admit, I've put that to good use over the years. I can't really explain it, but with some musicians, I can sort of "fast-forward" in my imagination and know how they will sound in the years to follow. On such occasions, when I can see into the future as I listen, I have absolute confidence that the young musician will develop into an outstanding player. I don't claim that I can identify every promising player I hear; sometimes, a musician I knew as a student blossoms into a wonderful artist, and I didn't see it coming. But with certain players, I seem to know after just a few minutes whether they have it or not. And based on that intuition, I have helped launch the careers of quite a few top-ranked players—particularly guitar players, among them (chronologically) Larry Coryell, Jerry Hahn, Mick Goodrick, Pat Metheny, John Scofield, Kurt Rosenwinkel, and Julian Lage. There is something very appealing about young players. They provide inspiration, energy, new perspectives, and above all, they bring what I call "the unpredictability of youth."

I discovered some new players simply from my vantage point at Berklee. The college is a magnet for promising musicians from all over the world, and just having the chance to hear them first allowed me to hire them first. But sometimes, the musicians find me.

In 1973, I went to Wichita, Kansas to make a guest appearance with the local college jazz band. As I kicked off the rehearsal, the woman organizing the event told me about a young guitar player who had gotten a lot of notice at the previous year's festival—so much, in fact, that they had invited him back. She suggested that perhaps he and I might play something together. I was skeptical, and in any case, I'm not usually into impromptu jamming. But this eighteen-year-old came in to rehearsal and said he knew a lot of my songs. He suggested a rather obscure composition of mine titled "Walter L.," and that was enough to settle the matter.

He was good. I could practically see the talent just pouring out of him. He asked what I thought about his prospects and what advice I could offer. I learned he had grown up not far away, in a small town near Kansas City, and that he was then at the University of Miami. Along with a few musical suggestions, I recommended that he move someplace with a lot of jazz activity—either New York or Boston—because he would have more opportunity to work with high-level players in those cities. We crossed paths again a few months later, at jazz camps in Oregon and Illinois, and I was sufficiently impressed with his talent that I recommended him to Berklee—as a teacher, not a student.

That was Pat Metheny.

PAT METHENY

Pat grew up in little Lee's Summit, Missouri, where his father managed the local Dodge dealership (Burton Motors, coincidentally). When he first got into jazz, Pat discovered my records from the '60s. As he describes it, this was jazz he could relate to as a Midwest teenager; his creative instincts just didn't jibe with the more traditional jazz styles of the time. He spent a year at the University of Miami, where he was quickly drafted to teach jazz guitar classes rather than take them. It was during this time that he heard about me playing at that college jazz festival in Wichita. He accepted their invitation specifically to meet me (and maybe even get to play with me), traveling by bus from Florida to Kansas—no small undertaking. Pat still has an old, scratchy recording of that first time we played together.

I have never known a musician more serious or dedicated. Among the many players I have hired through the years, only a few seemed destined to lead their own groups. The characteristic they all share is a curiosity about how everything works; nothing ever happens within ten miles of him that Pat doesn't notice. It's a trait I recognized right away, in that it reminded me of my own history with Shearing and Getz.

We stayed in touch after Wichita, and six months later, he moved to Boston. Typical of Pat, he wasted no time once he got there. He began meeting local musicians and was soon playing in Boston clubs, establishing a reputation as an up-and-comer.

Pat was unusually young to teach at the college level, but he had already taught in Miami, and I thought that given the chance, he would quickly prove his capabilities. I began a campaign of talking him up with Bill Leavitt, the chair of Berklee's Guitar Department, whose office was next to mine. As it turned out, Bill wanted to bring new blood into the department anyway. After meeting him, Bill hired Pat for the next semester, and he continued teaching at Berklee until he formed his own band a few years later.

Pat has always been incredibly practical and sensible—and also a tight guy with a dollar. He had saved all his money from his year teaching in Miami, and never touched it in the time he played with me. I don't know why he was saving it, other than maybe to start his own band. In the meantime, he lived a fairly Spartan existence. Boston often has severe winters and the one essential article of clothing is a warm winter coat, but Pat went around for several years in an old cloth thing; it eventually lost all its buttons, forcing him to hold it closed when he went outside. We used to kid him about it, but even after working in my band for quite a while, he refused to break down and buy a replacement. When he finally showed up in a new sheepskin coat, we all congratulated him.

The one area where Pat never skimps is music. He insists on having the best instruments, equipment, crew, and so on, and he spares no expense. When he toured extensively during the '80s and '90s, he traveled with two big trailer trucks of equipment that included his own concert grand piano, a complete sound system, and lighting—he even had an electrical box that attached to power lines at the pole, so they wouldn't have to depend on the antiquated electric service in older auditoriums. When I did a tour with Pat in 1991, he carried two Synclavier synthesizers, just in case one broke down. This is someone prepared for any contingency.

That's why I find it almost comical that he has such trouble choosing titles for his songs. He'll give them temporary names ("The One in A-Flat"), or just numerals. When he played with me, one of his tunes featured a lot of B chords and G chords, so we called it "B & G." It was named that for so long that even after Pat gave it a proper title ("Midwestern Night's Dream"), we call it "B & G" to this day. Whenever one of his albums nears release, the company has to chase after him for song titles until Pat scrambles something up; for a while he would call me for title suggestions. (Being me, I of course kept a list of words and phrases suitable for titles, in case I needed one.) I get a chuckle thinking about this guy who breezes through the writing of a dozen songs, then has to break a sweat to give them names.

Pat is amazingly focused, both in his musical pursuits and his personal life. He is among the very few musicians I know of who has never touched alcohol or tried any kind of drugs. (Among musicians I know personally, only Keith Jarrett also fits that description.) Pat has remained absolutely consistent through the years. He still has the same hairstyle and wears the same outfit on stage (jeans and sneakers, or maybe shorts and T-shirts in the summer) that he wore when starting out. But while he doesn't take risks in his personal style, he ventures widely when it comes to music. His success has afforded him the opportunity to collaborate with just about every musician he ever admired; sometimes, I think he started with a list of names and has been methodically checking them off. Some of these projects defy expectations, such as *Project X*, which he recorded with the "free jazz" innovator Ornette Coleman—one of Pat's jazz heroes, but a player whose own music flies in the face of the audience Pat has cultivated over the years.

One day, I got an e-mail from Pat saying he'd never had the chance to play with Chick Corea, and since he had so admired our duets, he wondered if we could all do a record together. It took more than a year to find time when everyone was available, but eventually, we went into the studio in New York—with Roy Haynes and the remarkable bassist Dave Holland—to make *Like Minds*. I booked five days of studio time, knowing that Pat and Chick often like to take their time when recording, but we moved along quickly and finished everything by the middle of the second day. As everyone packed up to leave, Pat said he wanted to look over some of his solos and would take advantage of the remaining studio time to maybe make some fixes here or there.

Pat used some of that extra time to sort through his solos and make a variety of small changes, most of which would hardly be noticed by most listeners. But here's the thing about Pat: being such a perfectionist as he truly is, his little fixes and adjustments may seem to go unnoticed, but the overall impact of the finished results is subtly better, smoother, richer sounding, and more compelling. When we work together on a record, mixing and editing, he always shows more patience than me when it comes to chasing perfection. But in the final version, I hear what he has done and know it was worth all the effort.

Pat's insights into both jazz and the jazz scene impress me, too. In 2001, he gave the keynote speech at the International Association of Jazz Educators Convention in New York. He spoke on "the state of jazz," and his delivery was so articulate, so insightful, you'd have thought he was an academic with a Ph.D., rather than someone with one year of college who had spent his life playing the guitar.

In our early days together, I was Pat's mentor and teacher, and I take great pride in his accomplishments, knowing I played some small role in helping him along the way. But after four decades, I find the roles very much reversed; now, I'm the one learning things from him, every time we work together. I consider his knowledge of record production more extensive than that of any other jazz musician. And he is one of those rare artists who knows his creative process so intimately, he can achieve exactly what he wants on each new project, no matter how far it veers from the last.

Within a short while of Pat's arrival at Berklee, I became aware of his great ambition to play in my band. I was quite keen to have him, too, but I already had a guitarist in Mick Goodrick, one of the best around. I didn't see how Pat could join unless Mick decided to leave.

A solution appeared one day when Pat brought over a 12-string electric guitar he had found in a local music store—a fairly uncommon instrument. The only 12-strings I had ever seen were acoustic, typically used in folk or country music; this electric version had a unique sound, quite different from the usual 6-string instrument. We both had been looking for a way to incorporate Pat into the band, and now we had it. The Gary Burton Quartet became the Gary Burton Quintet, and for the next two years, Pat played the 12-string electric, splitting the solo work with Mick on 6-string.

I quickly grew accustomed to the mix of two guitars. I especially enjoyed the thick, lush ensemble sound. As I've mentioned before, bands have a certain dynamic. You try different combinations of musicians, tweaking this or that to get the best balance of styles and talent. This one had real magic. The Quintet with Pat and Mick on guitars, and a rhythm section of Swallow and Bob Moses (who had rejoined the band) definitely remains one of my all-time best.

During the Quintet period, we made a record I also count among my best: *Dreams So Real,* my second project to feature music by Carla Bley (after *A Genuine Tong Funeral* almost a decade earlier). The time we spent recording the album in Germany set some kind of high-water mark given the amount of music we put on tape in those few days. Not only did we finish the album of Carla's music, much of it extremely complex and challenging, but we also stayed on to record Pat's first record for ECM, with me acting as producer.

Pat had begun to compose his own music by then, and we worked a lot to fine-tune his pieces and select which ones to include. He decided to make it a trio with Moses and bass guitarist Jaco Pastorius, whom Pat had gotten to know in Florida (and who would attain stardom the next year playing with Weather Report).

I had never before played the role of producer for someone else's record, and I approached it with enthusiasm. In retrospect, it seems risky to have tried recording two important projects without even a day off, but for scheduling reasons it made a lot of sense. We were already in Germany, we had studio time, and it made things more convenient for Manfred to oversee both records in the same week. I recall feeling pretty exhausted as we wrapped up the third full day of work on *Dreams So Real,* but Pat and Moses were totally energized as they dived into Pat's trio date. The sessions went smoothly, and I was proud of Pat, and also pleased with my own part as producer. My only regret was that when the record (*Bright Size Life*) came out, I saw that Manfred didn't give me a producer credit; in fact, my name appears nowhere at all on the record jacket. Up till then, Manfred had produced all of ECM's records personally; I guess he didn't want to break that streak.

In 1975, Mick decided to leave the band and return to his teaching career in Boston. The Quintet now reverted to a Quartet, and just in time, from Pat's viewpoint. He had increasingly felt limited in the role of "second guitarist." He also felt constrained from really stretching out when he soloed on the 12-string. But when he became the sole guitarist in the band, it was like making a fresh start. By that time, he had completed the conversion from newcomer to pro. His improvisation skills had grown immensely, and he instantly became the star of the band. Between our tours, Pat would play with his own groups, even as he planned the second record under his own name.

During this time, I experienced one of those travel nightmares that made me say, "Someday, when I write a book, I have to include this story." The quartet had played a jazz festival way north in Pori, Finland, several hours past Helsinki, and the itinerary had me going to Italy next, for two solo performances, before rejoining the band in Germany. We all left Pori early in the morning but still behind schedule, because we were sharing a bus with a couple of other bands, one of which—the Art Ensemble of Chicago—was running late. As a result, we got to Helsinki Airport with very little time to check in for our flights. I got my group squared away for their trip to Germany, and then got in line, with my vibes cases, to check in for my flight to Milan—where, it turned out, the Art Ensemble was headed as well.

I waited behind them in line while they checked in. When I heard them insist on sending their luggage via air freight, instead of as checked baggage, I spoke up and pointed out that they would need several days for customs clearance in Italy, which was notorious for being both slow and unreliable. My suggestion met with a blunt dismissal: "We know what we're doing, this is the way we always do it." But the air-freight issue was causing a serious delay, and our flight's departure loomed perilously close. You can probably figure out how this ends: the Art Ensemble finished up and rushed for the plane, but by the time I could check in and head to the gate, the flight had already departed. I was lucky to find another flight to Milan about four hours later—connecting through a different city—but unsure of whether I'd make it to that night's concert on time.

In spite of my delayed arrival on a different flight, however, the Italian promoter was waiting at the Milan airport to drive me to the concert, about three hours away in the town of La Spezia. But about an hour into the trip, we started having car trouble; several times, I had to get out and push to get the car started. We finally made it just in time for the concert.

My itinerary had originally called for me to continue by car to Rome the next day. But by now, the promoter's vehicle had truly expired. He put me on a train to Rome, which was so crowded that I had to sit in the aisle, on my vibraphone cases, the whole way. When the train pulled into the Rome station, more oddness: it was the middle of the day, and there was nobody around on any of the platforms. The other passengers detrained and walked into the station, leaving me totally alone with my instrument cases, sitting there at one of the busiest—but now emptiest—terminals in all of Europe. Where was everybody? More important, where was the guy who was supposed to meet me and take me to my gig? After a while, I spotted a porter in the distance and waved him over. He didn't speak English, but he understood I needed help with my baggage.

We went into the main part of the station, and it too was deserted. It looks like a bomb had gone off, I thought. Lucky guess: I soon learned there indeed had been a bomb scare, and the authorities had evacuated the entire station. The porter was now stuck with me and my baggage. But he brightened when I said something about renting a car (dropping the name "Hertz"), and indicated via various hand signals for me to follow him. We left the station and started wheeling the baggage trolley through the streets of Rome, a few blocks this way, a block or two that, and I started to wonder if he actually knew the way. But after about twenty minutes, we suddenly arrived at the local Hertz office. The attendant told me they had only one car left, and that I probably wouldn't want it because it was large and deluxe, but of course, that made it perfect for me—enough room for my vibraphone cases—and it even had air conditioning! After a lot of traffic confusion, I managed to find my way out of Rome and on the road to Pescara, the site of that night's gig, which I would share with Keith Jarrett.

Our performances went well enough, except for the usual dose of chaos associated with Italian concerts. After the show,

Keith and I returned to our hotel to find that due to a water shortage, the Pescarans turned off the water from midnight till 6 A.M. each day; thus, after a sweaty night on stage, no shower to be had. Keith hadn't yet organized transportation for the next day, so we drove back to Rome together in the rental car (and in fact, Keith kept it himself for several more days). With great relief, I bid farewell to the car and to Italy, and rejoined the band in Germany for some more "normal" touring.

All during my Italian travails, I was silently heaping expletives on the Art Ensemble of Chicago for causing me to miss that first flight—the precursor of all the trouble that followed. So, I can barely describe how I felt when, a little while later, I overheard someone talking about how the Art Ensemble had lost all their equipment on a flight to Italy months earlier. They were still trying to find where their baggage had ended up. Sweet revenge.

Italy seems naturally predisposed toward travel problems. On one mid-'70s tour organized by George Wein, we were traveling with several other groups—about a dozen musicians altogether—and the oddest thing happened at the Milan airport when we checked in for our flight to Lisbon. The counter clerk told us our plane had left already—an hour early! How could that be? Well, she said, everybody knows that when there is fog in Milan, all the flights leave an hour early. We had just missed our plane, and there were no other flights to Lisbon that day, which meant we would all miss our concert that night. What's more, we had no hotel reservations in Milan, and we quickly discovered that all the major hotels were full. So now, we had no place to spend the night, either.

Fortunately, I knew a small, boutique-style hotel where I had stayed the year before, and sure enough, they had just enough rooms for everyone. I remember Sarah Vaughan, who was among the travelers, saying to me, "Gary, you really got it together," which made my day. We returned to the airport the next morning—an hour earlier, just to be safe—and finally got to Lisbon. Since we were playing at a festival, the organizers simply rejiggered the program and added us all to that night's existing lineup. It made for quite a spectacular evening.

Sometime in 1977, I began to see warning signs that Pat's time in the band was coming to an end. I noticed that he took too long with his solos, sometimes playing too loud. He also argued with me over even my smallest suggestions about how to handle some of the songs. This caused problems, for me and for the music, but of course, I recognized the process. I had gone through this myself, before I left Stan Getz, and watched others in my own bands go through it as well. I realized (perhaps even before Pat) that he needed to move on. Pat was planning to leave, but not soon enough for me. I was increasingly unhappy with the tension that was building.

Pat had already made all the prelaunch preparations for a solo career; he only had to put it into motion. He had a record deal with ECM and had released a successful debut album, with another in the works. He had begun playing gigs with his own group, and had designated Ted Kurland as his agent and manager. Knowing that I needed to plan for Pat's departure, I looked at the schedule and saw we'd be working steadily through the spring, with a long break in May, followed by a tour of Europe. That would give me a month or so before the summer tour to break in Pat's replacement. From my perspective, it was better for Pat to leave the group sooner than later.

Pat was truly thrown by my decision. It upset him to have to leave before he had decided for himself, and it led to some terribly hard feelings. That parting of ways was a low point for us both, and it took quite some time to get over the experience. I think we each felt we hadn't handled it well. Our drummer, Danny Gottlieb, also left (with my blessing) to help Pat form his new band. They had known each other as students at the University of Miami, and I knew they wanted to continue playing together. And as I expected, the Pat Metheny Group achieved international success almost overnight.

It took some time, but I at last reunited with Pat via the Montreal Jazz Festival. That year, Pat and I were both scheduled to play. In fact, Pat had been selected as the "festival host," a post allowing him to perform a tune or two with each of several other musicians on the program. One of the festival directors called me at home and suggested that Pat join my band for one set, and I thought, "Why not give it a try?" When I arrived in Montreal, I recognized a feeling of apprehension. I hadn't even seen Pat in quite some time, and had no idea how this might go. While I was setting up my vibraphone, though, I heard a familiar voice say, "Hi Chief," and suddenly, it felt like just yesterday that we'd last played together. We had a great set that night, and we immediately started making plans to record. Within the year, we made *Reunion* for my new label, GRP Records. *Reunion* went to number 1 on the Billboard jazz chart, announcing to the jazz world that Burton & Metheny were together again.

CHAPTER 22

Wedding Bells Again

After Pat Metheny and Danny Gottlieb left in 1977, I reorganized the band with guitarist John Scofield, who I knew from his time as a Berklee student, and drummer Joe LaBarbera (based on Sco's recommendation). Despite Pat's departure, we continued to work steadily. I still enjoyed teaching and felt increasingly at home at Berklee, and at ECM, Manfred Eicher and I were making some of the best records of my career. I was also learning a lot about producing records. I had already made a dozen or so records as a leader when I joined ECM, but I hadn't paid much attention to the production aspects. Working with Manfred completed my education, when it came to recording.

My personal life needed some work, however. Three years had passed since my divorce, and I had begun to emerge from emotional exile. One day, I took notice of a student in my improvisation class. She seemed especially observant and very involved in the classwork, and I found myself looking forward to seeing her each week. A little later, during a gig at the Jazz Workshop, I saw her in the audience sitting with one of my vibraphone students. I chatted with her during the break and discovered she was really quite interesting. More important, she laughed at my jokes. I thought about calling her to ask her out, but I worried that as her teacher it might be inappropriate—even though Berklee's social structure was pretty casual in those days, and teachers did indeed date students. (In fact, several marriages between teachers and students at Berklee occurred during that era; thirty-five years later, as you would expect, there are rules to prohibit dating between students and college employees.) I finally got her phone number from my vibes student, then worked up my nerve to invite her to dinner that weekend—and held my breath, half expecting her to be insulted that I had called. But she said yes.

Her name was Catherine Goldwyn, and she had grown up in California. We immediately hit it off, and as I got to know her, I was all the more entranced. We spent every available minute together, and soon she began to travel with me on weekend trips to out-of-town gigs. On one such weekend, after a concert in Omaha, Nebraska, I suggested what I thought would be the next logical step in our quickly evolving relationship: I suggested we move in together. To my surprise, Catherine said she had no interest in that. She had tried that once before and had decided that the next time she lived with a guy, he would be her husband.

I hesitated a minute, did some fast thinking about how I really felt and our chances for the future, and then I told her getting married would be okay with me. I think that surprised her as much as she had surprised me. But after a short pause, she said, "Okay, let's do it." We had known each other for just six weeks, but it felt absolutely right to both of us.

Now, we had to break the news to our respective families. At thirty-one, I had already married once, so it was no big deal to tell my family I had met someone new and planned to marry her. But for Catherine, it was a very different situation: a twenty-two-year-old college student, she had suddenly decided to wed one of her teachers, who also happened to be nearly a decade older.

And at this point, I didn't even know about her family.

Catherine wasn't just a Goldwyn; she came from the Hollywood Goldwyns. Her grandfather, Samuel Goldwyn, was the famous movie-industry pioneer. Her father, Samuel Goldwyn, Jr., continues to oversee the Samuel Goldwyn Company to this day. Catherine's mother (who had divorced her father in the '60s) also came from a prominent family; *her* father was Sidney Howard, a Broadway playwright who was sort of the Neil Simon of the '30s and '40s. All this gave me at least a little pause. I'd be marrying into some genuine American royalty.

When I saw Catherine again a few days later, she told me that we were flying to L.A. the next weekend to meet her parents. She had broken the news to them over the phone as soon as we got back from Omaha! You can imagine the range of scenarios running through my mind regarding what might happen as we walked in her mother's front door.

Jennifer Coleman, Catherine's mom, turned out to be a real character—the kind of person sometimes described as "a little batty" (which I mean in the nicest possible sense). During her life, she had been a working actress, a mother of four, and ultimately a very accomplished painter, whose work hung in several L.A. galleries. She also was highly educated and spoke fluent French and German. I got on easily with her and her husband, John Coleman (also an artist). Whatever apprehension Jennifer might have felt about her daughter marrying a jazz musician, let alone her college professor, it didn't show. In fact, she was very enthusiastic about the wedding plans, and insisted that we have the ceremony in the very lovely garden behind her house.

The next day, we went to meet Catherine's father and his wife, Peggy. After the warm reception at Jennifer's, I wondered how it would go with her father. The Goldwyns met us at the door of their expansive house, all smiles and hearty handshakes, and the evening came off without a hitch. So, our "meet the parents" weekend was a success.

A year or so after the wedding, Mr. Goldwyn told me that when Catherine called to say she was marrying a jazz musician, he almost lost it. But knowing her independent streak, he realized that trying to talk her out of it would only strengthen her resolve to see it through. So, being a smart businessman, he decided to exercise some due diligence: he called two of his musician friends to see what he could find out about this Gary Burton.

First, he called Quincy Jones, who had composed film scores for several Goldwyn movies. A lucky break for me: I had played on one of Quincy's record sessions and also for one of his movie projects, and had gotten to know him pretty well. What's more, Quincy is a Berklee alumnus (arguably, the most famous), and he knew of my career because of the college connection.

Mr. Goldwyn next called Henry Mancini—another lucky break, since I knew Mancini as well, and in fact had recently spent a summer afternoon with him, on a yacht actually, cruising around Lake Michigan when we were in Chicago for a music-industry convention. Mr. Goldwyn told me that after receiving two reports practically describing me as someone who walked on water, he decided I was okay.

MUSIC FOR THE MOVIES

I have had a lifelong love of the movies, a passion that became fully entrenched when I first lived in New York. Since I worked mostly in nightclubs, I had my afternoons open, and since I didn't really have many friends yet (being new in town), I filled those afternoons with movie matinees. I checked the papers each week to see what new films had opened, and for most of the '60s, I saw literally every movie that screened in New York. Naturally, I hoped to someday take part in a movie scoring session. During my years with Stan Getz, I did get to appear in two movies, playing (what else?) "The Girl from Ipanema." But ultimately, I got to work with some of the greatest movie composers in the business—even though the results did not always meet expectations.

One day, I got a call from Quincy Jones, who learned I was coming to L.A. for some gigs; he said he really wanted me on his next scoring session. I was thrilled at the invitation. I arrived for the taping at Universal Studios in Burbank only to find two other well-known percussionists—Victor Feldman and Emil Richards, both of whom also played vibes—in addition to a full orchestra. I couldn't quite figure why Quincy needed me if he had already hired two other jazz mallet players for the session.

When Quincy got there, I noted that the orchestra had no written music. I watched as he viewed maybe ten or twenty seconds of the film on the monitor, then turned to the musicians and gave them instructions: *violins hold this note, cellists hold that note, everyone play this chord together; drums and bass, set up a repeated figure in medium slow tempo, something like this* (singing them an example of what he had in mind), and so on. Eventually, he had the full orchestra sustain one chord over a rhythm section groove. Then he turned my way and told me to play a few "bent" notes on the vibes, referring to an unusual technique of altering a vibraphone pitch by rubbing the bar with a hard mallet—a technique I had learned, ironically, from Emil Richards. That was all Quincy had hired me to do! And the guy who taught me how to do it was standing there with nothing to do but watch!

We went through the whole afternoon doing short bits of music this way. I had to admire Quincy's boldness: the very idea of recording a symphonic orchestra without any written music, just making up things on the spot, seemed crazy. Quincy remains one of my idols, and he has inspired me for years. But he didn't provide me the opportunity to do something great on a film score.

My next adventure in movie music came courtesy of Michel Legrand, whose work I have also long admired. Michel is justly lionized for his very beautiful music, much of it written for movies. When I got a call from him saying he really needed me for a soundtrack recording in New York, I immediately said yes, then entertained dreams of sounding like a million bucks as my vibes floated over a cloud of strings and woodwinds.

I flew down from Boston and made my way to Columbia Studios in Midtown, where I found a small group of musicians that included Lee Konitz, Johnny Coles, Barry Galbraith—all guys I knew. Michel arrived and handed out the parts, and I thought to myself, "Well, at least there's music to read on this one." But to my surprise, there were no notes on the pages—just squiggles and wavy lines all over the place. The film was a cops-and-robbers thing, and Michel's score called for sound effects to accompany the multiple car chases. We spent about eight hours making sliding and screeching noises as Michel watched the monitor and directed us. Toward the end of the day, the playback machine broke down and couldn't be repaired till the next day. Michel asked us all if we could come back; somehow, we all had other commitments. I talked to Lee Konitz about it later, and like me, he had anticipated the chance to play on some beautiful songs with a great orchestral background. Instead, we had spent a whole day making noises for car chases.

In 1997, I finally I got to play on a movie score in which I could take pride. It didn't involve a big orchestra on a massive Hollywood sound stage—just a small jazz group led by trumpeter/composer Mark Isham. He did a brilliant job coming up with tunes that were right for the movie and comfortable for the musicians. And better still (from my viewpoint), he reserved the entire closing credits—usually the longest segment in any movie score—for a solo vibraphone piece, giving me a real chance to show what I could do. The movie, directed by Alan Rudolph and starring Nick Nolte and Julie Christie, was *Afterglow*, quite a good film. I saw it at a local Boston cineplex and sat there long after everyone else had left, listening to myself play over the names of the best boy and the caterers and the accountants. I have to admit, that was a great evening.

Six months later, in July, 1975, in the garden of her childhood home, I married Catherine Goldwyn. As the oldest child—her three brothers ranged from middle school to late teens—she was the first to marry, so it was a big occasion for the family. And for me; my parents came from Indiana along with my brother and sister, as did a handful of our Boston friends. The guests, of course, included an assortment of Goldwyn family and friends, among them Jules Styne, the co-founder of MCA and Universal Studios (and his wife). I loved learning that Stein, another Hoosier, had started his career by booking bands at an Indiana ballroom.

Catherine's father had arranged for us to briefly honeymoon at a beach house in Malibu belonging to a film director he knew. We drove to the beach and found the house, which turned out to be a little creepy. This guy had a fascination with insects. Every tabletop, every wall, was covered with little plastic or metal replicas of insects: roaches, flies, spiders, a praying mantis, and more. Even his wallpaper had bugs printed on it. We laughed about it at first, and kind of settled into the house, intending to spend the rest of the week there. But after a few hours of looking at bugs—every time we opened a drawer or a closet, we found more insect replicas— we decided we couldn't handle it. I called the airport, and we caught a flight back to Boston that very night. (I only recently told Catherine's father about the honeymoon house and how we had sneaked out of town. He laughed and told me the guy had become a beekeeper in Illinois—a perfect fit.)

Friends have asked me about that time in my life, how it felt maybe sitting around the pool in Beverly Hills with movie stars and all. It was never like that. The Goldwyns have a long tradition of staying very down-to-earth. It began when Catherine's father was a young boy, and his own father required him to have a paper route so he would learn the importance of having a job. The family had legitimate fears about kidnapping, though, so they had the chauffeur follow him in the car while young Sam rode his bike around the neighborhood delivering papers.

Frankly, the most famous people I met through the Goldwyn family were the Goldwyns themselves. Catherine's father remains a Hollywood icon; her brother John produced many successful movies when he was Vice President at

Paramount, and now produces the television series *Dexter*;
and Tony Goldwyn is a well-known actor and director. During
Tony's college years in Boston, he often visited our house on
weekends. He was considering an acting career then, and he
and I spent a lot of time talking about life in show business.
After college, his career took off with a bang, and he has racked
up an impressive history of roles in movies, television, and on
Broadway, not to mention his successful work as a director.
(His first major role was as the murderous embezzler in *Ghost*,
and he has recently played the President on the network television series *Scandal*.)

Now that I had embarked again on married life, my little
suburban house suddenly seemed too small. Catherine and I
found a larger house at a bargain price in Brookline, closer
to Berklee, and better suited to our new life together. At first,
it all seemed ideal but busy: between touring and teaching,
I had trouble making time for my personal life. When the
1977 school year came to an end, I told Berklee I needed to
take some time off and didn't know for how long. I actually
thought I might not go back at all, but I kept the door open in
case I changed my mind.

Now, Catherine and I could spend more time together and
expand our social life. She had an uncle in Boston who was
well connected with the local intelligentsia, and sometimes
included us in his circle; once we found ourselves seated at
dinner next to the Harvard psychologist B.F. Skinner and his
wife. Dr. Skinner was famous for his theories about behav-
iorism, extending to the idea that through conditioning and
training, he could produce almost any desired behavior in a
subject. He had invented something known as "the Skinner
box" for training the behavior of lab rats. He then made a
rather fantastic leap to assume that whatever worked for the
rats would also work on humans. By the time we met, he was
being harshly criticized and regularly heckled at his lectures.

He certainly seemed harmless enough at dinner, and when I told him I was a jazz musician, he brightened a bit and said he had tried the saxophone when he was younger. But, he explained, "I just couldn't get the hang of that improvising business. I couldn't seem to let myself go"—how absolutely revealing, I thought, in relation to his psychological theories.

He and his wife seemed to really enjoy our conversation, and they invited us to their house in Cambridge to meet some of their other "young friends." They suggested a date for the following month, and we said, "Fine, we'll see you then." But when we rang the bell at their house on the evening in question, they weren't expecting us at all; in fact, they didn't even seem to remember us.

After three years, we decided to start a family, and as Catherine's pregnancy progressed, she extracted a promise from me: I had to stay home for a month prior to the birth, and for two months after, to help out. This would be a new experience for both of us, and she didn't like the idea of me running around the world while she coped with a newborn. I kept the band working as much as possible right up until November 1978, and then knocked off until February. I gave the guys plenty of notice so they could take other gigs, but not without concern; the band had never taken this much time off before.

I decided to forego something else as well: after thirteen years of smoking marijuana on a fairly regular basis, I decided to quit. I had never taken many chances with pot. For instance, I never carried it across any border when we toured outside the U.S. But as I prepared to welcome a baby into my life, I just couldn't picture smoking in front of my child. It was time to grow up. I worried that I would miss it, but once I'd made up my mind, I found it surprisingly easy to just forget about pot and get on with my life.

Around this time, I got a call from Steve Swallow. He was in Boston and wanted to drop by before driving home to

Connecticut. That's when he broke the news that after several years back in my band, the time had come for him to leave the group again, to pursue other things. I accepted his decision, of course. But I could hardly focus on our conversation because just before he got to our house, Catherine had gone into labor. The doctor told us that since it was our first child, we needn't rush to the hospital, so we had waited at home until Steve dropped by. But then, it started to snow heavily, so as soon as Steve left, we played it safe and headed for the hospital. Early the next morning, December 4, 1978, our daughter was born. We named her Stephanie, in Steve's honor. (Swallow returned to the band again later on. In fact, we continued playing together through most of the '80s.)

In addition to getting my own band back on the road, I continued touring each year with Chick Corea, and we recorded two more records: *Duet* (1978) and *Zurich Concert* (1980), the latter of which wasn't even supposed to be recorded. Chick and I had a concert at the Zurich Festival, and Manfred was there with his studio equipment to record guitarist Ralph Towner, another ECM artist performing earlier that night. Since he had everything already set up, he thought we might as well roll tape for our set as well. But neither Chick nor I were in good shape. We'd spent three weeks touring around Europe without a single day off (a schedule we would never dream of attempting today). We both had serious colds, and we didn't even get on stage till almost midnight.

We played to a packed house. Our friend Lee Konitz, the legendary saxophonist, couldn't find a seat in the audience, so he grabbed a chair from the dressing room and set it onstage behind Chick—probably the best seat in the house, actually. At the time, I thought the concert went "just okay." After all, it was late, and we were fighting a losing battle with our colds. Chick, unable to find any Kleenex, even had a roll of toilet paper with him at the piano so he could blow his nose between songs.

Later, Manfred sent me the tapes and when I took a moment to listen, I could hardly believe it. Somehow, this had turned into one of our best concerts ever. We were extremely lucky to have captured it on tape. I flew back to Germany shortly afterward to do the mix, and the album went on to win a GRAMMY, as had *Duet*—my second and third little gramophone statues.

I was delighted when I got a call in 1979 from George Wein, asking me to jam a few tunes with Bill Evans as part of the New York Jazz Festival. You'll recall that my first chance to play with Bill, back when I belonged to Stan Getz's band, didn't turn out too well. I don't normally care much for jam sessions, and neither did Bill. When we got together backstage, we found out the only reason we each had accepted was for another chance to play together. We talked about how each of us had admired the other's playing for a long time, and even raised the possibility of making a record together.

I knew a lot of the songs in Bill's repertoire and we quickly settled on two or three for the performance. Bill's trio at the time included Marty Morell on drums and my old pal Eddie Gomez, which augured well. But as we got underway, I felt like I couldn't seem to settle into the time feel and play freely. I thought maybe I was just spooked at playing with Bill and told myself to relax, but the second and third tunes didn't get any better. I came off the stage really confused. Bill and I said a few words as we parted, but we both knew it hadn't worked. There was no more talk of making a record together, I can tell you that.

About six months later, I got another chance to play with Bill, again thanks to George Wein, who booked my band to share a concert with Bill's trio at Carnegie Hall. George suggested we play some tunes together as a finale, and again we decided to try. I determined to get a different result this time. We picked some different songs and I gave it my all.

But damn if the same thing didn't happen again. Nothing felt comfortable. I couldn't seem to lock in with Bill's time. I didn't need three strikes to know this was doomed to failure. It's funny: sometimes you absolutely "know" the rapport with someone will be the best, and then it fizzles anyway.

Many years later, after Bill had passed away, I was flying to Japan for some concerts with Eddie Gomez when I recalled those times I tried playing with Bill. I asked him about it, and his answer was quite revealing. "Oh," Eddie said, "you mean the time-feel thing. Everyone who ever sat in with Bill's trio said they had trouble playing with us; it must have been something about the way we played together." Hearing that made me feel a lot better, but I still wish it had worked out.

As a musician, Bill was like a fish out of water—an introvert in show business. It's hard; I know because to a lesser extent, that describes me. And Bill was a classic introvert. Shy with people, awkward on stage, he played with his head down, almost never looked at the audience, and rarely spoke on stage. This relegated his career to mostly small clubs instead of major halls, because his unease on stage interfered with his ability to communicate with audiences. He was the most innovative pianist of his generation—a hero for most piano players at that time (and for many others of us, too) and a talented composer. His fresh style of melodic phrasing still influences players to this day. But he remained terribly insecure, and quite uncomfortable in his role as a jazz icon.

Bill liked Steve Swallow's songwriting, and he included a couple of Swallow compositions in his repertoire. When Swallow went to see Bill's trio at Keystone Korner, a jazz club in San Francisco, he talked with Eddie before the group began. Eddie said the trio had played Swallow's "Falling Grace" every night at the club, and he would most likely hear it the next set. But there was no "Falling Grace" that night.

Then, at the double bill at Carnegie, Bill mentioned that

he had been using another of Swallow's tunes, "Peau Douce," and that they would play it that night. Swallow sat out front during Bill's set, waiting to hear it, but no "Peau Douce." When he saw that Bill would be playing near his home in New Haven, accompanying the dancer Carmen de Lavallade, Swallow went to *that* performance, and there in the printed program, in black and white, was listed "Peau Douce." He felt certain he would finally get to hear Bill play one of his songs. But when they reached that spot in the program, Bill substituted another piece, his own "Blue in Green!" He was just too insecure to play a piece with the composer in the house.

After more than a decade of serious drug addiction, Bill finally gave up heroin in the '70s. I'm sure it wasn't easy, because he obviously had what we now call an addictive personality. The impetus may have been his arrest at JFK International Airport in New York. The airlines had just begun to search passengers for security reasons, and they found Bill's heroin supply as he tried to board a flight to Europe. Fortunately, he had a well-known entertainment lawyer who knew the judge personally, and the charges were dropped—on the provision that Bill would go into a treatment program. This was his chance to finally escape addiction. But Bill soon turned to cocaine instead, and all those years of abuse finally took their toll. Like John Coltrane, who had played with Bill in Miles Davis' band and died at age forty, Bill succumbed to liver failure, at fifty-one.

I've often wondered why Bill couldn't shake his addiction, even though he had to know it was killing him. Writer Gene Lees described Bill's addiction as "the longest suicide in history." Thankfully, I never needed drugs to escape my own insecurities—and I certainly have them. There are moments when I just can't deal with people. At such times, I'll sneak out after a performance rather than having to hang out and talk with people, as most musicians (including me) usually tend to do. There are some days when I just can't answer the phone or deal with anyone at all.

Shyness does not suit the musician's life. I think of my time in public, having to socialize with people, as part of my work. On those occasions, I play the part expected of a jazz musician. I doubt that people who know me would guess I find sociability so difficult. Sometimes, I think I even manage to be the life of the party. But I find it exhausting.

One of the most difficult trips I can recall was a so-called "Young Lions" tour of Europe. George Wein had produced several successful tours with older jazz stars, and now he wanted to try a group of younger players—although truthfully, we weren't all that young. I was in my late thirties, and most of the group was my age or older: Jimmy Owens on trumpet, Joe Henderson on tenor, Cedar Walton on piano, and Larry Ridley on bass. At the last minute, the original drummer had to cancel and we replaced him with Roy Haynes—who had just turned sixty. (Some young lion!) But I was happy to see Roy on the tour. It guaranteed one guy on the trip that I knew well. And I also looked forward to playing with Joe Henderson, an important musician and someone I had never met.

Be careful what you wish for.

Things got weird at the first get-together. The schedule had us rehearsing the afternoon of the performance, so we could work out what songs we would play and who would solo on the various pieces. I expected we would each suggest a tune or two, maybe even have some lead sheets to pass out to the others. From the drop, Joe acted strangely. Most of us knew several of his compositions—he'd written some great ones— but Joe said he didn't want to play any of those. However, he didn't have any new music with him, either. Whatever anyone suggested, Joe vetoed it. This went on for a long while, until about an hour before the gig, when it became obvious we were running out of time, and he grudgingly agreed to some of the choices. His behavior put everyone in a sour mood, and that didn't change much for the rest of the tour.

The first performance took place in a large sports arena in Vienna, as part of a jazz festival, where we shared the bill with bluesman B.B. King and a couple of other bands. Backstage, we learned that Austrian television, which was broadcasting the concert, had an experiment in mind; in addition to airing the concert, they were going to simultaneously film a scene for a television movie featuring several established actors. (I recognized German film star Kurt Jurgens, who played a doctor.) The script called for a shootout during a big concert, so they planned to stage a fake shooting in the audience at some point during the show. And they wanted the musicians on stage at the time to keep playing, as if nothing had happened. The "wounded" would then be rushed backstage for "treatment" by actors playing emergency medical workers. No one seemed concerned that the audience had no knowledge of this, or that they might think it was real. We musicians began to wonder what would happen if people in the crowd overreacted to the gunshots.

I made a point of watching all this from a seat in the audience, because I needed to see it with my own eyes. Sure enough, at some point during B.B. King's set, lights came on and gunfire erupted. People started yelling as the "wounded" actors were rushed out of the hall. All the while, B.B. and his band continued to play. It fortunately came off without any problems, but the next day, the newspapers were outraged and highly critical of the television production for putting the public at risk.

On that inauspicious note, our tour began, and things didn't get any better. Each night was a struggle with Joe. A couple of nights, he didn't even show up; it turned out he had gone to some other city to line up a cocaine buy. For part of the tour, he even had his drug dealer traveling with us. The last night brought the *pièce de résistance*, however. It was a midnight show at a festival in Bordeaux, France. After we had played the melody chorus of the first song, Joe noticed that Jimmy Owens had placed a small cassette recorder next to the piano. Joe gave him a hard look and asked what he was doing. Jimmy replied that he was taping the gig. In a dark voice, Joe said, "I don't tape." Jimmy took offense at this rebuff and said the tape was just for his own use, so no big deal. Joe once again voiced his objection, and that led to a loud argument on stage—all this while the rest of us kept playing. They went at it pretty good, Jimmy growing all the more insistent that he was damn well going to record us, Joe refusing to have anything to do with it. Then they moved their fight backstage where, through the thin curtain, the audience could clearly see their shadows gesturing wildly at each other. Meanwhile, the rest of us had reached the middle of the song and were counting on Jimmy and Joe to come back and play the melody to end the piece. I myself had never played the melody for this tune and I didn't really know it. We stalled for a while, and when we realized they weren't coming back, I made up some kind of final chorus to get us out. The four of us who remained on stage played the rest of the concert without Joe and Jimmy, and by the time we finished they had already left. I can't imagine what the audience must have thought.

Before the tour, I had considered Joe one of the great players of my generation, and I relished the opportunity to play with him, maybe even get to know him. I knew he had a reputation as something of a bad guy, sometimes walking out on concerts and leaving promoters and other musicians hanging. I had also heard a story from a bassist friend who'd had a bad experience with him, when Joe was looking to sublet his New York apartment. Wanting to move to New York from the suburbs, my friend agreed to a rental arrangement and a few weeks later arrived, with his wife and a U-Haul trailer full of furniture, at Joe's place. At that point, Joe demanded something like $10,000 to buy his furniture! He had never mentioned anything about the furniture before then, and it quickly became obvious he was just trying to take advantage of the situation. In the end, my friend turned the U-Haul around and went back home, rather than give in to Joe's scam.

Even knowing all this, I had looked forward to working with him. But not only did he act like a total prick during the tour; he didn't play that well, either. I knew that this kind of behavior, towards friends and fellow musicians, is commonplace among druggies. It all comes down to scrounging every dollar you need to feed the habit, and it brings out the worst behavior. But to this day, I can never listen to Joe's music without experiencing so many negative connotations that I have to turn it off.

By complete contrast, I got acquainted with B.B. King around this time. He's a charismatic guy, always charming, always complimentary. At first, I chalked this up to his show-biz persona, but I came to recognize him as one of the most positive and sincerely gracious human beings on the planet. We've crossed paths a number of times over the years, and it's always a pleasure to spend a few minutes with him.

B.B. even played on one of my records, a project I put together in 1992 featuring six of my favorite guitar players, entitled *Six Pack*. Pat Metheny wrote two tunes for it, and I invited Jim Hall, John Scofield, Kevin Eubanks, Ralph Towner, and Kurt Rosenwinkel to play. In addition, I asked B.B. to record a couple tracks. Although we had never played together—and, of course, he's not specifically a jazz player—I loved the idea of including him on the date. I recorded each of the guitarists over several days, but when the time came for B.B.'s session, he wasn't feeling well, so we had to record the backing tracks without him. He said he would add his parts the next time he came through New York. I had to leave for Europe, but two weeks later, Will Lee (who played bass on the sessions) came in to talk B.B. through the music we had laid down, and it all came off beautifully.

I hated missing B.B.'s session, but something nice came out of that evening. Between takes, Will mentioned my name and B.B. launched into a long monologue about what a great guy I was and how I was such a wonderful musician. Fortunately, the engineer had turned on a microphone and recorded the whole thing, which I found waiting in the mail when I got back home. The King of the Blues singing my praises—it's something I'll treasure for the rest of my life.

CHAPTER 23

A Trip to Moscow, and the Family Grows

For whatever reasons, I never live in any one place for very long. What with demands of work, financial ups and downs, getting married, getting divorced, whatever else—I sometimes feel like I'm always moving to another house.

Catherine and I lived five years in Brookline, during which time our family expanded with the birth of our son. We named him Samuel John Burton, after his great-grandfather. Now, we began to think about a change of scenery, and decided on Connecticut. Catherine had relatives in Stonington, a quaint seaside village in the northeast corner of the state, and after a couple of visits, the place completely charmed us. We found a spacious country house on a couple acres of orchards and gardens a mile outside the town. Stonington is known for its arts community and its eccentric crowd of expatriate New Yorkers. It is also a sailor's paradise, and I took full advantage of the ideal boating conditions. Since learning to sail in the late '60s, I have usually lived near the ocean, and I've owned a succession of boats over the years (both small and not-so-small). In fact, during my first summer there, Ted Kurland and I won the annual Stonington Catboat Race (with my then-new boat, the Fat Cat)—much to the chagrin of the local populace.

Shortly after the move, I made a trip to Russia with Chick Corea that remains sharply etched in my mind. It was 1982, toward the end of the Cold War, and it had been many years since the Russians had invited any American artists to perform there. I had traveled to several Eastern European countries during the '70s, which gave me some sense of life under Communism—specifically the gray, dark look of the cities in places like Hungary, Poland, and Czechoslovakia. I also carried the memory of a jazz festival in Prague, where in 1978, I was interviewed for over an hour by a writer who knew my music inside and out. He was preparing a lengthy article for an arts magazine about my career. A few years later, as I scanned an issue of *The New Republic* magazine, I ran across an article about Prague politics and was stunned to read that this writer had become a political prisoner. The article noted that he had written critically about the government, and also "had published a history of jazz musician Gary Burton!"

But in the early '80s, despite official disinterest from behind the Iron Curtain, the U.S. Ambassador to Moscow came up with a clever idea. Since no American performers could obtain Soviet visas at that time, he invited us to come to Moscow using diplomatic visas, as his personal guests. Once in the country, we would play informal concerts for invited audiences at the Embassy residence, and also meet some of the local musicians. It was *glasnost* under wraps.

Jazz has always held wide appeal around the world, and especially for those behind the Iron Curtain. Disparaged and discouraged by the authorities, jazz represented an artistic freedom at odds with Soviet repression; for decades, the daily broadcast to Communist Bloc countries of the "Voice of America Jazz Hour" proved extremely popular. So, things started buzzing when word got out that Chick Corea and Gary Burton would soon visit Moscow and Leningrad.

Upon our arrival, we were whisked to the Embassy

residence, a rambling mansion with plenty of extra space for guests. Ambassador Arthur Hartman and his wife, Donna, were gracious hosts and very savvy about how to handle the public-relations aspect of our visit. They arranged for us to meet local jazz musicians, at nightclubs and also at gatherings in people's homes, which offered a rare chance for Russian musicians to talk directly with American artists. They had heard our records for years. Now, they had a thousand questions. Mostly, they wanted to know how our lives compared with theirs. How did we find musicians to play with? How much did musicians earn? How did we get our concert dates? What if we wanted to change band members? They lived in a world the exact opposite of ours. They could only work with musicians assigned by the bureaucracy; they could only play for Goskoncert, the state-run concert agency; and they could only record for Melodiya, the government-sanctioned record company. The twenty-seven officially recognized jazz musicians—yes, they had a precise count at the time we visited—enjoyed guaranteed career earnings but precious little freedom when it came to making music.

We gave five performances in the Embassy ballroom (technically U.S. territory, by international agreement), each for five hundred invited guests. One night was reserved for local musicians and others in the arts; another night for government people and diplomats; another for press and business people, and so on. We also played one night in Leningrad at the U.S. Consul's residence (another island of U.S. territory in the midst of the Soviet Union). For the authorities, our visit was a mixed blessing. Officially, they expressed qualms about American musicians whipping up all kinds of excitement. On the other hand, quite a few of the government higher-ups wangled invites to our performances, trekking to the Ambassador's residence to hear some American jazz. As one Russian limousine after another deposited dignitaries on

"American soil," a staffer told me they had almost never seen some of those behind-the-scenes Kremlin bigwigs.

It all became newsworthy rather quickly. The NBC television crew based in Moscow taped one performance and also interviewed us for a story to air on the evening news in the States. *Pravda,* the Soviet national newspaper, interviewed me as well. But when NBC's videotape arrived in New York, it contained footage of Soviet soldiers marching through the city instead of a story on our visit. Apparently, some apparatchik, wary of publicity fallout from our Moscow trip, had intercepted and replaced the NBC tapes. Later, I received a translation of my *Pravda* interview. Most of the article quoted me stating my strong disapproval of the U.S. government's racist policies. Of course, the interviewer had never asked me about any government policies, and almost all of what they printed was totally made up.

Being a guest at the U.S. Ambassador's residence during the height of the Cold War was like living in a bubble. Everywhere we went, State Department employees accompanied us, making sure we could get around without interference. Conditions were hard for the local citizens, with even basic foodstuffs often difficult to come by. It was somewhat easier for the Embassy staff: they imported food from Finland, which was delivered once or twice a month by truck, and had a telephone line that dialed directly to the U.S., to stay in touch with people at home. Since this line had a Washington, D.C. area code, you could (if you knew the number) direct-dial into the American Embassy from any phone in the U.S. I have no idea how that was technologically feasible in 1981, but it would come in handy later on.

That initial visit with Chick went over so well, I received an invitation to return two years later with my whole quartet— pretty much a reprise of the first visit, with performances in Moscow and Leningrad and more opportunities to hang with local musicians. First, though, we had some travel issues en route to Moscow by way of Athens and Bulgaria (where we played before heading to Russia).

A mix-up with the Russian visas had one band member mistakenly listed as a female, an error we discovered only upon arrival in Athens. A discrepancy like that could cause problems when we got to Russia, but I knew one way to quickly fix the situation: get in touch directly with our Embassy contacts in Moscow, and let them know what had happened. At the time, it was virtually impossible to place an international call to Russia without a lot of red tape and delay. So, I told our State Department host in Greece about the direct-dial number—the one in Moscow with the Washington, D.C. number—which I had fortunately kept in my address book. She didn't believe me when I said it would ring directly at the American Embassy. But when she (hesitantly) dialed, it went through immediately, and by the time we flew to Moscow the next day, the Embassy staff had the visa situation straightened out.

Reuniting with the Moscow musicians was a real feel-good experience; some of them now seemed like old friends. I knew from my first visit that a number of the Russians had great talent, but they had to deal with challenges rarely seen in the States. For starters, they had trouble keeping their instruments in shape. Most of them owned decent instruments, but it was difficult to acquire things like saxophone reeds, guitar strings, drumsticks—all items that need to be replaced on a regular basis. Even something as basic as manuscript paper was hard to come by. So, just before my second visit, I filled two suitcases with hundreds of dollars worth of musical supplies donated by Wurlitzer's, a major Boston music store at the time. Whenever I met a Russian musician, I would ask what he played, then lead him to my stash of supplies and offer him reeds, or strings, or whatever he needed. I also took along a Polaroid camera—something illegal for Russians to own at the time—and had my tour manager snap pictures of me with the local players. Then, a minute or two later, I could hand them an autographed photo to take home. That blew them away; they had never seen such a thing.

During this trip, I was taken to a local university, where I heard two students play a piano/vibes duet on a challenging piece that Chick and I had performed during our previous trip. The vibes player especially impressed me, so I was astonished to find out he didn't own an instrument. He said he had built a mock vibraphone keyboard from blocks of wood and that he used this to practice the motions of playing, even though there was no sound. He only played "for real" on those occasions when he managed to borrow an instrument.

This stayed on my mind when I got home. A bit later, my friends from the Musser Company (which made my vibraphone) contacted me about playing at some music convention. I was willing to do it gratis, but when they asked me what kind of fee I wanted, I couldn't pass up the opportunity: I told them to give me a new vibraphone, adapted to 220-volt current (the electric service used in Russia), and they agreed. Now I just had to figure out how to get it to Russia and into the hands of Sergei, the vibist. Under Soviet rule, this would be strictly forbidden.

I got in touch with my contacts at the Embassy in Moscow, and they agreed to add the vibraphone to the "diplomatic pouch," which delivered items directly to the Embassy, free of restrictions and not subject to customs. I'd always pictured the diplomatic pouch as a leather shoulder bag stuffed with letters and documents, but in reality, there is no limit to the size or quantity of what you can send by that method: furniture, cars—even vibraphones. After the instrument arrived at the Embassy, we needed to get it to Sergei without the authorities booking him for fraternization with American diplomats or illegal receipt of a gift from America. The Embassy worked out a scheme to deliver the instrument to a school; one of the teachers would then contact Sergei to come and pick it up late at night. (I'm happy to say that Sergei still has that vibraphone. On a recent trip to Moscow, I borrowed it for a concert rather than schlepping my own.)

On a later visit to St. Petersburg (1992), I had a day off and was invited to check out a local jazz festival featuring several Russian bands. My host suggested I go backstage to meet some of the performers. No one there could translate except for a twelve-year-old boy who spoke surprisingly excellent English, so for about an hour, he helped me communicate with the musicians. When everyone had drifted off, I turned to my young translator and asked who he was. I thought he might be the son of one of the players. He told me he was Kirill Gerstein, and that he had played piano at the festival earlier that day. I missed his performance, but later, he dropped off a cassette at my hotel. His style reminded me of Keith Jarrett, and he was very, very good—so good that I spearheaded an effort (along with others at Berklee) to enable his entry into the U.S. When he turned fourteen, Kirill and his mother came to Boston, and we fixed up an efficiency apartment in a Berklee dorm so he could attend classes, making him the youngest student ever admitted to Berklee. He completed his studies, after which he developed a strong interest in classical music, going on to Manhattan School of Music in New York City for his Master's degree. Soon after that, he won the prestigious Rubenstein Competition in Israel, and just recently, at age thirty, he received the Gilmore Prize, the ultimate recognition for classical pianists (along with a $300,000 grant). Kirill is one of a very few musicians who started out in jazz and became a star in the classical world—one talented guy, and another reminder of the talent lurking everywhere around the globe.

Like most of my generation, I never expected to see the Berlin Wall come down (in 1989) or witness the fall of

Communism, let alone the mostly violence-free aftermath (the obvious exception being Romania). Having played often in the old Eastern Bloc countries, I'm heartened by the transformation from the bleak, sunless streets of the past to the modern, bustling cities of today. Since that first trip thirty years ago, I have gone back to Russia a total of twelve times, and I've seen firsthand the transition from Communism to a more open society. And every so often, someone still stops me and pulls out one of the old Polaroid photos I handed out long ago.

CHICK COREA

I once read a passage that described two kinds of genius. To paraphrase: In one case, you hear a great musician and think, "If I practice long enough and work hard enough, I could do that too." In the other, you listen and think, "I don't have any idea how to do that; I wouldn't even know where to begin." Those in the latter category are the rarest ones—the real deal—and they include Chick Corea, without doubt the most fascinating of the few geniuses I'm fortunate to have known. We have been playing together for over forty years, performing a couple thousand concerts, recording eight records, and winning six GRAMMYs together along the way.

Like me, he had very supportive parents—his dad was a musician in Boston—and they doted on Chick, an only child. He started playing at a quite young age and had an excellent teacher, who introduced him to classical piano music and helped him develop a first-rate technique. (From a strictly technical perspective, I consider him the best pianist in jazz.) Also, like me, Chick's career took off after he moved to New York, where he worked with Mongo Santamaría, Stan Getz, and singer Sarah Vaughan, not to mention his important period with Miles Davis in the early '70s.

In some ways we are quite opposite, though. When we first worked together, Chick prided himself on never reading newspapers or magazines, preferring to tune out the world and concentrate all his energies on music; by contrast, I'm a total news junkie. Chick tends to leave the small details to others, while I want to be involved in every step of every decision. But our differences seem to mesh into a perfect combination once we start to play.

I love Chick's quirky sense of humor. He always enjoys talking to the audiences, often rambling on about whatever pops into his mind. (I like to talk on stage, too, so we take turns at the microphone between songs.) One difference emerges when we play in countries where they don't speak much English. Then, I limit my announcements to briefly naming the composers and song titles, assuming the audience can't understand much more than that. But Chick talks about anything on his mind, for however long it takes, joking around, telling stories. It breaks me up, even as I wonder what the audience is thinking. Once, backstage at a concert in Istanbul, a young woman found her way into our dressing room and gushed about how she was a big fan of his music. She also told him she was a medium. Without hesitating, Chick looked at her very seriously and said, "You know, I used to be a medium, too—but now I'm a large!" I laughed about that for days.

When we both recorded for GRP Records in the mid-'90s, the label organized an all-star concert at the Beacon Theatre in New York. The plan called for the various GRP artists to work together in different combinations, rather than just playing with our own bands; Chick would play with his trio but also accompany singer Diane Schuur. Their rehearsal got off to a rocky start when Diane complained about Chick's playing. (Keep in mind that Chick has accompanied some of the greatest singers in jazz; his wife Gayle also sings and often collaborates with Chick.) The song was "Autumn Leaves"—a standard every jazz musician knows, so it should have been a breeze—but Diane stopped after about a chorus and asked Chick, in a haughty tone, "Is that what's on the music?" She had passed out her arrangement for "Autumn Leaves"—which, of course, none of the musicians really needed—and expected them to play it exactly as written. Chick protested that they should just play the song without sticking to the arrangement, but Diane then went full diva and insisted that he and the others play every note on the page! I watched from the side, knowing that Chick had only grudgingly agreed to play with Diane in the first place, as a favor to the record company. I half expected him to throw up his hands and walk off, as I probably would have done. But Chick was delaying justice for later. On the concert, he created a massive reharmonization of "Autumn Leaves," turning it into one of the most adventurous and modern interpretations you'd ever hear. To Diane's credit, she was a strong enough singer that all his wild diversions didn't throw her off, but I believe she got the message. She had played with fire at the rehearsal, and now she was getting a little singed at the concert.

Chick really came into his own when he began leading his own groups and composing his own repertoire, revealing his truly unique style as both a player and a composer. His work is universally admired. Young pianists often imitate his piano style, and scores of musicians have played and recorded his songs. But despite his instantly recognizable sound, you can't pigeonhole him. I think he's the most versatile musician in the history of jazz. He seems equally at home playing everything from bebop to electric fusion, classical to flamenco and tango, solo piano to duets and trios on up through big bands. But whatever the genre, he plays it with such conviction that you would think that genre was his favorite of them all. And like Duke Ellington, Chick is a prolific composer. He writes almost constantly and has published more than a thousand pieces in his career. Often, during our duet tours, he'll be engaged in his next project, composing music for a whole other lineup of musicians. He goes back to his hotel room after our concert and writes new music till 5 A.M. I have watched him do this for forty years and still find it amazing.

In the '80s, Chick and I talked about someday playing with a string quartet, and he began researching the format, listening to the string quartets of Beethoven and Bartók on his headphones and following along on the scores, all while we traveled in airplanes and cars. Eventually, he announced he was ready to start writing. We notified Ted Kurland, and he booked a tour: twenty-one concerts across the U.S. for Burton, Corea, and strings. With the tour scheduled to start in August, Chick set aside the month of July to compose an hour of string quartet music. I set aside the month to worry at home about whether he could do this in four weeks.

I waited a week and called to check his progress. Chick replied, "I haven't started writing yet, but I've found some great score paper. Don't worry." (Of course, that got me *really* worried.) I waited another week to call again. This time, he said, "I've finished the first piece and am working on the second, and you're going to love it. Don't worry." A couple weeks after that, I got to L.A. and headed for Chick's house to meet the string quartet for our first rehearsal. Sure enough, he had finished all the pieces, and the copyist was just putting the last touches on the parts. We started right on time and hardly made any changes at all in the seven movements of Chick's *Lyric Suite for Sextet*, which we recorded after the initial run of concerts. The music was challenging but gorgeous, and I still consider it one of our best efforts. We went on to tour the U.S., Europe, and Asia with the string quartet, completing sixty concerts in all—making the *Suite,* just possibly, one of the most performed works in modern chamber music.

Chick once told me how he composes so much music in such a short time. He sits down at the piano and writes a first song, and puts it aside; then he writes a second song and puts it aside. The first song, and maybe even the second, are often not that interesting, and he might not use them at all. But by the third song, he's gotten his creative juices flowing and can write song after song, almost without stopping. He writes till he is too tired to work any more, then goes to bed and continues when he gets up the next day. As long as he doesn't leave the house or talk to anyone or face any other distractions, he can keep the flow going till he finishes everything he needs. Like a handful of others I've met, he really understands how his own creative process works. For Chick, it is something he can literally switch on when he needs it.

The sheer volume of his output is prodigious, record after record, year after year, in all kinds of settings. He manages a grueling performance schedule, touring around the world every year, and still maintains his place as the most prolific composer in modern jazz history. Having performed a great deal of his music, I've found that in spite of their often difficult demands, Chick's songs are easier to learn—and easier to play well—than those of most other composers. I've encountered this attribute only one other time, in the legendary tango composer Astor Piazzolla. With both of them, melodies spring from a well of virtuosic playing, so you might think they wrote passages only another virtuoso could handle. But when a truly great composer writes even a complicated song, the melody has logical patterns that makes it easy to grasp, and it flows more easily than you'd have first thought.

People often ask what it is like to play with Chick, and this saying tends to pop into my mind: When you stand next to a lightning rod, don't be surprised if a stray thunderbolt comes along. I can't explain why, exactly, but more than with any other player in my experience, I seem to sense what Chick will do before he does it, and he seems to know where I'm headed before I even start my next phrase. Even so, he is full of surprises. He can still throw me a curve and send us off in a new direction entirely. This was true on our first duet album in 1972, and it remains true even when we haven't played together for a while. We frequently head off to do other individual projects, but we have never let a year pass without playing at least some dates together.

The duet setting is unique. When you play solo, it is like giving a speech to the audience. In a band, you're part of a panel discussion, with each player taking his turn to "speak" (solo). But in a duet, it's more like a one-on-one conversation between two friends. And there's something music has that conversation doesn't. When you talk with a friend, you have to take turns speaking. With music, you both can play at the same time, even as you "converse," which greatly multiplies the possibilities for interaction.

I used to think that someday our duo project would finally come to an end. After all, people evolve in different directions and move on to new things. Wouldn't Chick and I eventually lose interest after maybe fifteen or twenty years? But when we passed the thirty-year mark and continued coming up with new material—and were still so excited about playing together—I decided that maybe we'd just keep it going. The potential never seems to wane. As I was completing this book, we began work on another record (*Hot House*). Even then, I thought it might be our best yet; in February, 2013, it received two more GRAMMY awards for Chick and me, so I guess I was right: one for both of us, for "Best Improvised Solo," and one "Best Instrumental Composition" for Chick, for the song "Mozart Goes Dancing."

The Burton family enjoyed our first year living near the shore in Connecticut, but in 1982, some problems cropped up. I was often on tour, leaving Catherine stuck in the country with two small children, sometimes weeks at a time. We had friends in Stonington, but the house still got lonely when I traveled on extended trips. And things took a real turn for the worse when I came down with a serious illness.

I had finished some recording work in Boston, and as I drove back to Connecticut, I noticed a strange symptom—a sort of tingling on my face whenever I touched my forehead. I didn't know what to make of it, but the next day I got a sudden blinding headache. We called the doctor, and he told me I most likely had a case of shingles. He predicted I'd have some pain for a few days and prescribed some medication, confident that within a week, the worst would be over and life could get back to normal. If only it were that simple.

I went to bed but woke up an hour later with more pain than I had ever felt; I thought I was dying. I told Catherine to immediately drive me to the nearest hospital, in Westerly, Rhode Island, and as soon as they had admitted me, they gave me a shot of something that knocked me out. I then began a longer-than-expected hospital stay, most of it spent in a daze of painkillers. I'd wake up enough to start feeling serious pain, and then it would be time for my next dose. The right side of my face became a horribly swollen mass of open sores. The surrounding tissues got so distorted that my right eye was hardly recognizable. I could still see a little out of my left eye, but it had become so sensitive to light that we had to keep the room darkened.

Herpes Zoster, otherwise known as shingles, attacks when the chickenpox virus re-emerges after years of laying dormant in the spine. The condition occurs more commonly in elderly people, though I was not even forty and in good health—just my luck, I guess. Today there are treatments for shingles, even a preventative vaccine, but in 1982, the doctors could only offer palliative care and wait for it to pass.

After two weeks in the hospital, I went home and lay in bed for another two months, staying sedated and keeping cold compresses on my face, which felt like it was on fire. The nerves, damaged by the virus, continued to send out pain signals, even as I was gradually healing. By the time I recovered, I was left with residual pain and a variety of facial scars. A year later, I had plastic surgery to remove the larger ones.

I had to cancel quite a lot of work during those months. I kept thinking I'd get well enough for some gig scheduled a week or two later, but when the time came, I'd have to cancel because of the pain. Soon, I was getting close to the start of a major tour of the Caribbean and South America, which had been in the works for a year. By this time, I desperately wanted to get back to work. I certainly didn't want to lose a major tour like this one. And having to take care of me, along with a three-year-old and one-year-old, had left Catherine overwhelmed.

But as the tour loomed ahead, I still didn't know if I could make it. I still had a lot of pain and had to keep ice packs on my face most of the time. Laying flat on my back all that time, I had also grown quite weak. But Catherine really pushed me to make the effort, and Ted Kurland volunteered to go along for the entire trip to help me get through it. So, the morning of my departure, I staggered downstairs—for the first time since returning from the hospital two months earlier—and got into the back of a limo for the three-hour drive to JFK Airport in New York. I slept the whole way, groggy with pain meds.

I met Ted and the band at the airport, and we flew to the first concerts in Jamaica, Haiti, and the Dominican Republic. Those were the toughest to handle. I was so weak that I had to sleep all day, and only left my bed to play. At showtime, Ted would lead me to the stage. I kept a bowl of ice water just offstage, and whenever I had a break during someone's solo, I'd stroll casually to the side to press an icy washcloth against my face, just to calm down the nerves. Traveling from city to city didn't help at all. The slightest breeze on my face would set off the fireworks, and I was still very sensitive to light. At least, I could finally see again with my right eye, but I needed to keep my eyes shaded from the sun, so I wore dark glasses everywhere. My face was pretty scarred up. Several people asked if I had been in an auto accident, so when anyone commented about my appearance, I gave that explanation. It was easier than trying to explain shingles.

But during the tour, I slowly grew stronger and the pain gradually eased, and six weeks later, as the tour came to a close, I felt almost normal. It was good to get home and not have to confine myself to bed. As is typical with shingles, I had residual pain for several years, and even now I get an occasional twinge on the right side of my face. I remain forever grateful to Ted, who left his office for a month and a half to help me through that tour.

Soon after I got back home, I received a call from Berklee asking if I would give the commencement speech at graduation that year. Still struggling a bit with my symptoms, I almost declined, but then decided to tough it out, and I had a great time back among my friends at the college. On the drive home to Connecticut, Catherine told me she could tell I missed the scene at Berklee, and I realized she was right. And a week or so later, she suggested we move back to Boston. I resisted at first, since we had only lived in Stonington for two years, and I didn't want all the complications and disruption of moving again so soon. But she was right, and in the end, I agreed.

CHAPTER 24

Back to Berklee

The Burtons of Connecticut found a roomy house in a comfortable section of Boston called Moss Hill, and by the fall of 1982, I had returned not only to Beantown but to Berklee, too. The college offered me access to the talented young players that came through my band in the '80s, during which I experimented with different instrumentation: for the first time, I hired horn players. Instead of a guitarist, I brought in Japanese trumpeter Tiger Okoshi, followed a year or two later by alto saxophonist Jim Odgren. It posed an interesting challenge to again be the only chord instrument in the ensemble—the first time, actually, since my days with Stan Getz.

I had long believed I would never use a pianist in my band, given that I had such a great thing going with Chick. What other pianist could compare to the rapport I had with him? But then I heard Makoto Ozone.

I met Makoto in 1983, when he played a student concert at Berklee. He had a lot of technique, but I honestly didn't think about teaming up with him at that time; his style didn't seem a match for mine. A few weeks later, however, I attended a Berklee reception where Makoto happened to be playing in the background, while people stood around with their cocktails. I hovered near the grand piano all evening. Makoto knew a surprisingly large repertoire of very hip tunes, and his interesting interpretations really impressed me. There was a lot more to him than I had first thought.

After that, we started jamming together a couple of times each week. I urged him to play more contemporary songs, and he picked up on my suggestions very quickly. Soon, I knew I wanted to build a band around our emerging connection. Around then, he told me he would soon graduate and expected to move back to Japan, but I thought that would be a waste of his talent—so I offered him the chance to join my band when he finished school. We've played together off and on ever since, and have made a number of records. After another decade in the U.S., Makoto did return to Japan, where he remains a consummate jazz star but has expanded beyond the jazz world: he has built a second career performing classical repertoire as a guest soloist with orchestras around the world, while also hosting his own long-running radio show in Japan. For our 2002 CD *Virtuosi*, we rearranged works by classical composers—Scarlatti, Brahms, Rachmaninoff, and my '60s acquaintance Samuel Barber—in order to improvise on them. For that recording, Makoto and I received a GRAMMY nomination in the Classical field, a real honor for two jazz guys. I think the jazz community seriously underrates Makoto—probably because he is from Japan, and even though he comes to the U.S. and Europe regularly for concerts.

Eventually, I expanded my group with Makoto to a quintet by adding Scottish tenor saxophonist Tommy Smith, who has since become the leading jazz figure in the Scottish music scene. He has launched a university jazz program in Glasgow and done something truly remarkable: he has created, essentially single-handedly, a thriving jazz scene where none existed before. Tommy's National Scottish Jazz Orchestra is a topnotch band that puts on an impressive series of concerts each year.

Tenor saxophonist Donny McCaslin followed Tommy into the band and stayed a few years before going on to become one of the leading tenor players in New York. Donny was nominated for a GRAMMY in 2004—another young musician I'm proud to have given a start.

After almost nine years together, Catherine informed me she wanted to end our marriage. As she approached her thirties, she had grown unhappy; she felt overshadowed by my career and unfulfilled on her own, and she needed to find her own path. I was very attached to our family, and terribly disheartened at the thought of starting over. We continued to talk it over for several months, not wanting to rush into a decision this important; but in the end, she still felt the need to change directions in her life.

We split as amicably as possible, and I moved to a house nearby, but as in my first marriage, this breakup struck me as a giant failure on my part. And as before, the fears about my sexual identity returned to the surface. Rationally, I knew the breakup was not the fault of any one person nor caused by any one thing. There was no infidelity involved, and we were living up to our responsibilities as partners and parents. So, we weathered our first year of shared child custody as best we could. I spent as much time as possible with Stephanie and Sam so they wouldn't feel separated from me. In fact, since my new house was only a few blocks away, they could freely wander back and forth between our homes whenever I was in town. We must have done something right: some thirty or so years later, Catherine and I remain very good friends, still quite close to our now-adult children.

In spite of the stresses in my personal life, my return to Berklee went splendidly. It almost felt like I'd never left. I enjoyed teaching two courses in particular—*Advanced Improvisation* and *Music Business*—and I found the college's energy and creative atmosphere inspiring. This environment started at the top; Berklee has been blessed with excellent leadership since its founding by Lawrence Berk in 1945. Though educated as an engineer at MIT, Larry (as we all knew him) was also a piano player, and he turned his passion for music to building a music school focused on jazz and commercial idioms. His right-hand man during these years was Robert Share, who had a knack for guiding the day-to-day workings of the college through its early years of phenomenal growth. (That's the same Bob Share who had advised me to call my parents when I was a Berklee student nearly twenty-five years earlier.) By the '80s, Berklee's enrollment had reached 2,500 students, making it the largest music college in the world. (Today, enrollment stands at 4,000.) As Larry Berk reached retirement age, the Trustees voted to appoint his son, Lee—then serving as Vice President—to succeed his father as President of Berklee. It was a smooth transition, and the college continued to thrive.

But after the untimely death of Bob Share in 1984, Berklee sought to revamp the leadership structure to reflect the growing needs of the institution. Some new administrative positions were created. One of them, Dean of Curriculum, would now oversee the college's approximately six hundred courses, as well as the library, archives, and a variety of other related areas. I served on the search committee for this position, and we spent several months interviewing candidates.

During this process, I got a call from Lee asking me to meet him for breakfast the next morning. I'm not much of a morning person to begin with, and this was an especially busy week, as I was hosting Chick Corea, in town for a Berklee residency, while also managing my teaching schedule; an early meeting was the last thing I needed just then. I wandered half-asleep into the dining room at the Harvard Club, around the block from Berklee, and Lee started right in, telling me he didn't have much confidence in any of the people we had interviewed for the new post of Dean of Curriculum. Then he said he had decided I should take the job.

302

This was not at all expected. What's more, I couldn't even picture myself in an administrative job. I had no academic training; I didn't even have a college degree, having dropped out of Berklee to go on the road with George Shearing. But Lee insisted I take the job, so I hesitantly agreed to try. I secretly figured that after a year or so we would find someone better qualified, and I could get back to my teaching routine.

When I began my career in music, I had important mentors. Since then, as you'd expect, I in turn have mentored any number of young musicians. But as I embarked on this new role at Berklee, I quickly realized that the tables had turned once again, and I had another mentor of my own in Lee Berk. He turned out to be the perfect guide to becoming an effective educational leader. I was given an office next door to Lee's, and I began another on-the-job Berklee learning experience, just like when I'd started teaching fifteen years earlier.

I reviewed the course materials and documentation, all of which needed updating, and quickly saw that we first had to develop a computerized system for maintaining and archiving all the courses. While pondering the technical side of things, I also began thinking about my role as a leader at the college. What could I contribute in the way of new direction for Berklee? I don't think anyone, including me, would have foreseen the answer.

Berklee had long been known as a jazz school, even though its focus was broader than one genre. From the start, the school encompassed many types of commercially viable music, such as film scoring and traditional pop. In the '70s, rock filtered in, as younger teachers and new students cast their gaze across the stylistic divide—but we had no courses in rock music. Berklee had been the first school to give jazz an academic home, in the days when jazz was the music-world rebel that challenged the conservatory culture. I believed that now, we needed to do the same for rock. And I saw that, as with Nixon going to China, only an unlikely champion of this view—an established jazz musician, such as myself—could take the lead.

Some of the veteran faculty members feared that if rock came to Berklee, it would somehow ruin everything, so I needed a strategy to win over the old guard. I decided the best route was to count on musicians' natural instinct for bonding. I formed a group of about twenty-five faculty members, including not only younger ones interested in rock but also the crustiest old skeptics. I hosted monthly dinners with takeout Chinese or barbecue, knowing that musicians would be more comfortable hanging out at a party than sitting in an academic meeting. And most important, I brought guests to each meeting.

Because of my contacts with rock musicians during the '60s and '70s, I was able to get some well-known rockers to visit and give us their take on music education. These included two members of the band Boston, and also Felix Pappalardi, a '60s rocker turned successful producer. When asked what they look for in musicians, they all said they wanted players who could read music, knew harmony, could write arrangements, could play their instruments in tune—the same things you would want and expect in any type of musician.

After a year of meeting "the enemy" and learning they weren't so different after all, the older faculty's resistance to rock music just faded away. In the decade that followed, Berklee embraced rock with open arms. From that experience, my approach to leadership was clear. As Voltaire put it, "It is not enough to conquer; one must know how to seduce."

The next new opportunity that came knocking was music technology. Berklee had long used computers, of course, to manage administrative recordkeeping and scheduling. But in the early '80s, the use of computer technology in music remained in its infancy and still spurred controversy. Synthesizers had only begun to appear on the music scene, and initially, they were not that well received by most musicians. The use of computers for composing and recording still seemed like science fiction. Lee began pressuring me to increase our involvement with music technology, and the more I looked into it, the more convinced I became that it would have a huge impact in the near future.

We created an office of research to pursue these possibilities, but before it could really get established, it morphed into a new course of study we called Music Synthesis. Teachers as well as students began embracing the new technology. We installed studios, synth labs, media centers, workstations, and networks, and as fast as we built them, the faculty and students filled them to capacity. These days, Berklee is a model high-tech institution, and the world's absolute leader in music-technology education. I brag on many developments that took place in my tenure at Berklee, but I consider the crusades for rock music and music technology to be my most important contributions, and the ones that brought about the most profound changes at the college.

It turned out that in spite of my early apprehension, college administration suited me after all. I discovered just as great a creative challenge in this new post as I got from playing or teaching. Instead of instructing a hundred or so students in the course of a typical semester, as I did when on faculty, I now had an impact on thousands of students through the new directions I initiated and the programs I supported. In addition, I brought a different perspective to the school; coming into the administration from the unconventional background of a touring musician, I maintained a healthy skepticism for the worst of institutional life, but a fervent advocacy for the best.

We all want to make a difference in the world around us, and I found I could contribute by helping a few individuals "get over the finish line" of their college education. I believe that in addition to some combination of natural-born abilities, education is the second most important factor in determining one's success in life. I have always stood in awe of the power that education has to change people's lives. Working at the college, I occasionally came across deserving students who were maybe a year or two away from graduating but running out of money. (Actually, the first time I helped someone finish school, it was a Berklee classmate during my student years; I helped pay for his final year of college.) Over my thirty-three years at Berklee, I subsidized, in one way or another, six students altogether, allowing them to complete their education.

I think the motivation for my philanthropy resulted from my own sense of having missed out on a complete education. Considering my small-town roots, I was lucky enough to get some decent early schooling. It helped that I discovered the Princeton (IN) Public Library when I was about eleven, and from then on, I've continued to educate myself, supplementing what I learned in high school and at Berklee. Still, I've always wondered what else I might have gained from a complete college experience, say, at a school like Harvard.

Living in Boston, I was acquainted with quite a few people associated with Harvard—professors, grad students, and so on—and I always envied the comprehensive education provided by this most famous of American universities. So, when the chance came to become a Harvard professor for a year, I jumped at it. I didn't really have the time, but I loved the idea of doing something at Harvard. I taught in the Graduate School of Education, teaching music to non-musicians studying to be arts administrators. Surprisingly, this turned out to be a very interesting challenge—and another case of the teacher learning as much as the students. Every time I try something outside my usual area of expertise, I end up learning a lot that I can bring to my own work.

CHAPTER 25

Who Is Gary Burton?

As I entered my forties, someone asked me a thought-provoking question: What did I plan to do for the second half of my life? As I pondered this, I thought that I most wanted to fix anything that hadn't gone right during the first half.

In the years following my divorce from Catherine, I tried dating a few different women, but nothing serious developed. That got me thinking (again) about my sexual identity, and wondering for the umpteenth time just who—or what—I was. During both my marriages, I steered clear of anything that could cause me to confront this issue. That wasn't hard to do; I felt comfortable in both my marriages, which made it fairly easy to bury any alternative feelings. But now, I knew that I had to understand the crosscurrents that had churned just below the surface throughout my life. Fortunately, I found a terrific therapist, and after a year or so of exploration, I had the "aha" moment where I fully realized: I'm gay, and I always have been gay. I could hardly believe it had taken so long to see this. I had buried my true feelings for such a long time. I had kept them secret not only from everyone else, but from myself, too—all to avoid threatening the career I loved, and the life I believed society expected me to lead. Once again, I found myself in a familiar place—on the verge of making a career-risking move.

As the saying goes, when you come out of the closet, it isn't just once; you have to keep doing it, again and again, each time you meet someone who doesn't know your story. I would guess that 95 percent of my listeners don't know I'm gay. The musicians' grapevine being quite efficient, I usually assume that most of my jazz colleagues know by now, though I'm still surprised to occasionally run into a fellow musician who hasn't heard the news.

Even those who know I'm gay probably don't know the whole story, because so much confusion surrounds the question of gayness. Contrary to old-fashioned theories, we don't choose to be gay at some point in our lives. We are gay from the beginning, and the only choice concerns whether we accept that aspect of ourselves. Thankfully, here in the twenty-first century, it's increasingly common for young gay people to have the encouragement and acceptance they need to become comfortable with their orientation. With luck, they can enter adulthood with a lot less confusion and stress than I and others of my generation went through.

Starting my musical life in rural Indiana, growing up in the 1950s, launching my career in the '60s, the idea of homo-sexuality was simply off the table for me. (The word "gay" hadn't yet come into use.) I was a smart kid; I had a talent that opened doors for me almost from the moment I picked up the mallets. I wanted to avoid anything that might jeopardize that, no matter what the cost.

Still, I always knew I was different, somehow. I knew that I experienced the usual boyhood trials and epiphanies differently from my peers. At summer camp—a sea of boys living in close quarters, naked in the showers—some of us began acting on our newly discovered sexual feelings (pretty common stuff, actually). In high school, when everyone was expected to date the opposite sex, I usually had a girlfriend, but I didn't know what to make of my confused feelings. I believed I liked girls, yet I couldn't turn off my attraction to boys.

This ambiguity is common to many gays. Truman Capote once said he considered himself lucky because for him, there was no question: he knew from the beginning he was 100 percent gay and could immediately get on with things, and he felt sorry for the guys still wrestling with their identities well into their adult lives. That certainly described me. I reached my forties still thinking of myself as heterosexual, but with this "extra ability" to appreciate men too. At least, I fervently wished that to be true, and didn't let myself question it much. I wasn't intentionally lying to myself. I genuinely thought I had figured it out, and for quite a number of years, it seemed like the right explanation.

I tried to balance my sexual desires. As I've mentioned earlier, a high-school friend introduced me to sex (via mutual masturbation), and at our occasional sleepovers, we'd stay up half the night playing out our teenage version of gay sex. (We didn't know at all what we were doing, so it was pretty tame.) That kind of adolescent exploration is not so rare, and most people consider it a temporary phase on the way to hetero-sexual maturity. For years, I thought it would be like that for me, too. During that time, in fact, I sometimes wished I had no sexual feelings at all; I'd have preferred that to the confusion and frustration I experienced. And when I went off to Berklee, I did submerge the issue entirely, and remained asexual for two years. I was into music twenty-four hours a day and just pushed the whole sex thing out of my mind.

About a year after I moved to New York, I received my draft notice with instructions to report for my Army physical. I was expecting this, and also dreading it. This was 1963, and the Vietnam War had just gotten underway. But the big buildup of troops hadn't yet begun, which meant the demand for soldiers was still low—which, in turn, made it easier to convince the Army that maybe you didn't belong. I heard of guys who didn't bathe for a week, stayed awake for days, got as stoned as possible, then went in and acted psycho. I also heard another way to get out of the draft was to claim you were homosexual. I didn't think I could pull off a crazy act. Still, the idea of going near the homosexual issue terrified me.

But this was a very serious situation. I worried that I wouldn't be a good fit for the military. I was scared—not about combat (which really wasn't even an issue at that time), but rather about day-to-day life in the military. Bill Evans once told me that his years in the Army affected him drastically for the rest of his life, and at the time, I feared something similar could happen to me.

Even as I took the subway to the Induction Center in lower Manhattan, at 6 o'clock on a chilly morning, I still hadn't figured out what to do. When I arrived, I first had to fill out a questionnaire, and right there on page three was the question: Have you ever had any homosexual tendencies? The way it was phrased made it easier for me to answer. It didn't ask if I was a practicing homosexual (I wasn't). It asked if I had "tendencies." In other words, did I just think about it? I knew the honest answer to that was "yes," though it still petrified me to officially say so. Up till then, I had never talked about this to anyone.

I took a deep breath and checked the "Yes" box, then waited in a state of panic to see what would happen. Next came the colorblind test (I passed), and then, instead of proceeding with the others, a handful of us were called to step out of the line. We hadn't even gotten to the strip-to-your-shorts stage. I identified the others pulled from the line as either gay or drug-addicted (another question on the questionnaire), as we waited for our interviews with a psychiatrist. When my turn came, he asked how I met other homosexuals. I replied that as a musician who worked in nightclubs, I found it easy to meet people—true as far as it went, though I wasn't actually hooking up with anyone of either sex at the time. But that was all he needed to hear. He gave me a piece of paper to take to the exit room. After an hour, when the other gays and druggies had finished with the shrink, some tough-acting guy in a starched uniform walked in and angrily said, "Okay, all you faggots get out of here!"

I left the building drenched with sweat. I could hardly eat for a day or two, but I had done it. This was the first time I admitted to anyone I might be gay, although I still didn't have a good handle on it myself. So, I had "homosexual tendencies." But what exactly did that mean?

A few weeks later, I received a letter from the New York City Health Department inviting me to take part in a free therapy program for people with sexual deviancy! Wow. That meant the Army had violated my privacy and informed the City of New York that I was, in their words, a "sexual deviant." (I ignored the letter.) A couple weeks later, a second letter arrived, even more insistent that I should take advantage of this free program—after which someone called me at my unlisted phone number. (The Army must have provided that, too.)

But instead of telling them to leave me alone, I decided maybe I should check into it, because I really did have questions. I made an appointment and met with a young doctor who talked to me for a while and then asked if I wanted to set up a regular appointment schedule. I explained that because I traveled a lot, I couldn't really commit to regular appointments. In that case, he explained, I couldn't take part in the program, but he recommended I find a therapist on my own. And having gone this far, I was now indeed curious. Maybe, if I found a good shrink, I could finally talk about this stuff and get some answers.

My first therapist, Bill Fay, was really ahead of his time. In 1963, the mental health profession still classified homosexuality as a mental illness, but Bill was much more open-minded. He did ultimately characterize my homosexuality as merely a phase that I would pass through on my way to a heterosexual future; but that was a common theory at the time, and one that seemed believable to me. (Of course, I desperately *wanted* to believe it.) Bill helped me tremendously, even though we didn't achieve a real breakthrough in understanding my sexuality. I don't blame him for that. Therapy helps you find yourself—the therapist doesn't do the finding—and I just wasn't ready yet. Besides, I had more going on than sexual confusion, as I coped with the challenges of a fast-moving career and a late emergence from adolescence. In these areas, Bill's help proved invaluable.

Five years later, when I entered into marriage, I decided to end therapy. It seemed like it had served its purpose. I was beginning a shared life with someone I loved and felt very comfortable with, and I believed I had figured out how to live with my conflicting feelings. For those wondering how I dealt with my homosexual side during marriage, I can honestly say that I buried those feelings almost completely and fully committed myself to each relationship. I never felt tempted to stray. In fact, I found great happiness and a certain peace so long as married life was working for both parties. My homosexual nature just receded. It became an occasional fantasy part of my life, and I felt no compulsion to act on it.

So, why not just continue as a heterosexual? Good question, and one I've asked myself many times. But by my forties, there was that other good question—"How do you want to live the second half of your life?"—and it struck me as a very big one. It got me reviewing everything that had happened up to then, including two marriages that hadn't lasted, and realizing this was the time for me to change anything I hadn't yet gotten right. But having figured out the question, seeking the answer posed some hurdles. How would a forty-four-year-old divorced father go about starting a new life as a gay man? I had a lot at stake. I was a college dean and an established jazz musician with a career going full blast. I also had two young children living with me about half the time.

I read everything about gay life I could get my hands on, and I started to talk to those few people I could trust. First, I told Catherine, who was (and who has remained) very supportive. I remember her saying, "Don't worry about it affecting your career. This is the '80s; who cares?" (Funny: you'd expect that reaction now, but it was no sure thing at that time.) But in spite of her reassurances, I had serious concerns about what would happen if the news got out. Would the college have problems with a highly visible gay individual serving as a dean? Would the musicians I knew feel awkward about collaborating with me in the future? I knew that sooner or later, someone new might come into my life, this time a male partner. Was I prepared to let the chips fall where they may? I had already realized that I couldn't expect to keep secret any gay relationship that might develop.

I began to gradually explore the Boston gay scene. Being generally pretty awkward in social situations, I didn't have much experience at even heterosexual dating. Now I also had to incorporate this new identity that I didn't quite understand myself. But in time, I made a few gay friends and started occasionally visiting gay clubs, hoping to meet someone special and find a new relationship.

A talented and very likeable guy named Earl Dimaculangan became my boyfriend in 1989, and we were together for nearly seven years. Earl is one of those rare people whom everyone seems to like, which made him a perfect counterpart to my social reticence. He had gone to Berklee some years earlier, though I hadn't known him as a student. We met at a Berklee alumni event, after which he invited me to meet for a drink, and we started seeing each other regularly. We had dated for a few months when I decided to bring him to a reception at President Berk's house. Since the guests included a lot of faculty and alumni, I figured people would think we were just acquaintances.

But the next morning, after a routine faculty meeting, Lee asked me to stay behind for a moment. When we were alone, he said he wanted me to know that Earl was welcome at any Berklee function, any time, any place. That surprised me. I hadn't expected anyone to see us as a couple, but Lee picked up on it immediately. More important, he wanted to make his acceptance and his support crystal clear, which alleviated one big worry: I was on firm ground, as far as Berklee was concerned. (I had already faced the question of what I'd do if Berklee asked me to step down, and I knew my answer; out of respect for the institution, I would have moved aside if asked. Thankfully, I never had to.)

Now, I faced my next concern: how would my fellow musicians react? The music business differs from most lines of work, where you get hired and have a steady job. In music, you're hired over and over, essentially, as each new project, each new tour, each new record comes along. So, if anyone had qualms about collaborating with me, they might simply stop calling, and I would never know whether it was because of my orientation or because they just didn't have a project suitable for me.

I started by telling the guys in my band, individually, when the opportunities arose. To my surprise, all but one of them said, "Oh, I already knew that." Turns out I wasn't so discreet as I had thought—and clearly, it posed no problem for them. I had just completed the album *Reunion* with Pat Metheny, and we had a tour starting with the musicians from the record—a chance, I thought, to start sharing my story with some more high-profile players. The first night of the tour, after a rehearsal in Nashville, I broke the news to them at dinner. There was a moment of "Are you kidding or serious?" and then the conversation just moved on. So, no issue there, either.

By the time Terry Gross asked me about being gay on National Public Radio, I had gotten used to sharing my story with friends and colleagues. That made the leap to truly going public less scary than I expected. And I was glad to be completely out in the open, at last. Interestingly, when I tell people I'm gay, they often don't believe it at first. After all, I've been married, I have two children, and I spent decades in the public eye as a straight guy before "the gay thing" came up. But all the musicians I normally collaborated with have continued to work with me, and we have remained close friends. My family has been extraordinary, especially Catherine, Stephanie, and Sam. When Earl and I moved in together, they welcomed him as one of the family. And I was fortunate to have my first gay relationship with someone as popular and positive as Earl. Our time together gave me the opportunity to get settled into my newfound identity, with the love and support of a terrific guy along the way.

I felt like I'd gotten a late start on being the real Gary Burton—almost like beginning life again as a different person. But I have no regrets whatsoever about either of my marriages, and I adore my children. At times, I feel blessed to have lived both a straight life and a gay life—a rare unique experience that few people share.

CHAPTER 26

Tango Lessons

As I approached the 1990s, I enjoyed a sense of well-being that most of us know only a few times in our lives: the knowledge that at that moment, I had everything just how I wanted it. My work as a Berklee educator was going quite well, as was my playing career. My band worked steadily, and I continued touring and recording with Chick Corea. All this security allowed me to put my longtime fascination with tango music to the test.

Back in 1965, when I played in Stan Getz's band, we made a South American tour that included a three-night booking at Michelangelo '70, a famous club in Buenos Aires. We shared that weekend with a tango ensemble led by Astor Piazzolla. I had never heard anything like Piazzolla's music before. I didn't know it then, but he was the leading tango musician of his era and the greatest virtuoso of the bandoneon, the accordion-like instrument traditionally used in tango. In addition, he would soon emerge as one of the most important 20th-century composers. Steve Swallow and I stood at the bandstand every night, listening to his group and marveling at their music. I bought a stack of his records before leaving Argentina, and I loved playing them for musician friends in New York.

Almost twenty years later, Astor himself showed up at a concert Chick and I played in Paris (Astor's adopted hometown). We chatted a while, and he asked if I might want to try some kind of project together. By then, I had been a fan of his music for two decades. I had never once thought of playing tango myself, but I immediately said yes. When a couple of years went by without hearing anything further, I figured Astor's enthusiasm must have cooled. But one day, as I strolled through the lobby at Berklee, the receptionist waved me over to say I had a phone call from Paris—from Astor, it turned out, asking if I still wanted to play with him.

We discovered we would both be in Argentina about six weeks later, so we decided to meet then to talk about the music. I cautioned him not to start composing anything beforehand, because writing for the vibraphone differs from writing for piano or any other instrument. (Too many times, I've had to drastically rewrite vibes parts that proved unplayable.) But at my opening gig in B.A., Astor showed up backstage to animatedly say that after our phone call, he was so excited about playing with me, and could so completely picture all the music he wanted to write, he had forged ahead and finished all the composing. That scared me a little, and by then, I also had heard about Astor's reputation for sometimes volatile unpredictability. Swallow tried to convince me I should reconsider the whole thing, but I had gone too far at that point—and once again the "inner player" piped up to say, "Do it!"

Ted Kurland got busy and booked us on tours of Europe and Japan. More important, he also helped set up a record deal for the project. I originally approached Manfred Eicher at ECM, but he didn't think much of the idea; tango music didn't fit into ECM's range of styles. So, we instead made a deal with my old friend Nesuhi Ertegun at Warner Brothers. (Curiously, about a week before we were scheduled to record, Manfred reconsidered and asked if ECM could still do the tango album, but we had already committed to Warners.)

We decided to record our upcoming concert at the

Montreux Jazz Festival, the setting of my success as a solo performer fifteen years earlier. Since Montreux was only the fourth stop on the tour, we needed to learn Astor's newly written music in quite a short time frame. We met in Italy, where the tour would begin, with plans to spend two days rehearsing. The first day, we started around midmorning, practiced a couple hours, and then Astor announced it was time for lunch—one of those three-hour Italian repasts, followed by a nap. We never made it back to the rehearsal room. (That's when I discovered Astor didn't really like rehearsing all that much.) When the same thing happened the second day, I grew alarmed. We were all still struggling with the new music, and in my case, I was also trying to absorb a whole new genre. Fortunately, I had discovered by this time that Astor wrote beautifully logical melodies that were easy to understand, in spite of often being complex. And although he had never written for vibraphone before, I only had to make an occasional adjustment for technical reasons.

The night of the tour opener, at the Ravenna Festival, I came down to the hotel lobby dressed the way I typically prepared for a concert in that era—white trousers and a Hawaiian shirt—only to see that the musicians in Astor's band were all dressed somberly in black. Astor shook his head and said I couldn't appear like that. (I was getting fired before we played the first gig!) But after going on about it for five minutes or so, he shrugged and said, in essence: "Well, you're the jazz guy, so what the hell, you'll just look different." Rest assured, I went out the next day and bought black clothes for the rest of our concerts. (And as a matter of fact, I've continued to wear black on all my performances ever since.)

Despite the lack of rehearsal, we somehow made it through that first performance without what musicians call "a train wreck"—i.e., a major catastrophe—and proceeded to play concerts in Pescara (Italy) and Nice (France) en route to

Montreux. I spent the afternoon of the Montreux concert still practicing the more difficult passages in Astor's compositions, not at all confident I could nail them on the concert. To make matters worse, it turned into quite a long night. Miles Davis played first, and we didn't start our own set till after midnight. Everyone in the band was tired by the time we began, and I worried that the audience might be exhausted too, so I was pleasantly surprised to hear enthusiastic response all through our program.

Nonetheless, I didn't think we had played that well, and I remember telling Astor we should plan on rerecording everything again, in a studio, when the tour ended. After the concert, I ran into my journalist friend Neil Tesser backstage. He was there to cover the festival, and the first thing he said was, "Well, that wasn't your best night!" At the time, I felt the same way.

As the tour continued, I began to increasingly feel part of the tango milieu. Astor's wonderful musicians were genial from the beginning, but I think they withheld their judgment at first, waiting to see just how well a jazzer would master the details of tango. After the first week of the tour, however, the musicians took me aside and told me they now considered me a true *tanguero*—one of the greatest compliments I could have received.

Astor was unfailingly gracious and respectful to me and to all his musicians, but I did witness a couple instances of his legendary temper during that tour. In Zaragoza, Spain, at a free outdoor concert sponsored by the city, the audience included a lot of grandmothers and kids enjoying an evening of music in the park. Tango is often rather dark and gloomy—there's a reason the musicians wear black—and about halfway through, some of the younger audience members started to get restless, wandering around the park as we played. A few teenage boys happened across some stage props that included a large cross, apparently left over from some Easter pageant, which they put to good use. There we were, deep into a slow, somber tango, and here came the boys staggering across the lawn in front of the stage, dragging the cross like Jesus on the road to Calvary. I actually found it hilarious, and also pretty creative, and I had to stifle the urge to break out laughing. Astor, on the other hand, was furious. He spent a half-hour screaming in Spanish at the poor promoter for allowing such an insult. Astor later expressed his great embarrassment that I, a famous jazz musician, had witnessed this travesty, which he felt demeaned tango music as well as his stature as a performer. I just thought it was really funny, but I couldn't tell him that.

The following week, at our concert in Rome, the promoter attempted to pay Astor in Italian currency instead of U.S. dollars, as the contract specified. (At that time, the law prohibited you from taking Italian money out of Italy.) Astor got so mad that he made the guy buy a plane ticket and travel with us to Switzerland the next day—just to change the Italian money into dollars. There in the Zurich airport, the promoter exchanged his currency, paid Astor in dollars, and then turned right around to catch his flight back to Rome.

Some months after the tour ended, Nesuhi sent me the master tapes from Montreux. I wasn't too anxious to hear them. But when I did make the time to listen, I was thrilled to hear that, in fact, the group sounded terrific. What's more, we really had captured the excitement of that night at Montreux. (Neil Tesser later told me he had the exact same reaction when he first heard the recording.) I truly enjoyed mixing and editing the final version, and New Tango, by Astor Piazzolla and Gary Burton, remains one of my most important records. It continues to sell steadily even now, thirty years later—and I continue to tease Neil about his backstage critique to this day (although I agreed with him at the time).

ASTOR PIAZZOLLA

Astor Piazzolla's music is very complex and intrinsically modern—qualities I admire in jazz, as well, but tango is the national music of another country, and it took me a while to get over that. I had previously held a rather arrogant view of such local music. I thought of it as the equivalent of folk music, something simple and singable (with jazz, the "national music" of the U.S., being the rare exception). In fact, tango has an interesting history that closely parallels that of jazz. Tango came of age as a contemporary of jazz, born in the early 20th century in the bordellos of Buenos Aires, as opposed to the saloons of New Orleans. In the '20s and '30s, tango moved into ballrooms, where large tango orchestras played for dancing, just like the jazz big bands of that era. Tango orchestras with four (!) bandoneons, plus full string sections, played nightly in perhaps a half-dozen ballrooms around Buenos Aires. From the '50s on, both jazz and tango moved into the concert era, and both became more complicated and sophisticated. But while a handful of innovators spurred the evolution of jazz through the 20th century—Duke Ellington, Charlie Parker, Miles Davis, etc.—the analogous evolution of tango was almost singlehandedly the creation of Astor Piazzolla.

I sometimes compare Piazzolla to Ellington or to Aaron Copland. Like them, Piazzolla composed a voluminous amount of music, much of it now standard repertoire in the tango world. Beyond his genius as a composer, he was also the unparalleled master of the bandoneon, the national instrument of Argentina and the central instrument in tango ensembles. I can't think of a comparable performer/composer in modern classical music (although Chick Corea and Pat Metheny both fill that niche in the jazz world). Piazzolla's output was tremendous. He released some seventy albums of mostly original music, including an opera, symphonic works, theater music, and countless compositions for his touring group. What's more, Piazzolla's compositions are far more involved than typical jazz writing. Most jazz compositions require as little as thirty seconds to two minutes of written music, which is then used as a basis for improvisation. But in Piazzolla's work, each performance is entirely composed, encompassing six to twelve minutes of written music. In addition, the individual parts must be orchestrated as well.

I'm also amazed at tango's similarity to jazz in its melodic and harmonic content and in its emotional range. The point of departure is that tango does not rely on improvisation. And I continue to be struck by the knowledge and passion among tango fans. When we arrived on one tour in Japan, I was surprised to see about a hundred Piazzolla fans waiting at the airport, each waving a little Argentine flag. Piazzolla told me that the Japanese especially loved tango, and that they had schools that taught bandoneon—and even one Japanese company that manufactured a modern-day version of the instrument. Strangely, the American public has never really warmed up to tango. We've seen some successful tours by tango dance troupes, but Piazzolla himself never developed much of a following in the U.S. After our tour in '86, I asked him why he didn't play in the U.S. more often. He replied that he visited once in the '60s, for a concert organized by the Argentine Embassy in Washington, but that it didn't go over well, so he never came back. I told him he should try again, and he did manage to play a handful of dates in the East and Midwest in the late '80s. But he never really connected with the U.S. audience.

When Piazzolla introduced his *nueva tango* (new tango) in the mid '50s, the tango world was dominated by dedicated traditionalists, and this radical, contemporary style made him a controversial figure. Radio stations that played his records received death threats, as did Piazzolla himself. Not until the end of his life did he become the national icon that we know today.

I stayed in touch with Astor when our year of touring ended. At one point, I asked him if we could play together in Argentina; I really wanted to see what the tango purists would think of our music. But Astor laughed and said that if he brought a jazz musician to play tango in Argentina, they would kill him for sure! So it surprised him to see our record receive good reviews in Argentina, and as a consequence, he hoped to organize another round of touring, bringing our collaboration to South America after all. At the same time, he embarked on a new tango opera, which he considered his final epic work.

Unfortunately, none of this came to pass. A few months after he had returned to Paris, Astor suffered a massive stroke. I got a phone call from his sister-in-law in New York, telling me Astor was unconscious and near death in a Paris hospital. But a few weeks later she called again, with a story that was itself worthy of an opera.

When Astor's wife learned there was no hope of recovery, she said she had to take him back to Argentina. The Parisian doctors said that was impossible. Only the machines and the extraordinary efforts of the hospital staff were keeping him alive; no way could he get on a plane and fly to Argentina. But Laura insisted that if he had to die, he had to die in Argentina. Eventually, the President of Argentina, Carlos Menem, sent his personal jet to Paris, along with the equipment and personnel needed to transport Astor to Buenos Aires—and wonder of wonders, a few days later he woke up! He was mostly paralyzed, but the doctors held out hope that he might at least partially recover. I visited Argentina soon after and wanted to see him, but he wasn't doing well that day. I was advised that he wouldn't even know I was there, so no sense in making the trip. Astor never regained the ability to communicate with those around him. After more than a year of struggle, he mercifully passed away on July 4, 1992.

After Astor's death, I assumed my tango days were behind me. But in the late '90s, I was invited to take part in a Piazzolla festival in Buenos Aires. The bill included Chick Corea and Danilo Perez (the very talented jazz pianist from Panama), and besides playing some pieces with each of them, I played two or three tangos with a band organized by Astor's pianist son Daniel (which also featured his grandson "Pipi" on drums). As I relived my tango experiences on that visit, Marcelo Morano—a friend and Argentine promoter I have worked with over the years—proposed that we reunite the musicians from Astor's old band for a record. It sounded like an exciting idea.

However, they hadn't played together since Astor's death, and I feared it could become an organizational nightmare. I agreed that if Marcelo could get everyone together at the same time—and if we could get the best bandoneon players to play Astor's parts—then yes, I would gladly try it.

It took a year or so, but eventually, I found myself back in B.A., rehearsing with the same musicians I knew from a decade earlier—a very emotional experience that triggered many remembrances about Astor as we rehearsed and recorded new versions of his music. Sometime during that week, a couple newspapers got word that the Piazzolla band had reunited and was collaborating with me. This news prompted a call from the mayor's office requesting that we play a concert at the National Library, before we went our separate ways at the end of the week. That sounded like fun, and we relished the idea of performing music from the record for an audience. Even setting this up at the last minute, the logistics weren't too complicated. The Library had an outdoor space (seating about a thousand) where they regularly held public concerts, so we would play there. The concert was announced in the papers and on the radio just a couple of days in advance. With luck, I thought, we might have a decent turnout.

The night of the concert, we waited in the dressing room to go on—and waited; and then waited some more. The show was delayed for nearly an hour because so many people had shown up. The Library had a large projection screen on hand, used for political speeches and rallies, and they hastily set it up for the overflow crowd on the expansive lawn adjoining the building. When we finally started to play, we not only faced a capacity crowd in front of us; an estimated five thousand more watched the concert on the large screen. This was truly a happening for tango fans. And these people knew their tango. Most of the pieces were fairly complex compositions, and yet I heard people softly singing along as we played. During the concert, one of the band members turned to the others and said, "Poor *Tano*, he should be here for this" (using Astor's nickname, a shortened version of "Italiano," referring to his Italian heritage).

Astor Piazzolla Reunion came out in 1997, and because of its success, we toured Europe and South America and made a follow-up recording, *Libertango*, in 1999. We reunited for another tour in 2009, which yielded a television concert and DVD production. As a result, in Argentina, I am now as well known for my tango music as for my jazz. Part of me will always be in love with tango, and I continue to feel great kinship with those musicians. I also remain immensely grateful for the experiences I had playing with Astor. From him, I learned a tremendous amount—about music, about my own playing, how to play tango, and even how to play jazz—and I feel privileged to have known him personally.

Astor Piazzolla lives on through his compositions and his recordings, and because so many musicians perform his music. I take pride in having contributed in small measure to his legacy. In the late '90s, several biographies of Piazzolla were published—most in Spanish, but one also in English translation, where I was surprised and flattered to read that he considered his encounter with me a turning point in his career. Piazzolla was a national hero in the tango world long before I came along, but he credited our collaboration for introducing his music to a wider audience and lifting his career to a new level.

I believe that went both ways.

CHAPTER 27

Moving Forward

In 1989, nearly two decades after first meeting Manfred Eicher in Munich, I left ECM Records. It was a tough decision; I had made eighteen records with Manfred, including some of the best in my career. But now, I was coming up with ideas that did not fit into the ECM mold—such as the tango record with Astor Piazzolla—and Manfred didn't want to venture beyond those confines. To realize these ideas, I needed to change record companies.

Every label has certain stylistic specialties that constitute its trademark. At Atlantic, for instance, I once suggested a project using orchestra, and they explained that it didn't fit their style, and because of that, they couldn't market the record effectively through the radio stations they worked with. At ECM, I knew I could probably remain there for the rest of my career. If I had been a decade or two older, I might have done just that. Instead, I decided to take a chance on something new.

I reverted to a tactic I'd used before. I made my next record with my own money, and then decided whether I would sell it to ECM or do a deal with someone else. For the album, I chose saxophonist Michael Brecker, guitarist John Scofield, bassist Marc Johnson, and drummer Peter Erskine—a truly all-star lineup of contemporary players. The record, titled *Times Like These*, would actually have been acceptable to Manfred, since all these musicians had recorded for ECM at one time or another. But by the time I finished the sessions, I knew I would still need a new label. I had more projects in mind that would not work for ECM, and I knew the time was right to make my move.

Chick Corea had already left ECM and signed with a new label in New York, GRP Records. Since he kept raving about them, I talked to them first. And that was all I needed. We very quickly reached a deal for a seven-year contract. Back in 1973, I had taken the risk of leaving a major label to go with the fledgling ECM, which turned out great. ECM grew into one of the world's most prestigious labels, and my career shared in that success. Now, that pattern was about to repeat itself. During my time with GRP, the label rose from a small niche company to become a wildly successful jazz brand.

As I'd hoped, I got to try some new things at GRP. One of my first records for the label was *Reunion*, my 1990 collaboration with Pat Metheny. By then, I had also gotten interested in the new "smooth jazz" genre. Most of the records in this style struck me as being good at setting a mood, though short on compelling content. But now and then, I'd come across a smooth-jazz project that I liked, and I wanted to try it for myself. I got together with pianist and composer Bob James, whom I had long admired, and we assembled what I considered an intriguing collection of pieces. All of them had the easygoing feel of smooth jazz, yet each piece contained distinctive compositional elements. And I stayed away from the showy solo features or speedy tempos that I'd have typically included on my records.

The release of *Cool Nights* was greeted by a giant yawn. I had greatly misjudged the public response (neither the first time nor the last). I had hoped that my usual fans would see it as an interesting change, and that I'd make a lot of new fans in the process. But my usual listeners didn't like it at all, and few new ones materialized either. One of my all-time favorite record reviews, in *Down Beat* magazine, said, *"Cool Nights* is the best elevator music I've ever heard." The critic gave it a so-so review, grudgingly admitting that it did contain many worthwhile moments. For me, "the best elevator music" pretty much described what I had set out to accomplish in the first place, but the jazz audience didn't care. Larry Rosen (the "R" of GRP) told me that listeners had gotten used to hearing virtuoso improvisations from me, and they expected just that. I guess he was right. But to this day, I'll hear a track from *Cool Nights* as I walk through a department store or airport lounge—or yes, in an elevator—and think, "Someone out there likes it besides me." I'm not afraid of failure. I just want to try things. If they don't work out, I'll try something else.

I recorded seven records during my eight-year stay at GRP. Just as my contract was coming to an end, the label went through a corporate merger. I didn't really want to change companies again, but I didn't know any of the new people taking over the company. While I wavered about what to do next, I was contacted by Glen Barros, who had just become CEO of Concord Records in northern California. Glen flew to Boston to meet with me and Ted Kurland, and he proved extremely persuasive. Concord, which up till then was known for recording older jazz artists, had begun expanding in new directions, and Glen wanted me to be a part in it. I signed with Concord and made fourteen records over fourteen years with them. Chick came over to the label a year after I did, and that made it all the easier for us to work on duet records from time to time. (Except for a couple of brief periods, Chick and I have been label-mates since 1972.) In 2011, I signed with Mack Avenue Records, and so far have released two CDs on my newest label with the New Gary Burton Quartet, my latest touring group.

Around then, I made another important move, this time at Berklee. The college appointed me Executive Vice President in 1996, giving me responsibility for the entire day-to-day operation of the school. At first, I found it daunting. Learning to manage a large institution took a while. I read books on corporate management, hired consultants when I needed them, and trusted my own intuition for direction. It helped that probably two-thirds of Berklee's department heads and administrators came from backgrounds as working musicians, which fostered a certain level of kinship.

Keeping the normal business of Berklee functioning was one thing; my greater challenge involved getting 1,000 employees, 4,000 students (and their parents), alumni, and board members to understand and support our goals as an institution. We needed a vision for the future that people could identify with and rally around. At the suggestion of Lee Berk, we began the familiar corporate approach of creating multi-year plans. For each of these plans, my team and I would spend about two years identifying major initiatives and ways to better involve our community. Berklee is home to a lot of crazy creative people who really care about the place, and their abundant ingenuity allowed us to forge ahead with the innovative spirit that remains a Berklee hallmark.

At the same time, I continued to champion new programs at the college. One of these came about after I spent a month in northern Japan with a group of twenty autistic children and their mothers. I don't speak Japanese, but that really didn't pose a problem, since the kids didn't speak at all. I was one of several musicians who served as teachers or enablers, using music to get the children involved. We spent eight hours a day playing, singing, clapping, dancing, moving around— whatever we could do to arouse the children's curiosity (a real challenge with severely autistic children). Several times a week, I played jazz concerts with local musicians or spoke to groups of educators, but my primary mission was to work with the children. And they made amazing progress as they grew comfortable with us, with our instruments, with singing, and moving with the music. The educators and parents considered the program a big success, and it continued for several years.

Coincidentally, I returned to Boston to find that President Berk had come across a newspaper article about music therapy. Prompted by that, he asked me to investigate whether this might be something Berklee should offer. For the next two years, I researched the field and interviewed music therapists, and eventually I hit pay dirt. Suzanne Hanser, one of the leading music therapy educators in the country, expressed an interest in moving from California to Boston for family reasons, and we convinced her to start a music therapy major at Berklee—now among the largest programs in the country, and something in which I take great pride.

During my last few years at Berklee, another of my main ambitions was the creation of an online music school, something no one had previously accomplished. After researching it, I knew we would have some significant technological challenges. But I was confident we had the talent in-house to build this "college within the college," and I began a campaign to convince the Berklee leadership that this was something we could (and should) do. First, I had to convince the faculty that the new initiative would not threaten their jobs. I also had to sell the idea to the Board of Trustees, who would have to approve the funding. But we soon succeeded in getting the Board's approval, and Berkleeonline.com (our online music school) launched in 2002. A decade later, it stands as an unqualified success, both educationally and financially.

A lot of credit for these initiatives goes to Lee Berk, whose experience and leadership provided me with such a strong model. As for myself, the transition I underwent at Berklee— from overseeing a small ensemble of musicians to leading thousands of aspiring music students and their teachers—taught me a lot about people, and about what happens when diverse individuals participate in a larger community. Berklee draws students from all over the world, pursuing dozens of different styles of music ranging from jazz to rock to bluegrass and beyond, and hosts a faculty filled with expertise and passion. You can imagine the range of perspectives represented by all these people. More than anything else, I learned at Berklee that great things can result from that kind of diversity.

Whatever concerns I may have once had about leaving my mark, or making a difference, disappear as I review my time at Berklee and the changes I brought about. And if there were any doubt in my mind that Berklee recognized my impact, it too disappeared at a remarkable event that took place in 2010. The college asked me to organize a concert marking the fiftieth anniversary of my arrival at Berklee as a student—a half-century of on-and-off connection (but mostly on) with a single institution!

The idea called for a sort of "This Is Your Life" assemblage, bringing together many of the musicians I got to know through Berklee and who had played in my bands over the years. Flattered and excited about the possibility, I ended up with four groups of players representing different eras. We started with the New Gary Burton Quartet (first edition)—the group I formed in 1971 upon returning to Berklee as a teacher—with guitarist Mick Goodrick, bassist Abe Laboriel, and drummer Harry Blazer. Next on the program, an homage to my various quartets, with guitarist John Scofield, Joe Lovano, bassist Steve Swallow, and drummer Antonio Sanchez. We followed with a catchall group that included saxophonists Donny McCaslin and Jim Odgren, trumpeter Tiger Okoshi, and pianist Makoto Ozone, and finally with my Next Generations Quintet of the 2000s. The big surprise was my duo with Chick Corea—not a Berklee alum, but a Boston native (which counted for something). Having so many of my old friends on stage with me was a dream come true. I could never have imagined a greater homecoming, or a truer summation of my association with the institution that shaped so much of my life.

CHAPTER 28

Understanding the Creative Process

Artists are complicated, driven people, often conflicted over what and how to create, and always struggling to balance discipline and freedom. It's no wonder you hear so many stories about musicians' unpredictable or even lunatic behavior. To become a proficient performer requires tremendous discipline—hours and hours of regimented practice. But to become a true artist requires openness and spontaneity—the freedom to follow inspiration wherever it leads. When the regimentation gets oppressive, we must do things to reassert our sense of freedom and spontaneity. For any serious artist, this becomes a lifelong balancing act, and for performing artists, it includes unique challenges not faced by other creative types.

To begin with, performance idioms are time specific. The painter or novelist or composer can take as much time as needed to create something. He or she can return to it later, rethink it, make changes—work whenever inspiration hits, whether that's in the middle of lunch or the middle of the night. But a performer must schedule his or her creativity. I have to be ready to make music between the hours of, say, 8 and 10 P.M. this Saturday night. Like actors, dancers, and others in the performing arts, musicians must switch on the creativity when the curtain rises. We can't wait for inspiration to bubble up.

Actually we don't so much "switch it on" as just get out of the way. I describe this as taking a mental step back so that I become an observer while someone else does the playing. After all, my conscious mind is incapable of processing all the required information (what note to play, when to hit it, how loud it should be, etc.) while still maintaining melodic continuity—let alone keep up with the music's relentless forward motion. But my *unconscious* mind, miracle worker that it is, can instantly make all those decisions and keep the whole process flowing—as long as I don't get in its way.

Everyone employs this process in lots of everyday activities directed by the unconscious. The most obvious of these is speech. You don't think about nouns and verbs and adjectives when you talk to someone. Your brain has assimilated the rules of grammar and stored a sizeable vocabulary to draw from, so as you think of something you want to communicate, your unconscious mind instantly chooses the correct words and slots them into the right grammatical formation. At almost the same moment that you become aware of the sentence moving into your conscious mind, you speak the words—and sentence after sentence, the conversation effortlessly flows.

Improvisation works in much the same way. We assimilate the "vocabulary" and "grammar" of music. Then, when something (a certain chord sequence, perhaps, or some other stimulus) triggers the desire to play a melodic phrase, the unconscious mind assembles a musically relevant group of notes—a musical "sentence," if you will. And just like talking, we play that phrase at almost the same moment we become consciously aware of it. In the case of performers, the unconscious not only gives us the sentence. It also coordinates all the physical movements required to play it on our instruments.

This holds true for even a classical musician or an actor

playing a scripted role. They don't just go through the motions night after night. Even with all the notes or words in front of them, they can't just "phone it in." They have to lose themselves in the flow of the composition, or the dialogue, in order to bring a performance to life. It's the same for improvisers, except that we depend even more on the unconscious. Not having a script to follow, we don't even know what notes we'll play till the moment arrives.

People sometimes ask what I think about while I play. The answer may come as a surprise. Most of the time, certainly, I'm thinking about the music—just not in a specific or supervisory way. I'm not weighing which notes to play, as in "Should I play a B-flat next? Should I make it an eighth note? Should I use my right-hand mallet to make the attack?" I'm most likely thinking about the overall impact of the music. I'm picturing the mood I want the music to have—the emotional identity of the piece. Like an actor holding onto his character's emotional state, I am trying to maintain a grip on what I identify as the subjective feeling of the music.

Sometimes, my conscious mind acts as a critic. I talk to my "inner player" as the performance progresses, offering opinions on how it is going. ("Hey, this is too busy, no one can follow this," or "This is getting boring and repetitive, better do something different"—things like that.) I never tell myself to play any particular notes; that's the job of my unconscious. And sometimes—pretty often, actually—my conscious mind just wanders off to other things entirely. I may find myself thinking about what I have to do tomorrow, or the plane ride earlier that day, or the woman with the funny hat in the second row—whatever wanders into my thoughts. The rule is simple: I can consciously think about anything, just so long as I don't get directly involved in the improvising.

The unconscious mind functions in two specific ways that affect improvisation. First, it is a giant database. In the same way that it compiles vocabulary and absorbs rules of grammar (enabling us to form sentences when we speak), it also retains all the music we have learned over the years: the records we have heard, the songs we have played (and forgotten, at least consciously), the lessons we have practiced and prepared—they're all in the memory, stored in bits and pieces. This is the library that the unconscious mind accesses to pull together the desired notes, arranging them in a musically correct order for us to play. All new information, whatever we learn or hear, goes into this database, enlarging the possibilities for musical combinations.

The other function of the unconscious is less volatile. Again using speech as a comparison, the unconscious shapes one's individual style of talking—phrasing, syntax, volume— into a recognizable identity. That's why you can tell a friend's voice on the telephone from her first few words. It works the same way for one's musical identity. We each develop a unique style—based on phrasing, favorite bits of melody, and so on— that becomes a musical personality, which people often recognize just as quickly.

This personality (like one's speech pattern) doesn't alter from day to day; any change that does occur takes place only gradually over time. Some players have very distinctive phrasing, and a quality of sound, that makes them quite easy to spot. Others come across as more generic and aren't as immediately identifiable. But if you listen to any player on a regular basis, it becomes easy to describe their unique characteristics.

So, we have this database and this distinctive instrumental "voice," both of which feed the inner player—the unconscious mind—which handles the improvising for us. Sounds great, huh? Just stand back and let 'er rip. But this inner player is something of a loose cannon. It needs guidance. Left on its own, it pulls notes and phrases out of your memory bank that may fit from a technical standpoint but still fall short stylistically.

Like most musicians, I endured several frustrating years

watching my inner player choose some really corny licks and awkward phrases, which I would then play before I could jump in and block them. I finally realized I needed to somehow communicate with my inner player. It wasn't enough to try censoring something I didn't like at the last instant. I needed to let it know *beforehand* what kind of results I wanted.

But how does one offer guidance and direction to the unconscious? It doesn't speak English—nor any other language, for that matter; it communicates via images. In order to get the results I preferred (rather than just dealing with whatever potluck my unconscious retrieved), I needed to visualize how I wanted the music to sound. I learned that if I can *show* my unconscious what message I want the music to achieve, it can figure out how to deliver it.

For example, I might picture a steady, strong, comfortable groove. I might imagine soaring phrases that make perfect sense, and how great it will feel to play melodies like that. I immerse myself in the emotional mood that I envision for that song. This is the kind of communication the inner player understands. Over time, I became increasingly comfortable with this image-based language, so that I can now transmit my musical desires quite effectively. It's taken many years to become fluent. But I presume this is what happens with every accomplished player, and it's not as mystical as it may sound.

In addition to communicating with my inner player, my job is to communicate with the listener. Specifically, I want to convey two things: the structure and character of a song.

To understand structure, imagine showing a visitor around your new house. "There's the view of the garden," you'd say, "and here's the gourmet kitchen with the indirect lighting," and so on. It's the same with music. We're supposed to show the listener around the song. "Let me show you the compositional elements. Here's the time feel, and here's where the song transitions from section A to section B; oh, and look at this unusual chromatic passage over here." These are the high-lights, and we need to emphasize them in our improvising.

As for character, I use another analogy, in which each song is like a part in a play. The actor studies his part and figures out the personality and mood of the role. Does he portray someone dark and brooding, or does it call for wit and sophistication? The same holds true in music. We identify the emotional char-acteristics of the song and keep picturing that in our mind, as we first interpret the written melody and then improvise a solo—all the while maintaining the mood of the song.

The more information you can visualize and the more you can "feel" the song, the better your inner player will under-stand what the song is about—and how you want your inter-pretation to sound. The more information you provide to the unconscious, the more you will like what gets played. It's not enough just to play the "right notes" and avoid mistakes. You must capture the meaning of the music and then tell an interesting story, based on the song, in your solo. And only the inner player can deliver the goods. You have to work in harmony with the unconscious mind.

Although music is a sort of language, the majority of people who listen to music don't actually speak that language. When I play a concert, I assume that maybe 95 percent of the audience are non-musicians. Some of them may play a little, but they don't have enough knowledge or experience to identify the details of what we play—things like the tonality, melodic developments, compositional structure—as we whiz along at a snappy tempo. Rarely do you play for people who know enough to analyze what you're doing in real time, but when you do, you want to communicate with them, too. So ultimately, this means we need to reach two audiences: our peers, who understand every note, and the non-musicians, who hear the music a completely different way.

Fortunately, music can cut across this divide, communicating even to listeners who can't discern the nuts and bolts of its construction. Once again, the analogy to speech is valuable. Imagine yourself in a hotel lobby as a nearby group of foreign businessmen converses in another language. At first, you think, "I don't understand a word of this, so I can't possibly tell what they're talking about." But as you watch them, you begin to pick up a lot of general information. Start with the tone of their voices. If they are laughing and smiling, you know they're having a good time. You see one guy holding up a book and pointing at it as he talks, so you can guess he's talking about that book. Perhaps he's in charge of the whole group. When they start shaking hands and moving apart, you know the conversation has ended and they are saying goodbye. So without knowing a word of their language, you can make certain assumptions about their conversation, gain a general sense of their mood, and maybe even surmise the subject of their discussion.

Non-musicians perceive music in a similar fashion; they identify general characteristics and notice alterations in the flow. For most people, these characteristics determine the story that the solo tells. Is the tempo slow or fast? Is the melody busy or simple? Is there a steady pulse? What about the mood of the song—upbeat or sad? What about the colors—dark or bright? And do they change from section to section? Are there phrases that keep recurring? Does the solo build in intensity? All these characteristics make up the listening experience for the non-musician. And simply by being human, people contribute their own input to this experience. If a cat sits at the window watching cars go by, he maybe thinks, "Here comes something red; there goes something big and blue; there's a yellow something going slower than the others." The cat watches the ballet of traffic, quite entertained by the movement and colors, but has no idea what any of it means. A human sitting next to the cat will also see movement and colors, but because of your knowledge and memories, you can attach meaning to the shapes moving past. The sign on a truck says "Plumber," and you might imagine a storyline about a broken pipe downtown—or maybe about someone borrowing the truck to move a couch.

It doesn't have to be true, or even logical, but the human brain craves some sort of narrative. Unlike the cat, we need a story, compelling and interesting, and if we can find one in a solo, it enriches the listening experience.

Ideally, a highly skilled improviser creates solos that provide a feast for the minds of other expert musicians, but also an assortment of well-told stories for non-musicians to follow in their imagination. And while it may seem counterintuitive, I have come to value my connections with non-musicians more than the ones I make with musical experts. When I succeed at it, communicating with non-musicians comes close to true magic.

Younger musicians tend to focus on playing for their peers, intent on proving themselves to teachers and fellow musicians. But as they establish their self-confidence, most discover that the greater challenge lies in reaching the general audience—the listeners who are not musicians.

Personally, I want my entire audience to understand what I have to say in my solos. I'm like the country preacher. I'm not going to water down my message, but I will make it as passionate and clear and compelling as possible, as I try to bring them into my world.

CHAPTER 29

The End Game

As the new century approached, so did a new phase in my own life. By the year 2000, I was only five years from society's early "retirement age" of sixty-two. I had no plans to retire, of course. But my playing career now entered a period of stability, anchored by my ongoing collaborations with Chick Corea and Pat Metheny, and no longer buffeted by the head-long events of the 1960s and '70s. Reflecting now on the last decade or two, I wonder if I am still breaking new ground the way I did earlier in my career. I can always find new songs and new players to make music with, but these days, I tend to stay within a familiar comfort zone. This pattern is pretty typical for musicians as they mature, so it doesn't worry me too much. I find it helps me to have younger players around—for their energy and for inspiration—and to seek a variety of projects to keep me from getting stagnant.

It's always saddened me to see an elder musical giant still trying to perform long after he has lost his edge. Up to a certain point, an experienced improviser can cover up the decrease in physical and mental capabilities. I can tell you that after many decades of playing, we know every trick in the book to hide mistakes. We can adjust to the relentless grip of age. But we all reach a point beyond which the music becomes compromised.

I was very uncomfortable watching Lionel Hampton during

his final decade, after several strokes had robbed so much of his physical movement. In the end, he really couldn't play at all. He just waved his arms at the band and hit the vibes occasionally. But he also couldn't stay home in Manhattan with nothing to do, so he continued to gig (after a fashion).

Near the end of pianist Oscar Peterson's career, he appeared at Birdland in New York the same week I attended a meeting at Sirius Radio (where I hosted a weekly show at the time). For old times' sake, I went to see him. I already knew his playing wasn't what it used to be. Like Hamp, Oscar also had suffered a stroke, leaving his left arm dysfunctional. He still continued to perform, using just his right hand, which in Oscar's case would suffice. He was known throughout his career for his prodigious command of the keyboard.

I watched as Oscar was helped onstage and seated at the piano, and when the trio began to play, I immediately noticed that he struggled to play even mundane passages. He often fumbled over the keys, and generally played at about the level of an intermediate-level piano student. He also seemed out of it. He performed one song twice during the set, having forgotten he'd already played that one. And the set itself was one of the shortest in history. Oscar played only about thirty-five minutes before being helped off the bandstand and back to his dressing room. People had paid a hundred dollars a ticket (plus drinks) to see him, and several patrons were rightfully upset.

I knew Oscar's bassist, Dave Young, because we had both attended Berklee together in the early '60s, and I went over to say hello. Mostly, I wanted to ask him what was going on. He explained that Oscar would get bored sitting around his home in Toronto, so now and then he would put together a short tour, largely to get out and see some old friends. Impaired or not, he wanted to keep going. I guess I can understand that. But I wished he had just taken a vacation to New York instead of trying to play when he no longer could.

I'm determined to retain enough self-awareness so that I can realistically assess my abilities in the years ahead. I'm already aware of changes taking place due to age and health. I don't think I've yet hit the point where I need to quit, but I'm sure that eventually, the time will come. I just want to be clear-headed and strong enough to step back when it does.

My personal life also saw a welcome period of stability through most of the '90s, as my boyfriend Earl and I deepened our relationship while he launched a successful business. I felt I had at last discovered who I was, and that with Earl as my partner, I had developed lasting friendships and a social network unlike anything I had known before. Nonetheless, by 1997 our seven-year relationship had come to an end, and I found myself single once more. As with all of my breakups, life without a partner left me adrift and somewhat directionless. But this time around, I was no longer plagued by confusion over my sexual identity. In fact, I began dating with a passion, meeting new guys both locally and in some of the cities where I traveled. I think I was trying to make up for lost time, having not entered gay life till my forties. During this period, I met a lot of diverse and interesting men. (I once spent a romantic weekend in Chicago with a CIA agent.) It was a pretty adventurous time, and I have no regrets about it. But it didn't satisfy me; I felt incomplete. On the positive side, both of my careers were going well, and I had a supportive group of friends. But I was chasing after this missing piece—the new relationship waiting for me out there somewhere—and I always heard the clock ticking. Quite a few years would pass before I really felt whole again.

The universe, however, will sometimes come up with circumstances that completely divert your attention. In my case, I had other affairs of the heart to deal with.

At this writing, I have had a total of six heart operations, some minor and some major, and I know I will need to monitor my cardiac health from now on. The first event occurred in 1995, when I played a short Midwest tour with Makoto Ozone. We were in Chicago to perform at the Jazz Showcase and I had the afternoon free, so I used the time to walk around, exploring and people watching—a typical activity for me on the road. I suddenly started experiencing pain in my chest and in my left arm, along with shortness of breath: all the classic signs of a heart attack. Yes, I immediately knew what my body was trying to tell me. And what did I do? I did what everyone does at first: I tried to talk myself out of it. I stood in one spot for a few minutes till the symptoms went away, then walked slowly back to the hotel and laid down. I played the gig that night and the following night, too. I could play the vibraphone without setting off any chest pains. But I noticed the symptoms would return whenever I walked more than half a block.

Looking back on it now, I was insane to ignore these symptoms. I don't know what I was thinking. But I didn't relish going to a strange hospital in a city other than my own, and I didn't want to deal with whatever was necessary to check it out. And of course, I remembered the old show business slogan about how "the show must go on." I just couldn't pull myself away from my responsibility to make the gig. I never even mentioned my pains to Makoto, for fear he would insist I get to a hospital and forget about everything else. And in fact, we went on to play a night in Madison, WI, and another in Minneapolis, after we left Chicago. I made a point of walking very slowly and stopping frequently to rest. In the Minneapolis airport for the trip home, I had a very long walk to the gate and had to stop every fifty feet to keep the chest pains from returning.

By this time, I knew something serious was going on, and I went to my doctor as soon as I got home. Tests showed some degree of arterial blockage, and he told me to come back the next day for further evaluation. But at 5:30 in the morning I was awakened by serious chest pains and breathing difficulties; I was having a minor heart attack. Within a couple of hours, I had an angioplasty and a stent inserted to correct the blockage in one of my arteries. Looking back on it, I'm still amazed at my stupidity, going through almost a week of travel and gigs, all the time being maybe one song away from a heart attack.

Four years later, around my fifty-seventh birthday, the doctor conducting my annual physical informed me that I needed open heart surgery to fix a failing valve. Everything went smoothly, although this was a major operation. The procedure required the surgeons to stop my heart temporarily, during which time the heart-lung machine breathed for me and circulated my blood. I remember that afterward, my doctor made a specific point of saying I was only on the machine for 22 minutes, a fairly short time for such an operation. Much later, I learned the significance of that number.

I mentioned to the heart surgeon that I had a stack of books to read while I recuperated, and he jokingly said I wouldn't be doing much reading for a while. I quickly found out why. To begin with, my eyesight was affected for several weeks. I had generally blurry vision, and sometimes I would even see double. My sight eventually cleared up, but even then, I couldn't concentrate. When I tried to read, I found myself going over the same paragraph repeatedly, unable to remember what I had just read.

After a couple of months, I had recovered enough to resume my work at Berklee as well as my concert schedule. But although my mental focus had mostly recovered, it didn't bounce all the way back; it wasn't what it had been before the operation. At first, I chalked this up to my imagination, or wondered if maybe I hadn't fully recovered. But as the months passed, I realized this had become "the new normal." I found it harder to read music, to learn new pieces, or to memorize anything. I also found it more difficult to stay on top of the paperwork I had previously handled at Berklee. For a long while, I wondered if maybe this was just a symptom of getting older, until I ran across a magazine article that described my condition exactly.

According to the main study used in the article, 42 percent of patients who have spent any time on the heart-lung machine suffer a decrease in cognitive ability of 20 percent or more. The condition is called *postperfusion syndrome*, but the doctors commonly refer to it as "pump head." The more time on the machine, the greater chance of impairment. The fact that I had logged only 22 minutes worked in my favor.

Because the effects of pump head are typically slight, people don't notice it during most everyday activities. For me, it really only becomes an issue when I require focused concentration. I used to pride myself on my ability to memorize, to sight-read, and to absorb lots of complex information quickly. These things no longer come quite as easily now. I can only work on new music for about 20 minutes at a time. After that, the notes start to blur, and I can't remember what I'm playing or what comes next. I have to stop and walk around for a while before I can come back and practice some more.

The medical profession can't say exactly why this condition occurs and why it affects only some patients. But I still wish the doctors had explained the possible consequences beforehand. I'm sure I would have had the operation in any case. But I wouldn't have felt such confusion about the postoperative symptoms if I had known they were a possible consequence of the procedure.

In 2010, I went through an ablation, a fairly minor operation to correct a problem with my heart rhythm. The first attempt didn't solve the problem, and a year later I went in for a repeat operation, during which something went terribly wrong. As I found out much later, the surgeon mistakenly cut through the outer wall of my heart, causing my heart to stop almost immediately. The surgical team tried to stanch the heavy bleeding by jamming a needle into my chest and siphoning out the blood, which they then transfused back through an IV in my left arm. But they couldn't keep up with the bleeding.

An emergency call went out for a cardiac surgeon to take over. Fortunately, the doctor reputed to be the best heart surgeon in the area was in the building at that moment. He quickly prepped to perform a full open-heart operation (my second and hopefully last), in which he sewed up, and according to the medical report, also glued the laceration in my heart wall. (Glue? Who knew you could use glue inside the body? I'm assuming it wasn't Elmer's.)

A day later, I woke up expecting to go home, thinking that only a few hours had passed, and that my supposedly minor procedure had gone well. Imagine my shock to discover all kinds of tubes coming out of my bandaged chest, and to find I had lost an entire day. I later found out that during the entire time the emergency doctor prepped and I was wheeled into the cardiac operating room, I had no heartbeat. That's a long time with no pulse. I asked one of the team doctors how I had stayed alive. Had I in fact been dead, or what? He told me they'd kept my body functions going with manual CPR and a ventilator.

As a result of the operation, I also have a permanent blood clot in my left arm (most likely from the attempts to inject blood back into my IV). The blood circulation from my hand has had to find a new path back to my heart, flowing through secondary veins. Because of this, my left hand is permanently swollen to a slight degree and feels somewhat tight when I flex it. Sometimes, I get tingling and numbness in my fingers as well—not the best prognosis for someone who relies on precise hand movements. But mostly, I've learned to ignore these sensations when I play.

Those first days in the hospital, I felt very confused, both angry and scared. Once you've come back from the brink, I don't think you're ever quite the same. The knowledge of your brush with death stays with you. Like my first open heart surgery, the recovery was slow and stressful. And even though I hadn't used the heart-lung machine this time around, I discovered a new symptom when I returned to performing: I no longer could rely on my gift of perfect pitch, which I had taken for granted since the age of six.

Nowadays, when I try to identify notes just by hearing them, I sometimes get it completely wrong. I have the same kind of pitch recognition as the majority of musicians, something called "relative pitch." It means that once I start playing, I can recognize pitches sufficiently well—relative to each other—to make music. Losing my perfect pitch hasn't kept me from performing, but I do miss that old certainty about what I hear as I play.

Why did my operating-room trauma cause the loss of my perfect pitch? That's a mystery that will probably never be explained. The bottom line is that I lost one of my treasured (if not crucial) musical gifts.

In some ways, the heart surgeries and the aftereffects have exacerbated my reticence in dealing with people—not just fans or business associates, but even friends. Some days, I just can't answer the phone and need to avoid seeing anyone. I'm always aware that I have two pieces of metal in my chest that keep my heart functioning. That awareness comes with an underlying sense of vulnerability, and it has changed how I look at life. I always figured I could do anything I set my mind to. Now, I often wonder how big a role fate has played in getting me this far. There's good luck and there's bad luck. I've had plenty of the former, for sure—but some of the latter along the way, as well.

CHAPTER 30

Life Begins at Sixty

The old phrase "Life begins at forty" dates back to a different era, when people married young, raised the next generation, and by the time they reached early middle age, finally had the chance to reflect upon and renew their own lives. The focus of the phrase has crept higher and higher, and for many people today, "sixty" is "the new forty"—the time when they still enjoy health and energy, but also wisdom and experience, and can really make the most of their time. The whole idea is a cliché, of course, but clichés only get that way if they contain at least a kernel of truth in the first place.

As I approached my own sixtieth birthday in 2003, I felt a growing urge to start a new phase in my life. I had put in more than three decades at Berklee, as teacher, administrator, and vice-president, and had nothing left to prove there. I had achieved the goals I set for myself as a musician, many times over. I had figured out my sexuality, come to know myself, and knew how I wanted to live my life. But I was dreading the idea of turning sixty. It just sounded so *old* to me. My birthday falls in January, when the Boston winter is cold and dark and no boon to the spirit. On the spur of the moment, I got on a plane to Fort Lauderdale, just for the weekend, to shake me out of my funk.

That first evening in balmy Florida, I began thinking about the future. My Berklee contract was coming up soon for renewal, and I had reservations about committing to another five years at the college. I recalled reading that when Franklin D. Roosevelt was asked what he recalled about life before the White House, he said he "missed having the time to think things through." That just about summed up my feelings, having juggled two full-time careers for more than thirty years. I started to contemplate life as a full-time musician—and only a musician—once again.

Since it seemed to be a weekend for impulsive action, I decided the next morning to drive around checking out real estate ads, just to get an idea of the area. Fort Lauderdale is an extremely gay-friendly community, and while I didn't have a specific plan, I thought it would help to at least explore my options. After looking at a half-dozen houses, I saw an intriguing newspaper ad that read, "The Ellington at Victoria Park, Jazz Up Your Life." I wondered, could that be the Ellington I know? I drove out to find a new townhouse development just beginning construction—and it was, indeed, named for Duke Ellington. The property developer was a jazz fan—he had filled the sales office with jazz festival posters—and he had named the four basic home designs after Louis Armstrong, Count Basie, John Coltrane, and Miles Davis. I picked up the brochures and read through them on the flight home, and I arrived in Boston feeling a lot different about turning sixty.

A week later, I put a deposit on a Louis Armstrong townhouse. I have to admit, the jazz connection helped me make the decision. I felt I was on friendly turf. After all, what are the odds of finding a community to live in named after my hero, the Duke?

That fateful weekend set a lot of things in motion. I had one year left to finish things at Berklee, allowing plenty of time for a smooth transition. It so happened that Berklee President Lee Berk, whom I had worked alongside for almost twenty years, had earlier announced his own intention to retire. A national search was already underway for his replacement, with an administrative restructuring in the works as well. My decision to leave could be folded into the other changes. That spring, Bill Cosby received an Honorary Doctorate and gave the Commencement speech, as Lee and I both said farewell to the Berklee community.

When I returned to Fort Lauderdale some months later to close on the purchase of my new house, I heard a track from my record *Cool Nights* playing in the airport as I waited for my baggage. I took it as yet another sign that I was in the right place. When the school year ended in the spring of 2004, I completed my move to Florida and began the next phase of my career in earnest.

At the time I left Berklee, I hadn't had a steady working band for a while, and didn't quite know how to proceed. I did know I would have more freedom to travel, so the idea of putting a new band together had some appeal—especially since it would allow me to introduce another precociously talented young musician to the world.

A few years earlier, I had seen a pre-teen guitarist playing with a group of other youngsters on a GRAMMY telecast, in a segment promoting music education. Within ten seconds of hearing him, I knew he was loaded with talent. I checked with the GRAMMY office, found out his name—Julian Lage—and got in touch with him. We had a terrific phone call, discussing songs, harmony progressions, favorite records—all the usual musicians' shop talk. The difference was that I was talking to a twelve-year-old, and hearing him go on in his child's voice about such technical musical matters was straight out of *The Twilight Zone*. I could hardly wait to meet him.

I spoke with Julian's parents, and we arranged for him and I to play at that year's TED Conference (Technology, Entertainment, and Design) in Monterey, CA, not far from where they lived. Julian's musicianship exceeded even my high expectations. We played a couple songs together. Then Herbie Hancock, who was in the audience, joined us for another piece. Because it all went so well, I began booking some gigs that Julian and I could play together, starting with a jazz cruise across the Atlantic on the Queen Elizabeth II in the autumn of 2000.

When Julian turned fifteen, he sent me a new demo of his playing, which impressed me greatly—more so when he told me he had written most of the songs. It's rare enough for someone that young to play at a professional level, and rarer still for him to be a credible composer too. I knew the time had arrived for us to make a record together. Julian and his dad came to Boston for a few days so we could rehearse, and we set dates for the recording to take place in Berkeley, CA, near Julian's home. I also invited Makoto Ozone's trio onto the session, which took place in the fall of 2003.

Until then, because of Julian's age, his father had always gone along whenever we performed. But a week before the recording, Julian called—with his parents' blessing—to ask if he could be on his own for the recording dates. His father would drop him off the first day, then come back for him after we finished a few days later. I saw no problem, since we were staying at a hotel nearby and spending all our time at the studio anyway, and it offered the perfect opportunity for Julian to establish himself as an equal with the other musicians. He did just that. Though only fifteen, he wowed everyone and handled himself like a complete pro. I titled the record *Generations*, since it included three generations of musicians, with Julian and me representing the youngest and the oldest. I greatly admired his talent, but I think something else also intrigued me about Julian: a flicker of reliving my own entry into the music business at almost the same age.

Almost a year later, as I wrapped things up at Berklee, I now thought of putting together a new group with Julian.

I didn't know how regularly we could work together, with Julian still in high school, but we both wanted to give it a try. Julian's teachers were very accommodating. As long as he kept up with his schoolwork, they allowed him plenty of freedom to come and go. He managed to complete high school on schedule, and even to get some credits at junior college, as we periodically toured the U.S., Europe, and Japan. I filled out the band with several newly graduated Berklee students who fit in perfectly: drummer James Williams, bassist Luques Curtis, and Vadim Neselovskyi, an incredibly talented pianist and composer. Vadim grew up in Ukraine and eventually found his way to Boston for college, and he contributed (along with Julian) much of the repertoire for the new group.

After working for several years with what I called my "Next Generations" Band—the name taken from the title of our second album—I suddenly found myself entering a period of intense activity with both Chick Corea and Pat Metheny, which meant that I couldn't keep the band touring at the same time. But all the "Next Generation" musicians have moved on with their careers. Julian graduated from Berklee at twenty-one and started his own band, earning a GRAMMY nomination for their first recording. Vadim spent two years in New Orleans at the Thelonious Monk Institute. He now teaches at Berklee and has released a great record of his own. Luques stays busy in New York working regularly with several groups, and the same holds true for James, still based in Boston.

In Florida, I fell in love again. Having lived a single life after my relationship with Earl ended, I met Jonathan Chong at a popular gay club in Fort Lauderdale. We hit it off immediately, so we headed out to a favorite restaurant for dinner and started to get to know each other. Within a few weeks, we were a couple, and after a few months we moved in together. Love at first sight seems to be my style.

Unlike my previous boyfriends, Jonathan is not a musician,

and he knew only a modest amount about jazz before we met. In fact, many of our interests seem almost opposite. He's a gifted athlete, for instance, who plays a mean game of tennis; you're more likely to find me on the sofa with a book. At first, I didn't know if we would have that much to talk about, but after eight years, we're still talking. Thanks to Jonathan, I consider my life very complete.

My music continues to keep me as busy as I want (sometimes a little busier, actually). Chick and I won a 2008 GRAMMY for *The New Crystal Silence,* my sixth GRAMMY overall. My album *Quartet Live,* with Pat Metheny, Steve Swallow and drummer Antonio Sanchez, received a GRAMMY nomination in 2009. (We lost out to one of Chick's records that year, so at least it stayed in the family!) And just this year, Chick and I shared another GRAMMY win for our recording *Hot House.*

I have continued collaborating with Julian, too. In 2010, we formed the New Gary Burton Quartet with Antonio Sanchez and bassist Scott Colley, and we have toured on three continents. Our album *Common Ground* was voted one of the ten best jazz CDs of 2011 by *Jazz Times* magazine. We resumed touring in 2013 and have released a second CD, *Guided Tour.* Julian keeps getting better and continues to not only affirm my first judgment about his talent, but to inspire me as well. I expect I'll keep on making music with him, just as I have with Chick and Pat and Makoto, for a long time to come. Some combinations just work too well to give them up.

And although I thought I'd departed music education when I left Berklee, they reeled me back in. After seeing the great success of the online program I started, I couldn't resist getting in on the action. So in 2012, I launched my own course, *Gary Burton: Jazz Improvisation,* for which I created ninety-five videos to demonstrate and explain my improvisation concepts. I'm having a ball interacting with the students I meet online. I then extended my online presence by creating a jazz improvisation course for Stanford University's Coursera, the website that provides free college-level courses, where I now present my lessons to tens of thousands of students worldwide.

Early in life, I always had the support of my parents and siblings, and later on, the support of my own family. I'm tremendously proud of my children Stephanie and Sam, both fine young adults making their way in the world. And with the birth of Stephanie's son Tommy (whom Jonathan and I just adore), I recently became a grandfather. Jonathan's relatives have welcomed me wholeheartedly into their family, and I also have my extended gay family, made up of many enduring friendships built over the past twenty-five years. These relationships, and the support they bring, provide a warm and loving life almost entirely outside of my musical existence.

And that's as it should be, at least for me. I can honestly say that, contrary to the romantic notion of the artist who spends each waking moment "living the music," jazz is just a part of my life. Sometimes I feel like I'm playing out the role of a jazz musician. My neighbors and most of my non-musician friends have barely an inkling of the life I lead when I head for the airport, taking off for distant places—maybe to play for a president, or present a GRAMMY award to someone, or walk onto the stage of Carnegie Hall yet again. It sometimes seems that the real me is standing off to the side, just watching that *other* Burton, the jazz musician, do his thing.

Twenty-five years ago I told Terry Gross I was a jazz musician who happened to be gay. Later, I came to think of myself as a gay guy who happens to be a jazz musician. Perhaps it's more accurate to say I'm just a guy who happens to be gay and happens to be a jazz musician. Ultimately, I have no control over how the rest of the world sees me. And I've always known—regardless of my orientation, or my career as a college administrator, and in spite of the solos I may play, or the albums I have recorded—that when the last memory of Gary Burton fades from the public consciousness, it will probably be somebody saying, "Oh, yeah—that guy who played with four sticks."

And that's okay with me.

DISCOGRAPHY

RECORDINGS AS PRIMARY ARTIST

New Vibe Man in Town. Gary Burton, with Joe Morello, Gene Cherico. RCA, 1961.

Who Is Gary Burton? Gary Burton, with Chris Swansen, Phil woods, Bob Brookmeyer, Clark Terry, Joe Morello, John Neves, Tommy Flanagan. RCA, 1962.

Something's Coming. Gary Burton, with Jim Hall, Chuck Israels, Larry Bunker. RCA, 1963; Reissued by RCA France, 1993.

Three in Jazz. Gary Burton, with Jack Sheldon, Monty Budwig, Vernel Fournier. RCA, 1963.

The Groovy Sound of Music. Gary Burton, with Gary MacFarland, Ed Shaunessy, Steve Swallow, Phil Woods, Bob Brookmeyer, Joe Puma, Joe Morello, and string section. RCA, 1964.

The Time Machine. Gary Burton, with Steve Swallow, Larry Bunker. RCA, 1965.

Tennessee Firebird. Gary Burton, with Chet Atkins, Steve
Marcus, Roy Haynes, Steve Swallow, Buddy Speicher,
Sonny Osborne, Buddy Osborne, Ray Edenton, Buddy
Emmons, Henry Strezlecki, Charlie McCoy, Kenneth
Buttrey. RCA, 1966.

Duster. Gary Burton, with Larry Coryell, Steve Swallow,
Roy Haynes. RCA, 1967; Reissued Koch Records, 1998.
GRAMMY Nomination.

Lofty Fake Anagram. Gary Burton, with Larry Coryell, Steve
Swallow, Bob Moses. RCA, 1967.

Gary Burton Quartet in Concert. Gary Burton, with Larry
Coryell, Steve Swallow, Bob Moses. RCA, 1968. GRAMMY
Nomination.

A Genuine Tong Funeral. Gary Burton, with Carla Bley, Mike
Mantler, Gato Barbieri, Howard Johnson, Steve Swallow,
Bob Moses, Larry Coryell, Steve Lacy, Jimmy Knepper.
RCA, 1968.

Country Roads and Other Places. Gary Burton, with Jerry Hahn,
Roy Haynes, Steve Swallow. RCA, 1969.

Throb. Gary Burton, with Richard Greene, Jerry Hahn, Steve
Swallow, Bill Goodwin. Atlantic, 1969.

Live Concert. Gary Burton Quartet. Atlantic (Canada), 1970.
Canadian release only.

Good Vibes. Gary Burton, with Richard "T," Jerry Hahn, Eric
Gale, Chuck Rainey, Steve Swallow, Bernard Purdie, Bill
LaVorgne. Atlantic, 1970.

Gary Burton & Keith Jarrett. Gary Burton, with Keith Jarrett,
Sam Brown, Steve Swallow, Bill Goodwin. Atlantic, 1971;
Reissued Rhino, 1994. GRAMMY Nomination.

Alone at Last. Gary Burton. Atlantic, 1971. GRAMMY: Best Jazz Solo Performance.

Paris Encounter. Gary Burton, with Stephane Grappelli, Steve Swallow, Bill Goodwin. Atlantic, 1972.

Norwegian Wood. Compilation. RCA, 1972.

In the Public Interest. Gary Burton, with Michael Gibbs, Randy Brecker, Michael Brecker, Steve Swallow, and big band. Polydor, 1972.

Crystal Silence. Gary Burton, with Chick Corea. ECM, 1972; Reissued 1990.

New Quartet. Gary Burton, with Mick Goodrick, Harry Blazer, Abe LaBoriel. ECM, 1973.

Seven Songs. Gary Burton, with Mike Gibbs, Mick Goodrick, Steve Swallow, Ted Seibs, and string orchestra. ECM, 1974.

Hotel Hello. Gary Burton, with Steve Swallow. ECM, 1974.

Matchbook. Gary Burton, with Ralph Towner. ECM, 1974.

Ring. Gary Burton, with Mick Goodrick, Steve Swallow, Bob Moses, Eberhard Weber. ECM, 1975.

Turn of the Century. Compilation, double album. Atlantic, 1975.

Dreams So Real. Gary Burton, with Pat Metheny, Mick Goodrick, Bob Moses, Steve Swallow. ECM, 1976; Reissued 2008.

Passengers. Gary Burton, with Pat Metheny, Steve Swallow, Eberhard Weber, Bob Moses. ECM, 1977.

Duet. Gary Burton, with Chick Corea. ECM, 1978. GRAMMY: Best Jazz Instrumental Performance.

Times Square. Gary Burton, with Tiger Okoshi, Steve Swallow, Roy Haynes. ECM, 1978.

Easy As Pie. Gary Burton, with Jim Odgren, Steve Swallow, Mike Hyman. ECM, 1979.

Picture This. Gary Burton, with Jim Odgren, Steve Swallow, Mike Hyman. ECM, 1980.

Zurich Concert. Gary Burton, with Chick Corea. ECM, 1980. GRAMMY: Best Jazz Instrumental Performance.

Live at Cannes. Gary Burton, with Daniel Humair, Pierre Michelot, Ahmad Jamal Trio. Various Labels since 1981, but most recently Jazz World, 2007.

Lyric Suite for Sextet. Gary Burton, with Chick Corea, string quartet. ECM, 1982; Reissued 1992. GRAMMY Nomination.

Slide Show. Gary Burton, with Ralph Towner. ECM, 1985.

Real Life Hits. Gary Burton, with Makoto Ozone, Steve Swallow, Mike Hyman. ECM, 1985.

New Tango. Gary Burton, with Astor Piazzola, Pablo Ziegler, Fernando Suarez Paz, Hector Console, Horacio Malvicino. Warner Brothers/Atlantic USA, 1986.

Gary Burton & Berklee All-Stars. Gary Burton, with Jeff Stout, Bill Pierce, Orville Wright, Larry Monroe, Tommy Campbell, Bruce Gertz. JVC, 1986.

Works. Compilation. ECM, 1987.

Whiz Kids. Gary Burton, with Tommy Smith, Makoto Ozone, Steve Swallow, Mike Hyman. ECM, 1987.

Times Like These. Gary Burton, with John Scofield, Michael Brecker, Peter Erskine, Marc Johnson. GRP, 1988.

Reunion. Gary Burton, with Pat Metheny, Mitch Forman, Peter Erskine, Will Lee. GRP, 1989.

Artist's Choice. Compilation. RCA/Bluebird Records, 1989.

Cool Nights. Gary Burton, with Bob James, Bob Berg, Wolfgang Muthspiel, Peter Erskine, Will Lee. GRP, 1991.

Benny Rides Again. Gary Burton, with Eddie Daniels, Mulgrew Miller, Peter Erskine, Marc Johnson. GRP, 1992. GRAMMY Nomination.

Six Pack. Gary Burton, with B.B. King, John Scofield, Kurt Rosenwinkel, Kevin Eubanks, Ralph Towner, Jim Hall, Jack DeJohnette, Mulgrew Miller, Bob Berg, Will Lee, Paul Shaffer, Larry Goldings, Steve Swallow. GRP, 1992.

Right Place, Right Time. Gary Burton, with Paul Bley. SONOR, 1994.

It's Another Day. Gary Burton, with Rebecca Parris, Chuck Loeb, Alan Pasqua, Peter Erskine, Will Lee. GRP, 1994.

Face to Face. Gary Burton, with Makoto Ozone. GRP, 1995.

Collection. Compilation. GRP, 1997.

Keith Jarrett/Alone at Last. Compilation CD. Atlantic, 1997.

Departure. Gary Burton and Friends, with Peter Erskine, Fred Hersch, John Scofield, John Patitucci. Concord Records, 1997.

Native Sense. "Rhumbata." Chick Corea and Gary Burton. Concord Records/Stretch, 1997. GRAMMY: Best Solo Performance.

Astor Piazzolla Reunion: A Tango Excursion. Gary Burton, with Makoto Ozone, Pablo Ziegler, Nicholas Ledesma, Daniel Binelli, Marcelo Nisenman, Hector Console, Horacio Malvicino, Fernando Suarez Paz. Concord Records, 1998.

Like Minds. Gary Burton, Chick Corea, Pat Metheny, Roy Haynes, David Holland. Concord Records, 1998. GRAMMY for Best Jazz Instrumental Performance.

Libertango: The Music of Astor Piazzolla. Gary Burton, with Pablo Ziegler, Nicholas Ledesma, Marcelo Nisenman, Hector Console, Horacio Malvicino, Fernando Suarez Paz. Concord Records, 2000. GRAMMY Nomination.

For Hamp, Red, Bags, and Cal. Gary Burton, with Mulgrew Miller, Makoto Ozone, Danilo Perez, Russell Malone, Christian McBride, John Patitucci, Horacio Hernandez, Lewis Nash, Luis Quintero. Concord Records, 2001. GRAMMY Nomination.

Rarum, Vol. 4: Selected Recordings. Gary Burton. ECM, 2002.

Virtuosi. Gary Burton and Makoto Ozone. Concord Records, 2002. GRAMMY Nomination.

Music Stories. Gary Burton, with Thanos Mikroutsikos and Kamerata Orchestra. Blue Note Records, 2003. European release only.

Generations. Gary Burton, with Julian Lage, Makoto Ozone, James Genus, Clarence Penn. Concord Records, 2003.

Next Generation. Gary Burton, with Julian Lage, Vadim Neselovskyi, Luques Curtis, James Williams. Concord Records, 2005.

The New Crystal Silence. Chick Corea and Gary Burton. Concord Records, 2008. GRAMMY: Best Jazz Instrumental Album.

Quartet Live. Gary Burton, with Pat Metheny, Steve Swallow, Antonio Sanchez. Concord Records, 2009. GRAMMY Nomination.

Crystal Silence: Gary Burton/Chick Corea, The ECM Recordings 1972–79. Compilation ECM, 2009.

Common Ground. Gary Burton, with Julian Lage, Scott Colley, Antonio Sanchez. Mack Avenue Records, 2012.

Hot House. Gary Burton, with Chick Corea. Concord Records, 2012. GRAMMY: Best Jazz Improvised Solo.

Guided Tour. Gary Burton, with Julian Lage, Scott Colley, Antonio Sanchez. Mack Avenue Records, 2013.

NOTABLE RECORDINGS AS A SIDEMAN

After the Riot at Newport. The Nashville All-Stars. 1960; Reissued by Master Classics Records, 2000.

Jazz Winds from a New Direction. Hank Garland. 1960; Reissued by Sony Music Special Projects, 1995.

Last Date. Floyd Cramer. RCA/Victor, 1960.

Out of the Woods. George Shearing. Capitol, 1963.

Getz au GoGo. Stan Getz. Verve, 1964; Reissued by Polygram Records, 1990, and by Verve, 2007.

Bob Brookmeyer and Friends. Bob Brookmeyer. Columbia, 1964: Reissued by Sony BMG, 2005.

Getz/Gilberto #2. Stan Getz. Verve, 1965; Reissued 1993.

Reason to Believe. Tim Hardin. MGM, 1967; Reissued by Polygram Records, 1990.

Chick Corea/Gary Burton. Live in Tokyo. Laserdisc 1981; Reissued on VHS by Pacific Arts Video, 1992.

GRP All-Star Big Band. GRP, 1992.

Ingenue. k.d. lang. Sire/London/Rhino, 1992.

GRP All-Star Big Band Live! GRP, 1993.

Nobody Else but Me. Stan Getz. Polygram Records, Recorded 1964, Released 1994.

Symphonic Bossa Nova. Ettore Stratta and the Royal Philharmonic Orchestra. Elektra/WEA, 1996.

Charity of Night. Bruce Cockburn. Rykodisc, 1997.

Afterglow: Music from the Motion Picture. Mark Isham. Columbia/Sony, 1998.

Treasure. Makoto Ozone. PID, 2003.

ABOUT THE AUTHOR

Widely recognized as the most technically accomplished of jazz vibraphonists, Gary Burton also led the first true "fusion" band, combining jazz with rock and storming festival stages and rock palaces around the world in the late 1960s. By then, he had already toured the world with jazz icons George Shearing and Stan Getz—all before he turned twenty-five.

Photo by Michael Murphy

Blessed with musical gifts that were evident in his earliest years, Burton has spent nearly sixty of his seventy years as a professional musician, balancing full-time careers as a groundbreaking jazz artist and an innovative educator at the renowned Berklee College of Music. Through his bands, as well as through his partnerships with Pat Metheny and Chick Corea, he has forever changed the musical landscape of the late twentieth century. Now "retired" and living in Florida, he continues to tour widely and release new albums, and has engaged twenty-first–century media to create online courses in improvisation.

He is also a gay white man from rural Indiana, navigating his way through an urban cosmopolitan art form where machismo has ruled from the start. His has been a life spent "learning to listen" to his inner guide on this headlong and rewarding journey.

INDEX

Note: Page numbers in *italics* indicate photographs and are found in the photo section.

A

Adderley, Cannonball, 211
The Advocate, 196
After the Riot, 36
"After You've Gone," 13
Afterglow, 270
air drumming, 172
Aishe, Bernice (mother), 1–2, *P1*, *P4*
Aishe, Cecil
    (maternal grandfather), 3, *P1*, *P3*
Albam, Manny, 53
alcohol, 27, 108, 131, 144–45
All What Jazz (Larkin), 172
Alone at Last, 234, 239
    GRAMMY for, 240, 242
Alpert, Herb, 112
American Embassy (Russia), 284–87, 288
And His Mother Called Him Bill, 241
Anderson (Indiana), 2
    home, *P1*
Anthony, Ron, 77
Antony and Cleopatra, 185
A&R Recording, 70
Armstrong, Louis, 14–15, 17
Art Ensemble of Chicago, 259, 262
Astor Piazzolla Reunion, 326
Atkins, Chet, 34, 35, 38, 146–47
The Atlantic Monthly, viii

Atlantic Records, 233, 249
    recording with, 223, 228, 242, 248
audience
    communication with, 11, 337–40
    improvisation and, 337–40
autism, 330–31
"Autumn Leaves," 291
Avatar Studios, 80

B

Bach, Johann Sebastian, 237
"Back Home Again in Indiana," 226
Bailey, Mildred, 224
Balver Höhle, 200
the Band, 193
bandoneon, 317, 322
Bangkok, 157–61
Barber, Samuel, 300
    career, 185–87
    collaboration with, 184, 187–89
    homosexuality of, 186
    improvisation and, 187–88
Barbieri, Gato, 197
Barros, Glen, 329
Bartók, Béla, 292
Basie, Count, 171
Basin Street West, 144–45
Beacon Theatre, 291

Gary Burton – vibraphone
Scott Colley – bass
Julian Lage – guitar
Antonio Sanchez – drums

THE NEW GARY BURTON QUARTET
GUIDED TOUR

Gary's universally acclaimed career is rich with variety, collaboration and innovation. The vibraphone master celebrates his 70th birthday with this release, *Guided Tour*.

Guided Tour continues the distinctive legacy manifested in his group's facile, deep technique and the compositional contributions from each member.

Also available:

Common Ground
on CD and 180g double vinyl